BETRAYAL IN DALLAS

BETRAYAL IN DALLAS

LBJ, THE PEARL STREET MAFIA, AND THE MURDER OF PRESIDENT KENNEDY

MARK NORTH

AUTHOR OF *ACT OF TREASON*

SKYHORSE PUBLISHING
A HERMAN GRAF BOOK

www.skyhorsepublishing.com

10 9 8 7 6 5

Library of Congress Cataloging-in-Publication Data
is available on file.

ISBN: 978-1-62636-122-5

Printed in the United States of America

For Wendy,
une vie d'amour magique

In memory of Staff Sergeant Richard North, USMC
Battle of Iwo Jima, February 19–March 16, 1945
Courage

AUTHOR'S NOTE

THIS BOOK IS about justice, restoring governmental credibility, and closure for the American people in the death of President John F. Kennedy. We the people have long known that JFK died a victim of conspiracy and that our government knows more than it has been willing to reveal. What compels the government to continue to withhold the truth?

Betrayal in Dallas proves that President Lyndon Johnson and U.S. Attorney General Robert F. Kennedy knew from the beginning who the perpetrators of the crime were but prevented the Justice Department from pursuing prosecutions. Johnson did this to protect himself from disgrace and prosecution. RFK went along to protect his brother's secrets.

Johnson's and Kennedy's interests overrode the public's right to the truth in a time of national crisis. The Justice Department served their interest, as it does today, in preventing resolution of this matter.

But with the recent death of Senator Ted Kennedy (whom I made aware of the contents of this book) and the death of Johnson's protective widow, Claudia "Lady Bird" Johnson, the time has come for truth.

Betrayal in Dallas offers reconciliation between a people and its government and an opportunity for renewal of country and sense of purpose. In these troubled times, nothing less than the truth can clear the way forward.

Mark North
October 2010

CONTENTS

INTRODUCTION

DALLAS, TEXAS: NOVEMBER 22, 1963. President Kennedy lay dead. Vice President Lyndon Johnson, saved from imminent political ruin and imprisonment by the gangland-style execution, was both relieved and empowered. His close alliance with Dallas district attorney Henry Wade and the local Civello mob had paid off.

Within hours of JFK's death, Johnson would move to neutralize JFK's brother, U.S. Attorney General Robert Kennedy, nemesis of Civello's Pearl Street Mafia.[1] As soon as Johnson was on board *Air Force One* at the Dallas airport, he ordered that U.S. District Court Judge Sarah Hughes (whom LBJ had placed on the federal bench) be brought to the plane for the swearing-in ceremony.

At that moment, Hughes was the presiding judge in RFK's investigation and prosecution of the Dallas Mafia's illegal and highly lucrative bookmaking operation, *U.S. v. John Eli Stone, et al.* The U.S. attorney to Dallas, Harold Barefoot Sanders (handpicked by Johnson), like Hughes, had been bitterly opposed to Kennedy's attempt to destroy Stone's multimillion dollar gambling operation. But their hands had been tied by Kennedy's Organized Crime Task Force, which controlled

1. The first federal narcotics raids on the Dallas Mafia originated in the Pearl Street Market District. I coined the name *Pearl Street Mafia* to refer to the Civello crime family throughout this book.

the prosecution. Kennedy's people knew it would destroy the Civello mob by depriving it of most of its income.

The swearing-in ceremony, with a blood-splattered Jackie Kennedy standing at Johnson's side and Judge Hughes administering the oath of office, was a masterful demonstration of power. After the ceremony, to the relief of the Civello mob, LBJ had Sanders and Hughes stop RFK's prosecution of the Stone defendants. With Johnson's cronies now in control, the Justice Department knew their efforts would not succeed. LBJ had fulfilled his part of the bargain.

The Stone prosecution, temporarily halted by Hughes and Sanders until the "lone nut" cover story could be sold to the public, would have to be hidden from the American people over the long term, and local mobsters like Joe Ianni and Jack Ruby would have to be protected. But with the fanatically loyal Henry Wade in LBJ's pocket, there was little chance of failure. Over the years, Wade had worked closely with Johnson to help him obtain the presidency. His dream had now been realized. Judge Sarah Hughes was a longtime ally of the local Italian community and, like Wade, had turned a blind eye to the criminal activities of the Pearl Street Mafia.

There was little to fear from federal investigation. The most powerful agency in Washington DC, the Federal Bureau of Investigation (FBI), was controlled by Johnson's longtime confidant and neighbor, John Edgar Hoover. Like the Dallas Mafia, Hoover had been saved from ruin by Kennedy's murder. The Kennedy brothers had been planning his removal from the FBI directorship for years, and it would have been accomplished before the end of JFK's first term in office. With Johnson's executive order, Hoover would maintain his grip on power for another decade. His agency would prevent any effort to get at the truth behind JFK's execution.

Why another book on President Kennedy's assassination? Because the new evidence revealed in this book proves to a legal certainty everything you have just read. It is too late to prosecute JFK's murderers, but it is never too late for the truth. History has caught up with Lyndon Johnson, J. Edgar Hoover, and the Dallas Mafia.

1

THE ROAD TO TRUTH

When you know the truth, the truth makes you a soldier.

—Gandhi

I BEGAN MY INVESTIGATION into the mystery surrounding the murder of President Kennedy thirty years ago, after viewing the then-suppressed Zapruder film, which graphically details his death. As a historian and former Texas attorney, I came to realize that the Warren Report was mere subterfuge, designed to confuse the American people while allowing the Justice Department to avoid investigation and prosecution of those responsible.

To what purpose? Why allow the conspirators to go unpunished? And in the face of obvious conspiracy, why sacrifice governmental credibility to such an extreme degree?

Only after the deaths of President Lyndon Johnson, FBI Director J. Edgar Hoover, and U.S. Attorney General Robert Kennedy was Congress able to reexamine JFK's death. In 1979, the U.S. House Select Committee on Assassinations (HSCA) formally reversed the conclusion of the Warren Commission by admitting that Kennedy had been killed by conspiracy. Chief counsel to the HSCA Robert Blakey (a former U.S. attorney in the Organized Crime Division) stated publicly that "organized crime was behind the plot to kill John F. Kennedy."[1] Despite this, the Justice Department refused to proceed with investigation and prosecution. Portions of the HSCA's findings were classified and kept from the people.[2]

In 1991, my first book, *Act of Treason: The Role of J. Edgar Hoover in the Assassination of President Kennedy,* was published and became highly controversial. I was assailed by former FBI agents, the media, and elements within the research community. But my effort made two facts undeniable: Hoover had learned of death threats against JFK before the fact and withheld them from the Secret Service, and he was a longtime political confidant of Vice President Lyndon Johnson.

In 1992, Congress passed the Assassination Materials Disclosure Act. But once again, the Justice Department refused to move forward with the new evidence. Clearly, the Justice Department is paralyzed on the issue of truth in JFK's murder.

I face no such constraint. After years of investigation, I have discovered why JFK was murdered and why the Justice Department refused to pursue the killers. The evidence contained in this book will force the hand of that department by making public what they will not. The contents of secret Justice Department tapings of Mob conversations, recorded by RFK's people in Dallas in the months leading up to Kennedy's murder, should be released by the Justice Department. The tapes include incriminating conversations between Jack Ruby and other mobsters about to be prosecuted by RFK.[3] The people responsible for JFK's murder will become known for the first time.

A classified FBI report from the Dallas special agent in charge (SAC) to Director Hoover, which I obtained via the Freedom of Information Act (FOIA), reveals that by late 1961, RFK had set in motion a plan to destroy the Dallas Mafia. It reads in part,

> The Italians in Dallas were extremely "jumpy" due to the recent visit to Dallas of Attorney General ROBERT KENNEDY. The source stated that the Attorney General was supposed to have asked questions concerning Italians in Dallas and these Italians were convinced that the Government was conducting an intensive investigation into their activities and finances.[4]

RFK's covert operation was intended not only to break the Italian Mafia's Dallas operation, but also to make public their corruption of Vice President Lyndon Johnson, whom the Kennedys hated. Put to the wall by RFK, Johnson and the Dallas Mafia would stand or fall together.

2

UNHOLY ALLIANCE

Our opponents are ruthless, vicious, and resourceful. They will use every weapon at their command.

—U.S. Attorney General Robert Kennedy
Senate hearings on organized crime, June 6, 1961

BY THE TIME Lyndon Johnson made his second run for the U.S. Senate in 1948, the Dallas Mafia had become a powerful, corrupting force in the state of Texas. *The Dallas Morning News,* concluding Johnson would only worsen the epidemic of crime, warned that he epitomized the "lowest level in character and intelligence."[1]

In the run-up to the fall election, Johnson scrambled for every vote he could get. He was unpopular in conservative Dallas and sought out any faction he thought he could persuade to vote for him. This included the Italian-American community and their Mafia-controlled social organization known as the Anonymous Club (later called Zuroma Club). The club meetings (held in a rented house) were purportedly a weekly gathering of friends for a richly catered, traditional Italian dinner followed by drinks, cigars, and cards. The card games often involved a "heavy hand of poker" with Joe Civello and his associates. In effect, the Anonymous Club (consisting of twenty-five members) operated a gambling house under Texas state law. It was never raided because many Dallas-area law enforcement officials regularly appeared as guests.[2]

Lyndon Johnson's strongest Dallas supporter was an Italian-American activist named Pete Tamburo. Tamburo was a frequent guest and honorary member of the Anonymous Club. During the fall 1948 campaign swings through Dallas, Johnson undoubtedly was taken to the club as Tamburo's guest.[3] There, over whiskey and cigars, LBJ was introduced to members like the Dallas mob boss, Joe Civello. In his determination to win the Texas senate seat, Johnson proved himself willing to seek out every potential supporter, no matter who they were.

Pulitzer Prize–winning author Robert Caro, in *Means of Ascent*, volume 2 in his landmark Johnson biography, *The Years of Lyndon Johnson,* saw LBJ for what he became in his quest for power. In essence, Johnson was a "manipulator, a schemer . . . unprincipled and unscrupulous." A man without conscience.

LBJ's subsequent theft of the Senate seat through electoral fraud brought about public demand for federal investigation by the FBI. But Johnson was not worried. He and FBI Director J. Edgar Hoover had been close friends since the early Depression, practically next-door neighbors for many years. They dined together in the evenings and walked their dogs in a nearby Washington park.[4]

LBJ also understood everything that was going on inside Hoover's house. In a time when gay men were being ousted from public service, he had learned that Hoover and his aide Clyde Tolson were lovers. Johnson's secretary, Walter Jenkins, was also homosexual. Hoover knew this and protected Johnson by hiding Jenkins's arrests and private life from the public.[5] One hand washed the other, so to speak.

Because of their symbiotic relationship, Hoover had nothing to gain by investigating LBJ for voter fraud. A few FBI agents appeared in South Texas, but nothing came of it. When pressed, Hoover avoided the media over the issue of Johnson's electoral fraud by feigning bronchial pneumonia.[6] Behind the scenes, Hoover was quick to congratulate Johnson on his illegal seizure of power.

U.S. Attorney General Tom Clark, a former Dallas assistant DA, had developed a highly corrupt relationship with the Mafia. He derailed government efforts to deport them on a mass scale at the close of WWII. Johnson had helped Clark gain employment with the

Justice Department in 1937. As they were close friends, the attorney general simply went through the motions.[7]

Extremely ambitious, Johnson, after a little over a year in office, had become Senate Majority Whip. Early in the Korean War, as congressional efforts to deport Italian mobsters intensified, Johnson sought a fivefold increase in allowable numbers of aliens in the military, providing safe harbor against the Immigration and Naturalization Service (INS).[8] Johnson made Senate minority leader by 1953, the youngest in fifty years.

When the McCarran Act passed that year, the INS resumed its efforts to deport a powerful Dallas mafioso, Frank Ianni, based on his heroin trafficking convictions. Supposedly, only an act of Congress (i.e., private bill) could prevent his deportation. Although none came, Ianni was still spared. I filed a demand under the Freedom of Information Act to obtain Ianni's INS file, only to learn it had been destroyed.[9] Who intervened?

In a time when many mafiosi around the United States were turning to their elected representatives to save them from deportation, Senator Johnson was the logical choice. Known for his corruption and sympathies toward the Dallas mob (and the Anonymous/Zuroma Club), Johnson was recruited to stop the INS action against Ianni through Tom Clark's brother Robert. Bob Clark worked closely with Dallas mob attorneys Maury Hughes and Angelo Piranio. Bob's brother Tom Clark had also worked closely with Angelo Piranio, who had appeared with Ianni at the INS deportation hearings. Another Dallas mobster, convicted murderer Sam Savalli, had also sought out Johnson for help against the INS.[10] Senator Johnson stepped in to act privately as a sponsor, a character witness, in the mobsters' efforts to stop INS proceedings. The process in Ianni's case (and probably Savalli's) was known as an Application for Suspension of Deportation. It got the job done because neither man was deported. Both died years later in Dallas.[11]

Johnson's wife, Lady Bird, a former Dallasite named Claudia Alta Taylor, was, like her husband, an ardent Italophile. Prior to her marriage to LBJ, she had attended the University of Texas at Austin simultaneously with Frank Ianni's son Joe. They lived near each other off campus, and both were registered in the college of arts. Given the small size of the university at the time, they in all likelihood knew each other. Contrary to the public's perception of Lady Bird as a mere wallflower, she was an aggressive, ambitious woman who gravitated to power and partnered with LBJ to seize every opportunity. It was she who persuaded Johnson to purchase their home across the street from Hoover's house when they moved to Washington DC.[12]

Senate Majority leader by mid-decade, LBJ was recognized as the dominant force in Congress. He used his power in the Senate to promote the Italian population in Dallas by working to eliminate the hated quota system used by the INS to limit immigration.[13]

In the fall of 1959, Johnson arranged a private meeting at his ranch with Hoover and began working behind the scenes in the Senate for the purpose of seizing the party nomination for president.[14] Powerful Dallas officials like Judge Sarah Hughes, an avid gambler and favorite of the Italian community, and District Attorney Henry Wade, threw their weight behind LBJ.[15]

Because Wade was a conservative, the public knew little of his association with Johnson. But over the years, beginning with the tainted Senate election, they grew close, as evidenced by the dozens of personal letters between the two.[16] (These letters are reproduced in the Exhibits section of this book.) As they liked to put it, they were 100 percent for each other. His first year as district attorney, Wade began making trips to Washington, where he met privately with LBJ and attended political parties at his house.[17] With Hoover virtually across the street and a regular in the Johnson home, and Wade's status as a former FBI agent, the DA and the FBI director surely knew each other personally.

Wade closely monitored the Dallas political situation for Johnson from 1948 onward. He also traveled to other parts of the state in Johnson's behalf—conducting surveillance on political opponents. As early as 1955, he began urging LBJ to run for the presidency.[18]

When Wade ran for U.S. representative, Johnson wrote, "Let me know what you want or need from me. . . . I'm behind you in just about anything you undertake to do and I hope you know it."[19] Wade lost the election but kept his ambition.

In a 1959 letter, Wade made the decision to tie his political future to Johnson's. He wrote, "I have thought some about running for

Attorney General of the State next year, but now feel that I will remain here and do what I can in your behalf towards your nomination and whatever assistance I could be in your election. If there is anything that you would like for me to do, please call me. Your devoted friend."[20]

The district attorney gave Johnson his all in the presidential campaign and attended the Democratic convention in Los Angeles. When LBJ lost the party nomination to JFK, Johnson thanked an embittered Wade for his dedication, telling him, "I am deeply grateful to you for all your help and support. It is most rewarding for a man in public life to be able to count on friends like you."[21]

The Pearl Street Mafia counted on Wade as well. In early May 1951, the Dallas Police Department's vice squad staged a highly successful surprise raid on the Civello mob's primary bookmaking operation. Arrested were John Eli Stone, Isadore Miller, and Louie Ferrantello, close criminal associates of Jack Ruby. Ruby was not arrested in the raid, but the others were caught red-handed. Within a few weeks, the state of Texas had Ferrantello appear before its then-ongoing investigation into organized crime activity in Texas. Rather than testify, he took the Fifth Amendment over one hundred times and was cited for contempt of the legislature. One of LBJ's personal attorneys, Everett Looney (a man who had played a key role in Johnson's theft of the 1948 U.S. Senate election), came to Ferrantello's defense, appealing the contempt ruling.[22] It was a point not missed by Jack Ruby.

Ruby, by then a low-level bookmaker in the Civello mob, had come to Dallas in the latter 1940s from Chicago, where he had been a functionary in that city's organized crime operations. Ruby had undoubtedly been drawn to Dallas by LBJ's cohort Tom Clark. The Chicago thug had watched as Clark (a powerful and corrupt figure in the Truman administration's Department of Justice) had arranged the early prison release of several influential Chicago mafiosi. Once in Dallas, Ruby quickly perceived that the path to power and money lay in allying himself with the Pearl Street Mafia. In his association with Ferrantello, he became part of the Civello mob's bookmaking operation. He lost no time in compromising area law enforcement and, like other local mafiosi, avoided effective prosecution.

Despite the Dallas PD's arrest of Ferrantello, DA Wade failed to seize the opportunity handed him by the police department to destroy the Dallas Mafia's bookmaking operation. Stone and the others remained in business and developed the largest bookmaking operation in Dallas by the end of the decade.

Local Mafia boss Joe Civello's gambling lieutenant Joe Ianni also benefitted directly. Several months after the Stone raid, Wade allowed Ianni to avoid a murder prosecution for beating a local man to death in front of witnesses with a wooden club.[23] Thereafter, during the 1950s, the district attorney openly attended the Mob's Anonymous/Zuroma Club, ignoring the exponential growth of illegal syndicate gambling and narcotics trafficking in his city.[24]

Over the years, the populace of Dallas was traumatized by the endless procession of Mafia murders, bombings, and beatings. The sheer savagery of the violence reveals much.

> [He] . . . was found dead, his throat slashed ear to ear, his face bloody and battered from the jagged edge of a broken liquor bottle.
>
> [Another] . . . was riddled with bullets from two guns. All . . . were fired at close range. Six were .45 caliber, piercing the left side. A .38 caliber . . . bullet pierced the right side, passing through the body and embedding in the heart.
>
> [One man] had been shot in the chest and stabbed in the back. His throat was slashed on both sides, and the back of his head was crushed. . . . His hands were cut as though he had tried to grab his assailant's slashing knife. Part of one ear was cut away and there were many cuts and bruises on other parts of his body.
>
> The death car . . . was stripped to the bare wheels and chassis by the force of the blast. [The driver] was dismembered . . . and her torso hurled about ten feet into the front yard of the couple's home.
>
> A nitroglycerine bomb exploded when [he] pressed the starter button, killing him instantly. His 25-year-old wife, whose child would have been born within a week, was dead on arrival at a

> hospital. . . . It left their automobile a smoldering hulk and blew off [his] head.
>
> A young, female police narcotics informant's "body was found in a lake near Fort Worth, wrapped in chains and anchored with concrete." . . . Another was found "beaten and drowned in a roadside ditch."
>
> [A] Dallas narcotics hearing . . . backfired . . . after the . . . witness was discovered dead in a watery . . . ditch. . . . [He] had been brutally beaten with resultant skull and facial bone fractures.
>
> A bloodstained Cadillac . . . was found . . . in northwest Dallas County. . . . The car was locked, with the key in the ignition, and blood was oozing from the doors.[25]

In Johnson and Wade, the Civello mob found unholy alliance, a powerful combine that could only be broken by federal intervention.

3

THE BATTLE BEGINS

> [S]mashing the mob . . . "will get the highest, repeat, the highest priority after the inauguration."
>
> —John F. Kennedy, 1960

> [H]oodlums buy off the judge, they buy off the prosecutor, they buy off the sheriff.
>
> —McClellan Committee, 1961

BY THE TIME U.S. Attorney General Robert Kennedy arrived in Dallas, Texas, in mid-November of 1961 to launch the Justice Department's Organized Crime Task Force investigation of the Civello mob, he already had Louisiana Mafia boss Carlos Marcello (of Sicilian origin) under federal indictment.[1]

RFK believed that Lyndon Johnson was simply another corrupt politician—a man who had come from humble beginnings in small-town Texas and whose only motivation was the quest for power and the money it brought him. Under LBJ's ally, local district attorney Henry Wade—a street-savvy, longtime Dallasite—the Mafia's drug operations in the Southwest had mushroomed.[2] Though RFK knew little more, he knew enough to hold both men in contempt.

Robert Kennedy, while serving as counsel to the U.S. Senate's McClellan Committee in the late 1950s, had attempted to investigate the Mafia's operations in the state of Texas and Louisiana. He had reviewed the U.S. Senate's earlier Daniel Report about the Mob's narcotics trafficking operations along the Mexican border and the Gulf Coast. He had understood that Price Daniel, junior U.S. Texas senator to Majority Leader Johnson, simply took orders from LBJ. Kennedy had watched as Daniel made a mockery of the federal government's attempt to expose Civello's narcotics operation in Texas.[3]

Though it had been withheld from Daniel's final report, Kennedy had the file on a key Corsican heroin trafficker, Antoine D'Agostino. The Mob pusher had been seized by authorities in Mexico and flown to San Antonio, Texas. Presumably for purposes of his testimony at the hearings, the Federal Bureau of Narcotics (FBN) then transferred him to Austin where he was incarcerated in the jail only blocks from Daniel's committee (fellow trafficker and countryman Paul Mondoloni had escaped Mexican authorities and fled to Cuba). A French national, D'Agostino was a major supplier to the New York Mafia. The smuggler had coordinated shipments from illicit factories in France to Mexico and then on to the United States since the early 1950s, along with Paul Mondoloni. Mondoloni had evidently been arrested in Texas in 1953 but was somehow able to gain quick release and return to Mexico. The FBN's director had told Daniel during the initial Washington DC hearings that D'Agostino was a highly important figure. Another official had said the trafficker was "of first importance."[4] Despite this knowledge, Daniel ignored the opportunity to bring D'Agostino to the televised hearings and expose the workings of the Civello mob's heroin operation. Daniel, undoubtedly at LBJ's directive, waited until after the Texas hearings had ended to interview D'Agostino—in the Austin jail. That interview was excluded from the committee's report.[5]

From a variety of federal investigative sources, RFK knew that DA Henry Wade (a graduate of the University of Texas law school, like LBJ's underlings John Connally and Barefoot Sanders) had turned a blind eye to the Civello mob's narcotics operation over the last decade. The numbers were staggering. FBN reports had told Kennedy that almost 90 percent of the nation's illicit drug traffic flowed from Texas. As federal officials put it, Dallas was "alive with narcotics."[6] The Pearl Street Mafia, through its international suppliers, was running a million-dollar-a-month business.[7]

While serving on the McClellan Committee, Kennedy had learned that the Texas Civello mob and Louisiana's Carlos Marcello crime family operated in concert. Joe Civello, born and raised in Louisiana but now the head of the Dallas Mafia, was placed near the top of the committee's list of New Orleans–area mafiosi. RFK had subpoenaed Marcello and confronted him with the obvious, asking, "Are you an associate of Joseph Civello of Dallas?" Marcello took the Fifth Amendment against self-incrimination rather than answer.[8]

Kennedy, now the U.S. attorney general and armed with the knowledge that Civello and Marcello coordinated their operations, understood that ultimately, the Mob-corrupted Wade would have to go. But it would be much more difficult than he imagined. RFK did not grasp the depth and breadth of the DA's collusion with the Dallas Mafia. Over the years, Wade had been meeting privately with Civello, convicted killers, and heroin traffickers at the local Mob-dominated Italian-American Anonymous/Zuroma Club. Other officials were also guests of this club, including the county sheriff, members of the judiciary, and Johnson's handpicked, newly appointed assistant U.S. attorney to Dallas, Barefoot Sanders.[9] It was Sanders who met RFK at the Dallas airport upon his arrival and controlled his itinerary while in the city.

Johnson, through political ally J. Edgar Hoover, had gained detailed knowledge of Wade's criminal associations. FBI Director Hoover, an icon to Dallasites, maintained his status by carefully monitoring the private lives of former FBI agents such as Wade and avoiding any public association with them.[10] Through the weekly publication of an obscure Dallas-area Italian-American newsletter, *The Texas Tribune*, the FBI director had learned of Wade's involvement with Civello.[11]

By the time RFK came to Dallas, the situation had become obvious. Even the police department was publicly condemning Wade for his reckless track record of plea bargaining, suspended sentences, and failed grand jury proceedings.[12]

Despite this history, Wade had big plans. Through LBJ's new status as vice president, the DA sought a North Texas federal judgeship but lost out to local judge Sarah Hughes, a favorite with local Italians and a supporter of illegal gambling.[13] LBJ had arranged Hughes's new federal position, as he had Barefoot Sanders, in exchange for absolute loyalty.

Kennedy could not have known that LBJ had assisted Civello's cohorts during the 1950s, helping them avoid deportation under anti–organized crime drives instituted by President Eisenhower.[14] These were among the same men who frequented the Anonymous/Zuroma Club and dined with Henry Wade—men like Sam Savalli and Frank Ianni.

Robert Kennedy understood that the Civello mob's narcotics operation was funded by local illegal gambling. In Dallas, the money flow generated by the Texas oil boom ran into the billions. Gambling of every sort was made available in the city—and ignored by the district attorney. "When people want gambling ended, it can be ended," Wade said.[15] For the local populace, it was the best of both worlds.

RFK knew that by focusing the Organized Crime Task Force on Civello's gambling machine, run by Joe Ianni, he could disrupt the flow of revenue to the Civello mob. But he also knew that because of the popularity of gambling in Dallas, he had little chance of getting indictments with a locally impaneled grand jury. A small conservative town elsewhere in northern Texas would have to be used to prosecute the Dallas Mafia.

Though Kennedy did not know it, the Dallas police, a decade earlier, had arrested Joe Ianni for murder, only to watch Wade allow him to avoid prosecution.[16] From that time on, Ianni had operated with impunity. Within the local Italian community, he was both feared and respected.

Most Dallas gambling houses offered offtrack betting and were subscribers to the Civello mob's wire service, which delivered horse race and other sporting event results.[17] In turn, local bookmakers were required to pay a percentage of their profits to Civello's gambling lieutenant, Joe Ianni. Civello kept a portion of the take, forwarding the rest to mobsters at the national level.

When a confident RFK came to Dallas, he had already ordered the INS to put in motion a plan to deport Joe Ianni.[18] An investigation by the Internal Revenue Service (IRS) involving gambling taxes was also taking shape.[19] A part of President Kennedy's overall plan to exterminate the Mafia, this multiagency approach was unprecedented. What JFK understood was that Mob control was based upon money and its power to corrupt local law enforcement and elected representatives. The Kennedy brothers were prepared to go the distance.

Joe Civello's arrest and prosecution in Apalachin, New York, in the late 1950s had revealed the frightening dimensions of the epidemic of crime created by him and his Mob associates. National media interests labeled him an "anonymous officer . . . of an invisible government."[20] According to the FBN, Ianni and Carlos Marcello were like "corporation executives." The low-profile Civello fit the classic description of Mob boss, a "wine and cheese merchant" known to live quietly.[21] Well mannered, neatly groomed, and tight lipped, he lived in a small unassuming duplex (the other side of the duplex was shared with brother-in-law and number-two man in the Pearl Street Mafia Ross Musso) in a decidedly middle-class neighborhood in West Dallas. But like his peers, he traveled regularly to New York, Chicago, and Louisiana. There was an extensive history of phone calls to Marcello, who was, in the New Orleans style, more flamboyant but equally adept at appearing middle class.[22]

RFK remained in Dallas less than twenty-four hours. But while there, he briefed Barefoot Sanders about his plan to destroy Joe Civello's Pearl Street Mafia. Sanders, a former Texas legislator and a wily opportunist, wasted little time after the attorney general flew back to Washington DC. Within a few days, he had alerted Civello, possibly through his lieutenant Phil Bosco, to the Kennedy administration's plan. Powerless to stop the governmental onslaught, the mafiosi, and Sanders, could only watch as Robert Kennedy's war against the Mafia spread nationwide.

4

A WAR OF EXTERMINATION

In war there is no prize for the runner-up.

—General Omar Bradley

SHORTLY AFTER BEING appointed attorney general, RFK moved against the Mafia with new legislation. Said the *New York Times*, "The basic new technique Kennedy is using is to pick out . . . the most important criminals in the country—and throw against them the full weight of the many government agencies with investigative powers."[1]

Kennedy introduced eight bills. Several had been introduced before, but under Senate Majority Leader Lyndon Johnson and House Speaker Sam Taliaferro Rayburn of Texas (a confirmed bachelor like J. Edgar Hoover and intensely devoted mentor of LBJ), the legislation had always died in Congress. When LBJ later left Congress to seize the vice presidential spot, all the bills passed quickly in the Senate, with only three stalling in the House.[2]

Of the first four bills passed, *Interstate Travel* "made it a crime to travel or use any facilities in interstate commerce . . . to further an illegal gambling [or] narcotics . . . business."[3] Government analysts quickly labeled it "a frontal attack on organized racketeering" designed primarily to enable the prosecution of anyone using telephone lines to violate antigambling statutes.[4]

Transmission of wagering information "made it a crime for anyone in the business of betting to knowingly use a wire communication facility to transmit in interstate commerce any bets . . . or . . . collect money or credit as a result of bets."[5] This bill's passage would be, said Kennedy, "a mortal blow to their operation."[6] Analysts agreed, concluding it "would strike at the heart of organized betting on races and other sports."[7]

Transportation of wagering paraphernalia "made it a crime to knowingly . . . send in interstate commerce, or . . . in the mail within a state, any records, paraphernalia . . . or other devices used or to be used in bookmaking, wagering pools, or numbers games."[8] By making it a crime to ship such goods, a critical tool would be taken away from bookies.[9]

The last bill broadened the Fugitive Felon Act to incorporate all felonies.[10] Mafiosi fleeing across state lines to avoid prosecution for even minor offenses would now be pursued by federal authorities. The legislation was signed into law by President Kennedy in September, barely eight months into his administration.

Although the new legislation was the major accelerant in the war on the Mafia, RFK had struck the first blow against the Marcello machine six months earlier when New Orleans officials, emboldened by his tough rhetoric, moved against the mafioso. In March, criminal complaints were filed against Marcello and a lieutenant "for allowing prostitution on the premises" of their motels.[11]

The first week in April of 1961, Robert Kennedy did what no one thought possible when he had Marcello deported to Guatemala. Without warning, INS officials in New Orleans had seized the gangster, driven him to a waiting plane, and flown him out of the country.[12]

Interviewed in Guatemala City, a furious Marcello railed about the intensity of the government's effort behind his deportation: "You would have thought it was the President coming in instead of me going out."[13] A few days later, the IRS filed tax evasion liens against Marcello's holdings, totaling close to a million dollars. All would be sold if he did not pay up.[14] The same day, the president of Jefferson Parish, Marcello's home turf, called for a war on syndicate gamblers. Bookmakers were, for the first time, to be prosecuted.[15] In the days that followed, the IRS struck again, attaching liens to properties in other parishes.[16] Marcello's bank accounts were frozen. The mobster's attorneys complained that family members were "prevented from utilizing funds . . . for their own support and the support of their children, in . . . purchasing the necessities of life."[17]

In Guatemala City, officials came to the conclusion that Marcello had entered the country illegally, making him subject to prosecution there: "Outwardly calm, Marcello betrayed his nervousness by asking a newsman whether Guatemala 'allowed bond' if he were to be jailed."[18] His fears were justified. The next day, in front of his wife and daughter, who had flown in from New Orleans, he was arrested and thrown into the city jail.[19] A few days later, he was returned to his hotel room under house arrest. At that point, he attempted to flee the country with his family by plane but was refused a ticket. Marcello's family, separated from him by the authorities, was ordered out of Guatemala.[20] Marcello and his attorney were then seized by police, taken to the border of El Salvador, and dumped in the jungle. The two set out on a grueling seventeen-mile march. In the process of escaping local bandits that they encountered during this time, the middle-aged mobster at one point collapsed from exhaustion, breaking two ribs.[21]

In the United States, his Washington attorneys fared no better when a three-judge federal court upheld his deportation. The ruling was then affirmed.[22] The mafioso's associates realized that legal reentry was impossible, and Carlos Marcello was smuggled back into the country, where he surfaced in Louisiana in early June.[23] Refusing his attorneys' motion to prevent plans to deport him yet again, the district court judge said, "He is a convicted felon, . . . who deserves little, if any, sympathy from anyone."[24] The attorneys arranged for him to surrender in New Orleans, where he was incarcerated without bail in the parish prison and charged with illegal reentry.[25]

Just after the presidential election, New Orleans's *Times-Picayune* carried a letter that its editor sent to AG Kennedy, strongly urging him to deport Marcello. When RFK did deport him, the paper heaped praise upon him. RFK responded in a public statement, "[I am] very happy that . . . Marcello is no longer with us."[26] After the mafioso reentered the country, the paper again rallied behind the AG, describing the mafioso as the "head of . . . narcotics traffic in the South."[27]

Marcello's fear was heightened just days after being charged when the Justice Department announced that it had found another country that would accept him. In preparation for this transfer, he was taken from the jail by immigration authorities and flown to South Texas, where he was held in the alien detention center, cut off from family and counsel.[28] In Washington, his lead attorney, Jack Wasserman, denounced the move before the Board of Immigration Appeals in a tirade against President Kennedy and his brother. A bitter Wasserman declared, "It is persecution, revenge and blind justice. It is punishment without a trial by bureaucratic tyranny."[29] The third week in June, the mobster secured his release on bond and returned to New Orleans. There, he accused the administration of "prejudice, harassment . . . and persecution."[30]

The day before Marcello entered a plea of "not guilty" to the charge of illegal reentry, Robert Kennedy struck again with sweeping arrests of thirteen key operators in Marcello's bookmaking apparatus. These men coordinated the wire service scheme from places as far away as New York and Florida. The group was charged with "fraud by wire and conspiracy to defraud the United States."[31] A nationwide criminal enterprise, "the system . . . linked 20 cities by telephone, stretching from coast to coast and from Chicago to New Orleans."[32] In DC, a jubilant Robert Kennedy called it "the first breakthrough against organized gambling."[33]

The next blow came in early July when Carlos Marcello was subpoenaed to appear before Senator McClellan's Permanent Subcommittee on Investigations in Washington.[34] In August, a New Orleans grand jury began a gambling investigation in Marcello's home parish. Soon thereafter, the local crime commission called for war by the DA's office against Marcello's policy operations.[35]

A primary focus of McClellan's committee was Marcello's Nola Printing Company, which was the southern end of the Mafia's Chicago bookmaking wire.[36] Through interlinking wire services around the nation, Nola was able to obtain race results from as far away as Montreal, Canada. For a percentage, it supplied race results to Mob operations in southern Texas.[37] Disruption of the wire service shut off a major source of income, as Nola was also the dominant supplier of gambling paraphernalia.[38]

The president of Marcello's parish testified before the McClellan Committee, openly denouncing the Mafia crime family and local law enforcement: "I would like to see if the federal government can give us some help, since we are getting none from the sheriff or the state."[39]

The director of the local crime commission bluntly described Marcello as "a thug, holdup man and narcotics trafficker."[40] His previous arrests had included "assault with intent to kill a New Orleans police officer."[41]

Finally, in early September of 1961, Marcello and Wasserman appeared before the McClellan Committee—but only under threat of contempt. Challenging the government's right to even question him, Marcello took the Fifth over sixty times.[42]

Political powers in Dallas carefully followed Kennedy's assault on Marcello over the course of 1961. When RFK had testified before the McClellan Committee in May, he discussed a Mafia-related Texas gambling incident that occurred two years earlier. The incident should have triggered widespread media reaction in Dallas, but did not. RFK stated, "When a Braniff airplane crashed at Buffalo, Texas, . . . a collection man for a prime suspect of the Kefauver investigation, was killed. The . . . man was en route to New York with his boss's share of profits—an extremely large amount of money—from gambling operations in Texas."[43] The "collection man . . . was carrying a bag containing $100,000 which represented [that week's] collections from both Dallas and Houston." [44]

The findings of a Texas state investigation, the Murray Committee, were also brought up by RFK during testimony. Death threats had been made to committee informants in southern Texas. One city manager had been warned anonymously that if he cooperated, "someone was going to throw acid in his daughter's face."[45] Others had refused to inform, stating as a common reason, "I don't want to wind up in the canal."[46] It was a well-founded fear. According to the committee's report, "Stories of beatings, brutalities, terror and sadism were told."[47]

But some Texas officials were furious over the exposé. One said, "I told the Committee . . . that I shot some dice and played some poker when I wanted to, . . . something that is done all over the State

. . . when peace officers get together and have a convention . . . or anything like that. . . . I've seen Legislators do that, everyone else, in the Department of Public Safety, FBI . . . , deputy sheriffs, and policemen."[48] Said another, "It goes on in every big city in Texas."[49] Critiques of Texas, in fact, described Dallas's obsession with gambling as "almost a way of life."[50]

In reference to the Mafia in Dallas, one angry sheriff said, "There, people are killed like we used to kill chickens down on the farm. . . . [Y]ou have gang killings and you have 20 unsolved murders."[51]

Over the course of 1961, there had been indications that Mob operations in Dallas were expanding. Aside from the exponential growth in narcotics-related property crime, there were reports that drug traffic was growing in outlying areas.[52] In February, the Dallas PD broke up a policy game that was running citywide, only to see nearly all those arrested receive suspended sentences.[53]

The day before President Kennedy signed the anti-Mafia legislation in September 1961, *The Dallas Morning News* attacked the move. "It means a constant increase in federal power. FBI Director J. Edgar Hoover steadfastly has resisted this power. He insists that control of most crimes remains the job of local . . . law enforcement authority."[54]

In Louisiana, Marcello reeled under the newly legislated power of RFK. The New Orleans press reported, "The bookies . . . were walking around . . . shaking their heads, wondering what they were going to do. [A]ll of them agreed that booking bets without wire service was about on par with selling shoes without soles."[55] Simultaneously, the New Orleans Crime Commission published a list of Marcello-controlled gambling houses, including street addresses, and provided copies to the county grand jury, DA, and parish president.[56] Echoing President Kennedy, AG Robert Kennedy, in a Chicago speech, branded Marcello and Civello a "malignant threat" to society.[57]

In obvious contempt for Marcello, the very day JFK signed the new anti-Mob legislation, the New Orleans federal court denied the mafioso's motion for dismissal of the illegal reentry indictment.[58] Carlos Marcello's attorneys responded with a bitter attack, terming his deportation order meaningless. The mafioso, they defiantly stated, was entitled to "self help."[59] In the weeks that followed, the attorneys launched an appellate assault upon the INS. The agency was dismissed by the lawyers as a criminal operation. The New Orleans press described the appeal "as bitter a document that has been filed against . . . the government."[60] The hearing that followed, "a three hour argument marked with sharp exchanges," was stopped "four or five [times] to call a halt to the clashing attorneys."[61] Wasserman denounced the INS as "two faced and double crossing," its actions "the darkest and foulest chapter in deportation history."[62] He then tried to criminalize the Kennedy administration, labeling it through its actions "guilty."[63]

If Marcello's attorneys thought the counterattack against the INS was going to prove his salvation, they were dead wrong. Several days after the hearing, the New Orleans federal grand jury handed down two more indictments, for perjury and conspiring to defraud the United States. A warrant for Marcello's arrest was issued.[64] Soon after, the INS appeals board in DC upheld the pending deportation order.[65]

Robert Kennedy summarized the damage done to Marcello and Civello in 1961 with enthusiastic confidence in a special year-end task force report to the President. Marcello's Nola Printing Company had been closed down. In a reference aimed at Dallas and its fixation with wagering, he proclaimed that football gaming had dropped sharply. Racketeers were shifting to Canada. Montreal, with its large Italian and French communities, was becoming a Mob-infested city. Robert Kennedy described administration efforts against the hard narcotics trade as "the deepest penetration the federal government has ever made in the illegal international traffic of drugs."[66]

The FBN agreed, announcing that several major narcotic conspiracy investigations were successfully conducted with police authorities of Canada, Italy, France, and Mexico.[67] In December of that year, some eleven members of one large operation were convicted.[68] In the American Southwest, it was announced that Texas had added new major penalty provisions to its anti-narcotic laws.[69]

The year 1961 was one of triumph for the Kennedy administration in its war on organized crime. In an ominous reference to officials like Lyndon Johnson and Henry Wade, Attorney General Kennedy warned publicly, "Those who ally themselves with big crime are a disgrace to the country."[70]

5

HE KNEW BOBBY WAS OUT TO GET HIM

No enterprise is more likely to succeed than one concealed from the enemy until it is ripe for execution.

—Niccolò Machiavelli

THE FIRST YEAR of JFK's administration had ended badly for Lyndon Johnson. Hoover had fallen into disfavor, and Texan Sam Rayburn, U.S. Speaker of the House, had died. With his passing, LBJ lost an intensely devoted friend and powerful ally. The Pearl Street Mafia, for the first time, was without congressional protection.

The new year brought increasing focus on LBJ's home turf from the Justice Department, driven in part by the Kennedys' contempt for the vice president. During the presidential campaign, JFK had referred to Johnson in private as both a "chronic liar" and a "riverboat gambler."[1]

To those around him, Johnson's declining political situation had become obvious. An aide's description of LBJ poolside told all: "He looked absolutely gross. His belly was enormous and his face looked bad, flushed, maybe he had been drinking a good deal. [I]t was a tremendous frustration . . . , just tremendous. . . . He knew that Bobby was out to get him."[2]

It was well known in Dallas that LBJ had long coveted the presidency. "It was his life dream," said one news editorial.[3] Rayburn had pushed hard for his nomination in 1960. But the press, understanding Johnson for what he was, had already concluded that he was "a man who has manipulated the way to command . . . without being quite certain that he has what it takes [to lead]."[4]

An accurate assessment, LBJ clearly understood that the system of government provided more than one way to the top, and so he had not hesitated to accept the vice presidency.[5] Were Kennedy to become unable to serve, the crown would fall to LBJ.[6]

Early in 1962, anti-Mob bills that had stalled in the previous session of Congress were reintroduced. RFK again appeared in hearings. A proposal was made that was designed to destroy the gaming device industry by eliminating the distribution of pinball machines, which had largely taken the place of slots.[7] Planning ahead, Kennedy argued for structuring the bill in such a way that the Mafia could not find a loophole. "I think the provision . . . will allow us to . . . cover different kinds of machines that might be devised later," he said.[8]

RFK also sought the power to "require 'any person' engaged in business involving gambling devices and knowing they have been transported in interstate commerce, to register with the Attorney General"—a ready-made list for purposes of criminal indictment. He said, "We believe it will . . . be an important factor in cutting organized crime down to size."[9]

There was another provision designed to take away the right against self-incrimination by granting immunity from prosecution. In effect, it would require that defendants reveal where they obtained gambling devices. Low-end retail businesses housing the machines would be forced, for the first time, to implicate suppliers.[10]

With the passage of additional legislation aimed at shutting down wire services, Mob bookmakers turned to telephone WATS lines. In response, Kennedy prepared a report recommending that the FCC require Bell to divulge the names of all WATS subscribers, as well as records of all calls made by their customers.[11] RFK's report also called for legislation to increase the penalties for use of electronic devices that circumvent the phone company's recording system.[12]

Kennedy recommended legislation designed to greatly broaden the government's power to conduct wiretapping on a national scale. One Kennedy supporter termed it "the single most valuable weapon in the fight against organized crime."[13]

Additionally, an amendment was proposed to the newly passed anti-wire service law, making it a crime merely to relay the racing information.[14] The amendment would establish a basis for eliminating illegal offtrack betting of the type offered in New Orleans and Dallas by ensuring the prosecution of Mob bookies.[15]

In an effort to bolster his legislative agenda, RFK penned an article entitled "The Baleful Influence of Gambling" in which he said that "if we can reduce the gambler's income, we will take a . . . major step toward cutting off the funds which are now being used to bribe officials and finance the narcotics trade."[16] Bringing focus to the situation in Dallas, Kennedy said his greatest concern was the "Mafia's power to corrupt . . . public officials, and . . . gain political control of an area."[17]

RFK's war on the Mafia infuriated elements in the national media aligned with Marcello and Civello, and he was repeatedly attacked over his efforts to destroy organized crime operations.[18] Mob-corrupted officials—and there were many—made it clear that they had little use for Kennedy's anti-Mafia programs.[19] In spite of these attacks, RFK's legislation continued to wind its way through Congress. The crucial pinball bill, which had stalled in the House the previous year, won committee approval in the spring of 1962.[20]

As a result of RFK's efforts, a snowballing reform movement in southeastern Texas began sweeping corrupt officials from office. Indictments were being handed down. Responsible elements of the national media began to focus attention on the area, labeling Mob operations and official corruption a "rotten mess."[21]

In Louisiana, Carlos Marcello's legal struggle suffered a series of debilitating setbacks. Four separate motions filed by his lawyers, which were designed to kill his illegal reentry indictment, were dismissed by the court.[22] His attorneys again attacked the basis of the deportation order by trying to get the court to throw out his Depression-era narcotics conviction. In a bitter reference to Marcello's deportation, one of his attorneys "told the court that Marcello 'wants the same opportunity to do to the government, what the government did to him.'"[23] Shortly thereafter, RFK's task force struck again. Three horse race bookmaking operations were shut down in a March raid on the New Orleans area, resulting in the arrest of six,[24] the same week the southwestern mob's wire service supplier Illinois Sports News came under indictment.[25]

In Texas, the state legislature launched an investigation of corruption in the refereeing of college sporting events.[26] The legislative committee's chief counsel understood that bookmaking operations were tied to the Marcello-Civello network. It was reported early on that a "major gambling syndicate, including a well-known professional gambler of the Dallas-Fort Worth area, is involved."[27]

One of the individuals subpoenaed before the committee, Sig Dickson, proved extremely important. The Dallas bookmaker was suspected by the Texas Department of Public Safety (DPS) to be "the go-between for the bookies and referees."[28] Proof of his ties to the network became known when investigators uncovered records of regular long distance calls to Marcello's layoff bookie Gilbert Beckley. The year before, when RFK's task force broke up Marcello's bookmaking operation, one of those arrested was Beckley. Under indictment and prosecution during the Texas point-shaving investigation, he had relocated to Miami, Florida. It was through that Florida operation that Dickson did business. The committee called Beckley "one of the largest bookmakers and gamblers in the United States."[29]

Dickson avoided subpoena until the very last day of the Texas hearings, which were held in Austin. In retaliation, the committee cited him "for Contempt of the Legislature . . . for failure to answer questions propounded to [him] by the Committee."[30] Like other mobsters, Dickson repeatedly took the Fifth.[31] But he readily gave interviews to the Dallas press, which "concluded that [he] was a 'church type person.'"[32] Bowing to political pressure, the committee ceased investigation after the July hearing, and no action was taken on their findings. There were no hearings in Dallas.[33]

During the course of the Texas hearings, Robert Kennedy's assistant attorney general Herbert Miller, in charge of the criminal division, spoke about organized crime in Dallas and revealed only a rudimentary knowledge of the situation. A few months earlier, *Life* magazine had called him "a man with virtually no previous experience in criminal law."[34] And in public hearings the year before, he had warned congressmen, "I am a neophyte in the job I have now."[35] Other portions of his testimony made it clear he was not exaggerating.[36] Why then had RFK placed him in charge of the criminal division? Prior to his job with the Justice Department, he had been "counsel to the . . . board of Teamster Union monitors."[37] Robert Kennedy's obsession with prosecuting Teamster boss Jimmy Hoffa had driven the choice. In the end, it would prove to be an unfortunate lapse in judgment.[38]

The demand for large-scale syndicate gambling was growing (as the Texas House General Investigating Committee had concluded). There were repeated efforts at the state level to legalize large-scale pari-mutuel betting.[39] In Dallas, DA Henry Wade encouraged this mind-set by continually failing to effectively prosecute gambling offenses. One criminal, convicted on three counts of felony bookmaking, was sentenced to only thirty days in jail and handed a nominal fine. Another received even less.[40]

In the summer of 1962, Robert Kennedy infuriated Johnson by initiating prosecution of LBJ's close ally, Texas con artist Billie Sol Estes. Circumstance had created the opportunity for RFK. Early on, the Kennedy administration had found itself in the position of investigating Estes while continually struggling to avoid incriminating LBJ. The case centered around Estes's massive multi-million-dollar illegal transactions in federal cotton allotments, mortgages on nonexistent liquid fertilizer tanks, improper influence within the U.S. Department of Agriculture (USDA), and political interactions with the vice president. Making Kennedy's prosecution of Estes more difficult, the USDA official who had investigated Estes's operations early in the Kennedy administration was murdered in gangland fashion in the FBI's bureau district which included LBJ's home turf.[41] The Texas DPS published statewide a description and sketch of the suspect, but he had somehow escaped.[42] The implications of Estes's ongoing prosecution and his close connection to Johnson further damaged Johnson's power base. In another unfortunate development for Johnson, a political break with Texas attorney general Will Wilson made the two bitter enemies.[43] When Wilson announced his plan to run for governor in 1962, Johnson responded by injecting his Gatsby-like creation, John Connally, into the governor's race. This infuriated Wilson, who publicly denounced LBJ. "Mr. Connally knows nothing of Texas' problems. His sole interest is in gaining control of the Texas Democratic Party for LBJ. [T]he two are inseparable, the one a carbon of the other."[44] Indeed, Connally, who had helped LBJ steal the 1948 senate election, was little more than a bagman. Wilson stated prophetically that the placement occurred "to pave the way for [LBJ's] political aspirations." And he added that if Connally were elected governor, it "would be the tightest political machine ever set up."[45]

In an attempt to bring down Johnson, Wilson tried to obtain a copy of the USDA report on Estes, but he was stopped cold. In a public statement in response to Wilson's effort, Johnson's protégé Barefoot "Sanders said . . . it had been decided that the matter would be delayed . . . pending a study," prompting Wilson to appeal directly to JFK for access to the report.[46] But the matter had become too volatile for the administration to discuss publicly. Dallasites, most of whom loathed LBJ, were not surprised at the revelations of his corruption and the increasing strain it brought to the administration.

Later that year, Connally won the governor's election. LBJ's ally Waggoner Carr took the Texas attorney generalship, and Wilson was able to accomplish little during his last months in office.[47]

In June, the President signed National Security Action Memorandum No. 161. Its effect was to strip FBI director J. Edgar Hoover of the chairmanship of the Interdepartmental Intelligence Conference, a key position in the control of internal security matters.[48] Adding insult to injury, Kennedy gave control of the position to his brother Robert.[49] With Hoover's compulsory retirement at age seventy coming near the end of Kennedy's first term in office, the process of forcing him out had begun. The Dallas media responded quickly. Readers were told to send telegrams of support to Hoover and "pray that he has many more years of service."[50] Hoover publicly expressed his thanks to Dallas "for the cooperation . . . rendered."[51]

LBJ's bond with Barefoot Sanders intensified over the spring and summer of 1962. Johnson said in a memo to him, "I have been confident all along that your service as U.S. Attorney for the Northern District . . . would be such as to write a distinguished record for others to follow."[52] From 1961 on, Sanders had been briefed regularly by the SAC of the FBI's Dallas field office regarding RFK's growing investigation of the Civello mob. He had learned that Kennedy was also planning to deport key bookmaker Phil Bosco. Because of the public record of Sander's association with Bosco at the Mob-controlled Zuroma Club, formerly known as the Anonymous Club, which ran a week-to-week poker game controlled by Civello, Johnson's confidant faced ruin were the mobster to be brought down. Undoubtedly, Sanders expressed his fears to LBJ.

The administration's assault on the Mafia raged over the summer. At the end of June, the U.S. House passed anti-pinball legislation, paving the way for Senate approval and enactment into law that year.[53] In an early July article, RFK publicly called for all-out war on the Mob. He revealed to the American people the existence of files compiled by his Organized Crime Task Force, to be used to deliver a final crushing blow to organized crime. Referring in the same article to the breakup of a large "Italy to New York to Canada" narcotics operation, RFK proclaimed, "We were able to dig up the roots as well as chop down the tree."[54] He noted with satisfaction that dozens of mobsters had been arrested, a number of whom were then murdered by their peers in an effort to contain the damage.[55] During the first half of the year, there were no less than six major drug busts impacting the Mafia and their suppliers.[56]

In New Orleans, Marcello continued the uphill struggle to overturn his old narcotics conviction.[57] In an ominous sign of his growing frustration with the system, he said in court, "I still don't know my rights."[58] In late July, the IRS struck again, filing tax liens on two pieces of Marcello's property.[59] In August, New Orleans district attorney Jim Garrison's office launched a drive on the Marcello-controlled French Quarter. The announcement came after an assault by a Marcello henchman on a state's witness in a Mob-related prosecution. The local press reported that the witness had been "sadistically beaten . . . in the face and head with a blackjack" and warned, "If you keep your mouth shut, nothing will happen to you. You're lucky, because the big man would just as soon have you dead."[60] It took thirty stitches to close his wounds.[61] An angry assistant DA vowed the "'contemptuous beating . . . ' was the 'straw that broke the camel's back. [I]t shows utter contempt for the law. It shows things are out of hand.' The drive will not be of 'three or four days' duration, but will go on for 'three or four years.'"[62]

Narcotics trafficking was to be Garrison's office's prime target.[63] On the gambling front, in near simultaneous fashion, the federal court ordered an October trial for several of Marcello's lieutenants under indictment in the Beckley prosecution.[64]

In Dallas, the Pearl Street Mafia suffered a major setback when the operators of Illinois Sports News were convicted under the new federal legislation. It brought an immediate halt to the distribution of the service racing sheet in the Dallas area.[65]

To Texans, Johnson's lack of influence with the Kennedys was becoming obvious. An increasingly angry and desperate LBJ concluded that only a drastic change in tactics could save him. He turned to his old friend and close ally U.S. Texas representative Albert Thomas of Houston for help. Thomas had the ability to bring President Kennedy to Texas. The representative was heavily involved in the development of the space center in Houston and was chairman of the U.S. House subcommittee's aerospace budget.[66] LBJ, as chairman of the national space council, worked in close coordination.[67]

Thomas was also chairman of the Independent Offices of the House Appropriations Committee, a committee critical to the success of the administration. JFK was well aware of Thomas's power. Obsessed with the success of the space program, Kennedy was forced to cater to him.[68]

In the summer of 1962, Thomas began an effort to get JFK to speak in Houston. To the Texas representative's advantage, on July 20, something unprecedented occurred in Congress. By the mere flip of a coin, Thomas became the first member of the House ever chosen to chair the all-powerful Congressional Appropriations Conference, providing a solution to the stalled negotiations between the Senate and House.[69]

But in early August, as the war on the southwestern Mafia raged, as Kennedy pressed to eviscerate Hoover, the pressure on LBJ intensified. It was a desperate situation calling for desperate measures. On the afternoon of the ninth, Johnson flew to Austin and was driven to his Texas ranch. Upon arrival, he did something that would be virtually impossible for a vice president to do today. He dismissed his "staff [and] secret service contingent" and, in an act equally unprecedented, disappeared for five days. Reportedly, it was to rest. But with his official *Daily Diary* left unattended, and a Secret Service staff he considered to be little more than spies for RFK now absent, there would be no record of where he went or with whom he met.[70] The time had come to act. He would stand or fall with the Pearl Street Mafia.

Marcello, Civello, Johnson, and Hoover had now perceived a common and mortal enemy in JFK. All had the strongest motive to see Kennedy fall. Marcello and Civello, with their murderous track record, had the means to make it happen. And in Dallas, with the investigative shield provided by Wade and Hoover, Marcello would find the *opportunity to do to the government what the government did to him.*

6

A CORRIDOR OF ESCAPE

[W]e are not going to be able to do . . . the job against organized crime . . . where you have a breakdown of local law enforcement.
—U.S. Attorney General Robert F. Kennedy, 1962

At least wait until November before you shoot him down.
—Vice President Lyndon Johnson, Dallas, Texas, April 23, 1963

THE CONTRACT KILLING of President Kennedy and the hit men's escape without detection could only have occurred in Dallas. Pearl Street mob boss Joe Civello had every reason to allow the use of his city. The Kennedy administration's war on the Mafia was fast coming home—the Mob's congressional protection now gone. The last barrier between Civello and federal prosecution was the Johnson/Hoover machine. The summer of 1962 had seen the beginning of the end for LBJ, and Hoover would soon follow.

At the hands of Kennedy, Civello had seen the arrest and prosecution of close associates. The year before, a West Coast ally had been convicted on federal extortion and anti-racketeering charges.[1] That same year, one of Florida mob boss Santo Trafficante's couriers had been arrested in Dallas.[2] Worse still, in August 1962, a key Chicago mafioso, previously shielded because of his ties to LBJ's crony Tom Clark, had come under investigation by the IRS.[3]

Civello had watched with growing apprehension as public attacks on the vice president from within his own party grew in number. One such assault was made by Texas attorney general (and former Dallas district attorney) Will Wilson. Though he was on his way out of office, he was vigorously advocating reform of state corruption statutes. Likening the Texas political situation to a field poisoned by "Johnson grass," Wilson began calling for statutes enabling an attorney general to initiate the removal of a district attorney who failed to prosecute Mob corruption or was taking bribes.[4] He had also contacted the U.S. Senate's Permanent Subcommittee on Investigations in an effort to obtain federal legislation giving the Texas AG access to tax returns of local officials and mafiosi in Texas.[5] Although Wilson was leaving office in January 1963, were the Johnson machine to collapse, he would surely run again for governor.

Despite the growing threat created by RFK's war on the Mafia, Joe Civello knew that his city offered something that no other Mob-controlled municipality could provide. Under the cultivation of the Pearl Street Mafia, the city of Dallas offered the typical climate of both official corruption and general mentality of lawlessness—combined with a collective obsession with gambling. But coupled with that was the extraordinary fact that the DA was both a Mob ally and close confidant of the vice president—himself a proven friend. This combination of circumstances made the city the right place to kill the President.

John Kennedy would not be killed by Civello's own henchmen. With the Stone investigation underway, Civello knew it would simply be too dangerous to act directly. For a murder of such magnitude, outsiders would have to be used. Standard to a Mob contract of Civello's day was the concept of disassociation. The Mafia family in the city where the hit was to occur relied on a family in another city to supply professionals to do the job. RFK was aware of this and discussed the concept during federal hearings on organized crime and narcotics. "[I]f they want to have somebody knocked off, . . . the top man will speak to somebody else who will speak to somebody else and order it. The man who actually does the gun work . . . does not know who ordered it. . . . You are going to have to get everyone along the line . . . to talk," said Kennedy.[6]

With Civello providing the kill zone, it fell to Carlos Marcello in New Orleans to obtain the assassins. But he did not dare supply hit men from his own territory. It would require importation. With Marcello's and Civello's fluency in Italian and control over the southwestern drug corridor's ports of entry, they were equipped to do just that. The drug corridor, with its long-proven track record as a route for smuggling narcotics into the United States from Mexico and Canada, was the avenue of choice. Hit men could be brought in, positioned to do the job, and then safely removed. Marcello himself had used the corridor when he was smuggled back into the United States from Central America the year before. Exactly how he got back into Louisiana, investigators were unable to learn.

Civello had numerous ties to the northeastern U.S. and Canadian drug cartel. Arrested with him at Apalachin, New York, in the late 1950s was mafioso John Ormento, a key lieutenant in the New York City Lucchese crime family and close associate of Antoine D'Agostino. The Lucchese mob, through men like Ormento, had "specialized in distributing huge quantities of heroin in local and interstate commerce."[7] According to narcotics reports, "He was involved in the . . . traffic with . . . members of the . . . Cotroni organization of Montreal . . . , which smuggled . . . heroin into the United States."[8] An FBN report on Ormento identified his close criminal associates. They included "Rocco Pellegrino [and] Joseph Ianni of Texas."[9] Ianni ranked near the top in the Pearl Street mob. His father, Frank, was Pellegrino's cousin. Two of Rocco's allies had assisted for a time with Dallas drug operations after Civello's arrest at Apalachin during the Eisenhower administration. Pellegrino, the report went on, "was [the] source of supply of narcotics for Italian violators in Dallas."[10] The portion of the report concerning Civello identified him as "the leader from the Dallas area. Controls all rackets in Dallas and vicinity."[11]

Ormento was also associated with the Tampa, Florida, Mafia chief Santo Trafficante, who controlled Mob operations throughout central and southern Florida.[12] According to reports, "The Port of Miami [was] a receiving point for heroin from Europe." And "residing in the Miami area [were] . . . leading racketeers from . . . New York City. . . . Among these [was] . . . Rocco Pellegrino."[13]

By the early 1940s, Lucchese and Ormento were getting drugs via the southwestern end of the drug corridor.[14] "The narcotics received . . . were obtained in Mexico . . . through the aid of several Jewish racketeers. . . . Lucchese . . . directed these activities but remained insulated from possible incrimination by delegating the implementation of these illicit operations to . . . Ormento."[15] Prosecuted with Civello, Ianni, and others in the latter Depression era for heroin trafficking were several Jewish mobsters under the control of Dallasite Louis Ginsberg.[16]

The Lucchese organization also relied on the northern end of the drug corridor and used Salvatore Shillitani to control the distribution of heroin from Montreal, "which ended up in Chicago."[17] As pointed out during federal hearings, the city was "the secondary distribution point . . . with traffickers . . . furnishing . . . cities such as . . . Dallas, Houston, [and] New Orleans."[18]

By the 1960s, Shillitani had become closely associated with Antoine D'Agostino, the mobster whom Price Daniel and LBJ had kept hidden from public view during the U.S. Senate's narcotics investigation the decade before. According to federal testimony, D'Agostino's criminal associates included Frenchman Paul Mondoloni.[19] Localities the two frequented were "Marseilles, . . . Montreal, . . . New York City [and] Mexico City."[20] Hearings also listed D'Agostino and Mondoloni as key members of the French Canadian "Cotroni mob of Montreal."[21]

"French traffickers . . . found it necessary to establish an operating point in Mexico City because of seizures in . . . Montreal. . . . [L]arge amounts of heroin were sent to the United States by way of Mexico City."[22] By the 1950s, the Marcello and Civello mob families were Mondoloni's connection in southern Texas. It was no coincidence that when his lieutenant D'Agostino had been arrested in Mexico City in mid-decade he was temporarily held in Texas.

From the beginning, Kennedy's war on narcotics operations brought heavy assault on the Lucchese family. In late 1960, members of the Lucchese-Cotroni operation, including John Ormento and Joseph Valachi, were put on trial in federal court in New York.[23] There was a mistrial the following April, but the Kennedy administration retried them. On July 10, just a few days after JFK had replaced the director of the FBN with a man of his own choosing, Ormento was convicted along with others and sentenced to forty years in the penitentiary.[24] The vicious nature of Ormento and his associates quickly became obvious during trial proceedings. "The defendants disrupted the second trial with violent outbursts, open threats and attacks. . . . To maintain order in the courtroom, it became necessary for the Government to deputize as marshals several Federal agents."[25]

As the proceedings wore on, the mobsters became more violent. "During the last three weeks . . . thirty deputy marshals guarded the courtroom. . . . No one was permitted to occupy the first three rows of spectator's seats. No one was permitted to enter the courtroom once the trial was in session. Visitors were searched. . . . [O]ne of the defendants while testifying picked up the witness chair and hurled it at the prosecutor. [He] . . . was subdued by marshals[,] . . . shackled and gagged for the remainder of the trial." Another defendant made "repeated outbursts of vituperation," at one point "entering the jury box and pushing jurors about." Ormento was cited for contempt for "screaming and yelling in the vestibule of the judge's robing room and banging on the door." At sentencing, the judge said, "After more than 25 years . . . in courts throughout the country . . . , I have never heard or seen anything to equal such an outrage, . . . such violence in the courtroom."[26] And to Ormento, the judge said, "You are . . . an incurable cancer on society. You are totally undeserving of any mercy."[27]

Ormento and the others appealed their convictions. In denying release, the court warned, "There would be danger to the public, the witnesses, to the jurors and to the court personnel if bail were granted."[28] In short, Joe Civello's associates were capable of murdering federal officials. One month later, federal investigators publicly linked Ormento to Civello via disclosure of "phone calls [made] immediately prior to the [Apalachin] meeting."[29]

Under RFK, close to half of the Lucchese mob would be eliminated through death, arrest, and prosecution. Pellegrino was fighting deportation proceedings.[30] Sources of heroin were being cut off. There were numerous arrests of Sicilian and Corsican mafiosi, many of whom were based in Marseilles.

In August 1962, key associates of Ormento, Pellegrino, and Trafficante were indicted in New York on federal narcotics trafficking charges.[31] Members of the group were credited with dumping "400 kilograms of heroin" into the United States over a twelve-year period.[32] Much was made of the important role played by "criminals of Corsican origin," men such as Mondoloni.[33]

In order to destroy the Montreal–New York operation, President Kennedy understood that he would have to eliminate the Corsican-Sicilian power base. Government missions were sent to various Mediterranean nations to convince leaders to ban the production of opium.[34] At the first White House Conference on Narcotic and Drug Abuse in September, John Kennedy unveiled his plan for the "elimination of illicit traffic in drugs." He announced that "the Bureau of Narcotics is being expanded to other parts of the world, a program which will be implemented before the end of the year." Robert Kennedy, as chairman of the conference, said, "This . . . can be a historic beginning, for it embodies two important principles which for too long have been missing in this field: Reliable information and sustained cooperation."[35]

Following words with action, in October, the "investigative jurisdiction and operating procedure" of the FBN was expanded, with plans to open a field office in Mexico City in January 1963.[36] The addition of that office would give the FBN a base of operations from which to launch crippling strikes against the Cotroni-Mondoloni drug cartel. Marcello and Civello, as two of their U.S. distributors, became prime targets of the FBN.

Marcello's gambling operative Gilbert Beckley also had ties to mobsters in eastern Canada. Like Marcello, Beckley was questioned by investigators in Washington DC. "You have been named as one of the largest of the big time gamblers, bookmakers, and layoff operators. You have operated in Montreal. . . . Do you wish to make any comment on that?" said one.[37] Beckley took the Fifth.

By midsummer 1962, Marcello and Civello had set in motion the plan to murder the President. Understanding that the vice president was a confederate of the Dallas Mafia and the corrupted Henry Wade, LBJ had been recruited—either directly during his unprecedented five-day disappearance in August or indirectly via intermediaries who conveyed Johnson's determination to rid himself of his nemesis, RFK.

LBJ, confident in his decision, was ready to get away, relax. And what better place than Italy? There, the common folk would welcome him and Lady Bird as if they were royalty coming home. But in the twisted mind of Lyndon Johnson, it would be more than that. It would a fitting tribute in recognition of his unquestioning allegiance with the Mafia. Like Machiavelli, he had made his pact with the devil.

7

FORCES OF DARKNESS

Hell is empty and all the devils are here.

—Shakespeare

LYNDON AND CLAUDIA Alta Johnson made the trip to Southern Italy the first week of September 1962. During their stay, LBJ was surrounded by local dignitaries and people of influence. He addressed groups affiliated with organizations in the United States and met with representatives of the Rome chapter of Boys' Town.[1] The youth organization had friends in the Dallas, Texas, chapter—one was Mayor Cabell.[2] The Dallas mayor was also a frequent guest of the Zuroma Club and was close to Joe and Sam Campisi. The Campisis maintained a public image of respectability while secretly acting as underlings to Civello and Ianni in the control of gambling operations. Media reports suggest that Sam Campisi, a close confidant of Jack Ruby, was also in Rome the first week of September.[3] Whether Campisi was there simply by coincidence or intentionally, to meet with Johnson and observe his involvement with the Italian people, will never be known. But LBJ's actions spoke volumes to the Dallas mafioso.

The tone and image of LBJ's public appearances while in Italy were no different than those of a visiting and immensely popular head of state. When he deplaned in Rome, he said, "This is a meeting of friends with friends to plan with confidence and enthusiasm for the future."[4] As he traveled via motorcade to his hotel, "many Romans recognized the Vice President. . . . Along the route there were handclasps, applause and cheers. [He] left his car and shook hundreds of outstretched hands."[5] Two days later in Naples, he repeated the performance. "[He] stood up in his open car to wave, shake hands and . . . shout 'Viva Napoli!' At the United States Consulate . . . the Vice President emotionally addressed several hundred working-class Neapolitans who after two years of waiting had obtained United States visas."[6] Johnson said, "This is one of the most genuine and thrilling experiences of my life."[7] The opportunity to ally himself with Italian immigrants to the United States had not been missed.

He also spoke of his wartime experiences. "I was last in Naples at the end of World War II. I came here in June 1945. Those were distressing days. . . . But then, like now, your people could not be deterred, they did not waiver in the face of adversity."[8] While a U.S. representative at war's end, Johnson had toured Southern Italy on a fact-finding junket in connection with the House Committee on Naval Affairs.[9] His public report left little doubt he was deeply affected by the terrible conditions.[10] Native Dallasite Sam Campisi remembered Johnson's WWII trip, which was reported by the Texas press at the time. It had also caught the attention of the Anonymous/Zuroma Club. In essence, the Dallas Italian-American community knew that Johnson and his wife genuinely sympathized with the plight of their countrymen.

The people of Rome loved Lady Bird. While her husband promoted himself with various politicos, she toured extensively, doing the same. "Mrs. Johnson . . . visited an Italian Baptist orphanage that has the support of many Texas Baptists. . . . The children's chapel . . . , just outside Rome, was built . . . with funds contributed by Texas Baptist women."[11] Fixated with all things Italian, Johnson's wife reveled in the attention officials lavished upon her.

While in Italy, Vice President Johnson met with officials and signed a mutual benefit accord with the Italian premier that was designed to put an American-Italian satellite (Telstar) in orbit.[12] However, some U.S. congressmen were angered by LBJ's action. They had grown weary of Italy's policy of noncooperation in the area of INS efforts at deportation of men like Marcello. Even before Johnson's return to the United States, momentum was gathering to cut off aid of the type that LBJ had just arranged.[13]

In his last speech before leaving Italy, LBJ spoke of his commitment to its people. "Never has the opportunity been greater . . . to work side by side."[14] After the Johnsons' departure (in clear response to U.S. congressional interests that had taken issue with Italy's lack of cooperation with the INS), one Italian "editorial . . . cited [the] Vice President's words to reproach 'those, who for party's interests, cast shadows and suspicion on Italian foreign policy.'"[15] There could be no doubt about Johnson's loyalty to the Mob.

After his return to Washington DC, Johnson flew to his Texas ranch on September 11. From there, he traveled to Houston. In response to a request by Representative Albert Thomas, President Kennedy had agreed to come to Houston in promotion of the space program. He arrived on the night of September 11 and the following day addressed a large crowd at Rice University. "I regard the decision . . . to shift our efforts in space from low to high-gear as among the most important decisions I expect to make in the office of President. . . . During the next five years [the National Aeronautics and Space Aeronautics] expects to . . . direct or contract for new space efforts at a rate of $1 billion a year from this space center alone," said JFK.[16] With Kennedy's commitment to the space program came the absolute requirement for cooperation from Congress. And Thomas, with his control over funding, was the key player.[17] Upon the President's return to Washington, he met with the press about his Houston trip.[18] "This was a non-political trip," claimed JFK.[19] But it was clear to all that without Thomas's cooperation, the space program wasn't going anywhere—a fact clearly perceived by LBJ.

After Kennedy completed his Texas speech, LBJ made a sudden change in plans. As reported by the media, "Leaving Houston . . . , the President made the visit to Saint Louis, the last of four stops, unaccompanied by Vice President . . . Johnson, who had been . . . scheduled to go to Saint Louis."[20] According to the press, LBJ "stayed behind to attend a Sam Rayburn . . . [memorial] ceremony."[21] But the ceremony was not for several days, and the vice president again went off record. For the next five days, his whereabouts and activities were unknown.[22]

The day after Johnson went off record, there were sweeping IRS raids on syndicate gambling operations in New Orleans, Austin, Beaumont, and Dallas. The raids in New Orleans had been large scale, hitting seven different operations almost simultaneously. Marcello was livid.[23]

On September 18, 1962, Johnson resurfaced, flying directly from his ranch to the United Steelworkers' convention in Miami, Florida. There he addressed, and aligned himself with, organized labor at the Fontainebleau Hotel, a watering hole of Marcello's Florida counterpart, Santo Trafficante.[24]

With Marcello's and Civello's August decision to kill President Kennedy, there followed two independent private conversations verifying that fact in the month of September. The threats, one made by Marcello in Louisiana and the other in Miami by Trafficante, both spoke in terms of a planned hit in the works.[25] Trafficante's took place just after LBJ's Miami address.[26] During a sharp exchange about politics with a prominent Cuban exile, the mafioso said, "Have you seen how his brother is hitting Hoffa, a man who is a worker, who is not a millionaire, a friend of the blue collars? He doesn't know that this kind of encounter is very delicate. Mark my words, this man Kennedy is in trouble, and he will get what is coming to him . . . he is going to be hit."[27]

Just after September 21, the second conversation occurred, this time near New Orleans.[28] Marcello, reeling from the latest IRS raid on his gambling operation, was in a violent mood.

> The conversation . . . turned to . . . the pressure law-enforcement agencies were bringing to bear on the Mafia . . . [Marcello's] words were bitten off and spit out when mention was made of . . . Robert Kennedy . . . "Livarsi ne petra di la scarpa! . . . Take the stone out of my shoe! . . . Don't worry about that little Bobby son of a bitch," he shouted. "He's going to be taken care of!" Carlos . . . knew that to rid himself of Robert Kennedy he would first have to remove the President. . . . No one at the meeting had any doubt of Marcello's intentions. . . . Moreover, the conversation . . . also made clear that Marcello had begun a plan to move. He had . . . already thought of using a "nut" to do the job.[29]

Unknown to Marcello, one of those at the meeting, Edward Becker, was an informant for an ex–FBI investigator working for the Los Angeles, California, field office. That office tracked the meeting with Marcello.[30]

LBJ, working in concert with Thomas, began to push for yet another trip to Texas by President Kennedy.[31] But with the Cuban missile crisis and close of the congressional session, there was no chance JFK could be forced to return before spring 1963.

Time was beginning to run short. With each passing month, Johnson's position became more precarious. His Texas allies sensed his growing impatience with his status as vice president. Henry Wade had become obsessed with LBJ's acquisition of the presidency, repeatedly addressing him as "Mr. President" in personal letters.[32]

RFK's attacks on Johnson continued to grow in intensity. The vice president's herculean effort to distance himself from, and downplay the importance of, the Billy Sol Estes scandal continued to make headlines.[33] Much of the prosecution during this time was handled in Dallas via grand jury investigation. Though Kennedy's people were in charge, Barefoot Sanders remained involved and kept LBJ informed.[34] Apart from the Estes case, there were also mushrooming federal investigations into corrupt practices by corporate interests within the Texas oil industry.[35] That industry had closely supported Johnson, and he was expected to reciprocate. Johnson's inability to stop RFK's investigation of powerful entities in Texas such as the Mafia and oil corporations was a clear sign of his waning power to those around him. In early 1963, when JFK proposed changes to tax laws which would damage the oil industry, it was too much for Johnson, and he instructed Governor John Connally to attack the legislation.[36]

In a calculated move to gain control of JFK's agenda, Johnson made plans to come to Dallas to promote the space program.[37] He arrived in the city on April 23. There, before the media, he took an aggressive and very hard-line position on the space race as well as Cuba.[38] When asked by the press about removing Castro, he responded, "We must do everything short of starting a third world war. . . . Cuba is a subversive threat."[39] It was also reported that "in spite of . . . speculation to the contrary, Johnson gave the impression that he was available for nomination for a second term as vice-president."[40] In a surprise announcement to reporters, LBJ stated that President Kennedy would be coming to Dallas in the fall. When asked about widespread criticism of JFK, he said, "At least wait until November before you shoot him down."[41] During a reception that same day, Johnson met with local officials, including his close confidant Henry Wade. Unable to restrain themselves, the two embraced for the cameras.

To Barefoot Sanders, who had coordinated LBJ's visit to Dallas, Johnson appeared unusually euphoric in the days that followed his trip.[42] Why? Only days before, Johnson's longtime confidant Representative Thomas had publicly disclosed that he was terminally ill and would not seek reelection. When JFK learned of it, he immediately called Thomas and attempted to change his mind.[43] In order for Kennedy's cherished moon project to remain on schedule, Thomas's every request would now have to be met. Said an anxious JFK to the media, "It is impossible to exaggerate the importance of the leadership . . . [he] has exerted in the House."[44]

Johnson, sensing the opportunity to gain control of Kennedy's agenda, had seized the opportunity created by Thomas's plight. In publicly committing JFK to a November appearance in Dallas, he had given the Mafia what it needed most. The President would be brought into the killing zone.

8

SHADOWS FALL—THE STONE WIRE

> Profits from illegal gambling are huge and they are the primary source of the funds which finance organized crime, all throughout the country.
>
> —U.S. Attorney General Robert Kennedy

> I'll tell you one thing; we're . . . not on . . . a fishing expedition.
>
> —U.S. Attorney Arnold Stone, Organized Crime Task Force
> Dallas, Texas, October 2, 1963

LYNDON JOHNSON'S APRIL announcement that JFK would come to Dallas had not come a moment too soon for the Pearl Street Mafia. Things were heating up. In early January 1963, at Robert Kennedy's directive, Assistant U.S. Attorney General Herbert Miller instructed the regional office of the IRS in Dallas to investigate Joe Civello's largest bookmaker, John Eli Stone, for income tax evasion.[1] The Dallas field offices of the FBI and the Bureau of Alcohol, Tobacco, Firearms and Explosives (ATF) were ordered to work with the IRS.[2] Wade began to sweat.

Director Hoover, well aware that Stone answered to Dallas Mafia boss Joe Civello through lieutenants Joe Ianni and Philip Bosco, was given weekly briefings by the Dallas SAC.[3] Taking down Stone would not be easy. A violent man with a long track record in Dallas, his arrest record included a charge for assault to murder.[4] Like Ianni and Bosco, he was always armed. Dallas FBI agents were instructed to use extreme caution when approaching any of the three men.[5]

John Eli Stone and his brother James Stone used the phone lines of a downtown Dallas cleaners, the Enquire Shine and Press shop, owned by the Miller brothers Isadore and Dave, as the "wire" to coordinate the handling of bets in their illegal bookmaking operation. Each day, John Stone got the "line" through a Mob contact at a hotel in Las Vegas. He then relayed the information to Isadore at the Enquire. Stone then called Bosco and provided the same. Operatives used the Enquire to place bets and pick up any winnings.[6] The IRS discovered this and placed both physical and electronic surveillance (called misur, short for "microphone surveillance") on the Mob operation.[7] It was quickly learned that Dave Miller worked closely with bookmaking operative Jack Ruby. The latter owned a strip club called the Carousel, located two doors down from the Enquire. Ruby gave Miller permanent passes to the club, for him and his close associates.[8] In addition, Ruby directed customers wishing to place bets to Miller. Ruby also placed bets directly for customers and was observed by federal investigators entering the Enquire on a regular basis in 1963.[9] Like Stone and his Italian counterparts, Ruby was always armed.

The Stone brothers and the Miller brothers soon learned the Enquire was under federal investigation by RFK's Organized Crime Task Force and stopped handling operations over the shop phone.[10] John Eli Stone was netting close to $200,000 per year after Civello's cut and began using public pay phones at prearranged locations to continue his operation.[11]

With RFK's investigation accelerating, tension within the Civello mob was running high. Joe Ianni and his brother-in-law John Carcelli became enemies, supposedly over the latter's handling of a local Mob-controlled liquor store.[12] Their falling-out occurred even though Carcelli was a valuable asset to the Dallas Mafia by virtue of his assistance in President Truman's fraudulent pardon of Joe's father, Frank (a convicted heroin trafficker), during the latter 1940s. Despite Carcelli's status as a member of the Civello mob, on March

31, 1963, Joe Ianni or one of his cohorts confronted Carcelli at his home and shot him in the chest with a handgun. The killer then put the pistol in Carcelli's mouth and fired a round into his head. Carcelli's wife (Ianni's sister) was evidently close by and may have witnessed the murder. She immediately called Mob boss Joe Civello. After a tense conversation, she called the Dallas police. Although the police believed Carcelli had been murdered, the death was ruled a suicide the same day. Incredibly, Joe Ianni, his potential murderer, was the official informant at the coroner's inquest, providing the information used to rule the death a suicide.[13]

Carcelli's killing may have involved something more. Violation of the Mafia code of omertà by talking to law enforcement officials dictated death—often by shooting the victim through the mouth. His murder raised the possibility that Carcelli had become an informant in RFK's war on the Dallas Mafia. By 1963, the Dallas FBI and other law enforcement agencies had, in fact, developed informants to keep pace with RFK's drive on the Mob.[14] Pallbearers at the funeral included Ianni's gambling lieutenant Phil Bosco. The Dallas press did not report the cause of death.[15]

District Attorney Henry Wade declined to investigate Ianni as a likely suspect in Carcelli's murder. The mobster had successfully avoided prosecution since 1951, and Wade's reasons for allowing that, whatever they were, still held.

Hoover, realizing that the situation in Dallas was intensifying (and knowing that President Kennedy would be visiting the city in November), made the decision to remove that city's field office SAC and replace him with a highly trusted underling who had served at FBI headquarters in Washington DC. By the third week in April, Gordon Shanklin was in place.[16]

The crushing power of RFK's Organized Crime Task Force, so successfully brought to bear against the Marcello mob in New Orleans, was now rapidly increasing pressure on the Dallas Mafia. At Hoover's directive, Shanklin ordered FBI special agents Robert Barrett and Robert Gemberling of the field office's organized crime unit to initiate surveillance on John Eli Stone, his brother James Stone, and Isadore "Izzy" Miller.[17]

RFK's task force agents also put electronic surveillance (misur) on pay phones used by the mafiosi. Charles Bus, an ATF special investigator, began following John Stone. On June 19, while Stone was using a pay phone outside a grocery store, Bus heard him arranging the "line" from Las Vegas. The agent prepared an affidavit for the investigation, which read in part, "I overheard him talking with someone whom he called Izzie. . . . I heard Stone say that he would call and get a line. . . . I heard him dial and tell someone that he wanted to talk to Las Vegas. . . . He then . . . received the baseball line for that day. . . . [A]fter that, he telephoned someone and gave them the line. . . . At the end of that conversation I heard him say that he would call 'Bosco.'"[18]

With that information and phone tap evidence compiled by the task force, search warrants for the Enquire and apartments of the mobsters, rented under assumed names, were obtained on June 27. Forty-eight hours later, arrest warrants for Isadore Miller and the Stone brothers were issued to the task force. James Stone was taken first and then his brother John, near the Pearl Street district, followed by Miller in his apartment.[19] Mob defense attorney Charles Tessmer was quickly retained.[20]

Stone's fellow bookmaker, Phil Bosco, was also under investigation by RFK. His operation, which paid a percentage to Civello, was run in similar fashion. Dallas PD, aware that Kennedy was building a case against Bosco, saw their opportunity. On July 17, they raided his "front," a local gas station, and arrested him.[21] While he was in custody that day, the Dallas FBI interviewed him, but an enraged Bosco refused to talk.[22] Through his attorney, bail was soon arranged.

Two weeks later, *The Saturday Evening Post* ran a revealing article about Mafia narcotics trafficking and Civello's associates which, according to a Dallas FBI informant, triggered a meeting between Civello, Ianni, and other mafiosi. Civello, reeling from the arrests of Bosco, Stone, and the others, raged against the system and Kennedy's war on the Mob.[23]

In early September, the task force's investigation widened with federal grand jury hearings in Wichita Falls, northwest of Dallas. Robert Kennedy, knowing he could not get indictments in Dallas because of the pro-Mob mind-set, had chosen the smaller conservative city. Johnson's confidant Barefoot Sanders, infuriated by Kennedy's tactic, tried to prevent the hearings by going directly to RFK's assistant, Herbert Miller.[24] But his demands were dismissed, and the hearings went forward. All was not lost, however, as Johnson made sure that his loyal servant, U.S. Fifth Circuit Court Federal Judge Sarah Hughes, Northern District of Texas, was appointed to preside in the case. Clearly prejudiced in favor of the defendants by virtue of her bias in favor of illegal gambling, the appointment of the diminutive but powerful Hughes was a fundamental failure of judicial procedure and ethical codes.

Hughes had the suspects in the John Stone investigation, as well as Phil Bosco, called before the grand jury. U.S. attorney Arnold Stone, speaking to the press, "declined to say whether or not the investigation . . . had a national aspect. . . . [E]fforts will be made by the Department of Justice to ascertain where in the United States layoff money was being sent when Dallas gamblers became overloaded with bets. . . . [T]hose summoned . . . were expected to take the Fifth Amendment."[25]

A sense of doom seized Civello's operatives, who realized that Robert Kennedy was now positioned to completely destroy their lucrative bookmaking operation. DA Wade could not protect them as he had in 1951. But Joe Civello and Lyndon Johnson remained calm, confident in what was to come.

9

EXPOSURE AND DENIAL

He who helps the guilty, shares the crime.

—Publilius Syrus

IN THE WEEKS leading up to President Kennedy's visit to Dallas, the local media engaged in a collective denial of the presence of the Pearl Street Mafia. In Washington DC, federal hearings on the Mob were about to begin. Reality was coming home to Dallas.

With RFK's war on the Civello mob intensifying and gaining momentum, U.S. attorney to Dallas Barefoot Sanders, in a desperate attempt to trivialize the Stone grand jury proceedings (and save himself from disgrace were his association with the Zuroma Club to become known), issued a public statement about the Mafia.

"[T]he Dallas area has been 'most fortunate' in avoiding the influence of organized crime. . . . [T]he spread of syndicated vice has not yet come to the . . . area because of the effective working relationship between all lawmen involved in stopping crime. Criminals and racketeers regard this as no safe haven for their activities," claimed Johnson's minion.[1] His statement was an outright lie. Sanders regularly reviewed the Justice Department's Crime Condition Reports, which flatly stated that the Civello crime family consisted of twenty-five members.[2] The attorney knew the reports were accurate because he had met most of those listed during his visits to the Zuroma Club.

Just days before Kennedy's attorneys arrived in Wichita Falls, Sanders prepared a document summarizing and inflating his few accomplishments as U.S. attorney in an attempt to ingratiate himself with his mentor, LBJ. The day of his public statement, he sent a copy to Johnson, who confidently responded, "Somehow I get the feeling that your reports will be even more impressive in the future."[3] LBJ was well aware of Sanders's involvement with the Zuroma Club and Phil Bosco and knew his protégé could be directed to do anything the vice president demanded once President Kennedy was killed.

On the same day of LBJ's response to Sanders, September 20, JFK addressed the United Nations about the space program and suggested the possibility of a joint U.S. and Soviet moon mission as a gesture of goodwill.[4] Johnson and Representative Thomas reacted quickly. As reported in the press, "Mr. Thomas wrote to the President asking him to clarify his 'position.' . . . [He] said that the press and many private citizens had interpreted the speech 'as a weakening of your former position of a forthright and strong effort in lunar landings.' In reply, the President vigorously denied any such intent."[5] "My statement . . . was an extension of a policy developed . . . with particular leadership from Vice President Johnson, . . . then the Senate Majority Leader," said JFK.[6] But Thomas was not placated, and JFK quickly finalized the impending Texas trip.[7] To reassure Thomas and the people of Texas that he wholeheartedly supported United States supremacy in the space race, the President agreed to conduct a statewide tour, including motorcades. Houston and Dallas, with their burgeoning aerospace industries, were the top priority. On September 26, the White House confirmed the timing of the trip.

Rumors were already flying about the Democratic Party's presidential ticket in the coming year and the growing belief that LBJ would not be Kennedy's running mate in 1964. Party nominating caucuses were set to begin within a few months. The Mafia knew that Kennedy's murder had to occur prior to the party's nominating convention, at which JFK was planning to announce a different running mate for the 1964 election.[8]

Two days after the White House confirmed President Kennedy's trip, RFK opened public hearings in Washington on organized crime. The Joe Valachi hearings (Valachi was a heroin trafficker in the New

York Mafia who had turned government informant) were designed to educate the public about the reality of the Mafia's existence and their international drug cartel and how criminal organization was flooding America, via Texas, with hard narcotics such as heroin and cocaine.[9] The exposé, with its disclosures about Lucchese in New York and Paul Mondoloni in Mexico City and how their drug operations worked, only spurred Mob commitment to do away with the President.

Attorney General Kennedy testified to make sure the public understood both the gravity of the situation and what the administration was doing about it. "Syndicate leaders and their associates have been identified and all are now under investigation. . . . [M]any more cases are in the indictment or investigation stage. . . . More than a score of Cosa Nostra members have been convicted recently on narcotics charges."[10] And on pending anti-Mob legislation, he said, "Senator, if those three bills were passed, the wiretapping . . . plus the immunity bills, then I would think that the need for this kind of hearing five years from now would not be necessary."[11] Senator John McClellan, who chaired the Valachi hearings, said, "I am thinking in terms of making it a crime, making it illegal to belong to a secret society or organization."[12] Kennedy responded, "We will be glad to work with the staff of the committee."[13] The opportunity to render the Mafia a criminal enterprise in and of itself would eliminate the need to prove involvement in actual crimes by its members, thereby greatly simplifying prosecution of anyone arrested.

The attorney general then revealed to the public the relationship of the Paul Mondoloni drug cartel with domestic Mob operations. He stated that "in the field of narcotics, there is no question that those who operate here in the United States operate with their counterparts in other countries."[14] For added effect, he brought Joe Valachi before the cameras.[15] The mobster disclosed detailed information about Mondoloni's and Antoine D'Agostino's associate Salvatore Shillitani. Drug trafficker John Ormento and Joe Civello were publicly linked. An FBN agent said, "Ormento . . . is in . . . gambling, drugs, and he was at Apalachin, and he made a number of telephone calls . . . to . . . Joe Civello, in Dallas."[16] The testimony about the Mob's connection to Dallas was closely followed in Texas.

The Dallas media, still in denial about the presence of the Pearl Street Mafia, attempted to counter the Kennedy administration's growing focus on Mob activity in their city. One article said, "A suspected Cosa Nostra chieftain lives in Dallas . . . but he has been linked with no underworld associates or rackets here."[17] But by then, their protestations had taken on a hollow ring.

During the hearings, Valachi had also acknowledged that RFK's proposed immunity legislation (compelling testimony) would force mobsters to reveal information implicating their Mob bosses in criminal acts.[18] In addition, new wiretapping laws passed to gain evidence against bookmakers via their telephone conversations would, Valachi said, "wipe out the business."[19] Dallas bookmakers like Bosco and Stone had, in fact, shifted to the use of public pay phones in an attempt to adjust to the new tactics implemented by Kennedy's Organized Crime Task Force.[20]

Senators expressed outrage over the INS's seemingly endless struggle with Carlos Marcello and other hard-core cases. "We know that they are here in violation of the law. They should be deported."[21] As RFK had learned firsthand with Marcello, it was proving to be a tough fight.

Another official testified at the hearings about the Mafia's command structure. "The appearance that organized crime gives is very deceptive. It is like an iceberg. . . . [They] frequently have a very beguiling manner. . . . [When] you see where they stem from and how they came up, you have a much better picture. . . . [Most] of these people have come above that violence, they are not in it."[22]

As if on cue, shortly before the hearings ended, "narcotics agents arrested [Frank] Costello and charged [him] with violations of Federal narcotic laws."[23] Costello, a key New York mafioso, was Carlos Marcello's mentor and was far removed from daily Mob operations. Following that, "a Federal grand jury returned indictments against 41 members of [a vast narcotics distribution organization believed to control 80 percent of the illicit narcotic traffic in Chicago.] [A]rrests . . . followed."[24] Shillitani was among those arrested, many of whom were French nationals.[25]

On the last day of public hearings, Senator McClellan provided prophetic closing commentary: "The shocking narratives that we have heard here . . . generates, I think, an immediate sense of urgency."[26] Time was quickly running out for John Kennedy.

10

THE FACE OF EVIL

> If an injury has to be done to a man, it should be so severe that his vengeance need not be feared.
>
> —Niccolò Machiavelli

ATTORNEY GENERAL ROBERT Kennedy pressed the attack on the Mob. Despite his youth and inexperience, he knew that the Organized Crime Task Force approach to destroying the organization was working. By eliminating their sources of income, syndicate gambling and narcotics trafficking, it was only a matter of time before he achieved complete success. He had the Mafia by the throat and was slowly choking it to death.

The October 1963 arrest of Salvatore Shillitani meant inquiry into the Marseilles-Montreal-Chicago-Dallas-New Orleans narcotics smuggling corridor. The indictments of Shillitani and his cohorts directly threatened the heroin supply source of Carlos Marcello, Joe Civello, and Chicago mob boss Sam Giancana. This prosecution only increased their loathing of Attorney General Robert Kennedy.[1]

With the close of the Valachi hearings, the reaction in Dallas was swift, and it followed the familiar pattern. One newspaper editorial wondered if the hearings were just "hot air."[2] Law enforcement officials said the city was "a barren field for any crime syndicate to begin operation of gambling, narcotics traffic and prostitution."[3]

Another article stated, "[T]here may be members of organized crime in Dallas practicing their trade elsewhere, but not in Dallas."[4] It was indeed the perfect place to murder the President.

Even though RFK's prosecution of Stone and his cohorts was not taking place locally but in Wichita Falls, the Dallas media understood the lethal nature of the threat that the prosecution posed. Exposure and verification of the Civello mob's long-term criminal operation in Dallas was what city officials had long been denying. A major scandal was in the making.

Journalists for both of the Dallas newspapers anxiously monitored the Stone grand jury proceedings in Wichita Falls. Stated one press report, "[I]nvestigators of two federal agencies told how they sat a block away and listened to the conversations of a bookmaker then under surveillance as he talked with gamblers in Las Vegas."[5] RFK's assault was gaining momentum and was described as "a full scale investigation into gambling and racketeering in the North Texas area."[6] It was lethal prosecution in the making.

In Wichita Falls, reporters were there when Philip "Bosco was called into the Grand Jury room."[7] From Bosco, RFK had the opportunity to gain a detailed understanding of the Pearl Street Mafia. But true to omertà, Bosco took the Fifth against self-incrimination. He was brought before Judge Sarah Hughes, who "exempted [him] from criminal prosecution . . . and instructed [him] to return to the grand jury room and answer questions as propounded to him by [Arnold] Stone."[8] But Bosco "again refused to answer . . . , again took the Fifth Amendment, and asked to consult [a] prominent Dallas criminal lawyer."[9] Reluctantly, Judge "Hughes scheduled a contempt of court hearing" to placate RFK's prosecutors.[10]

At the hearing, RFK's lead task force attorney, Arnold Stone, read into the public record the questions Bosco had refused to answer: "Do you know Johnny Stone? Did you ever bet with Stone by telephone? Did you ever use the telephone in betting and wagering? Did you ever employ any person for the purpose of offering the facilities of the telephone for gambling? Did you ever receive from John Stone or James Stone or Isadore Miller wager or bet information to be used in the business of gambling?" In conjunction with Attorney Stone's effort to prosecute the Civello mob, he brought in IRS intelligence unit officials to present surveillance films of the Dallas Mafia's bookmakers.[11]

The same day, Dallas mob bookmaker Albert Meadows was arrested for "violation of federal gambling laws."[12] It was as important as the subpoenaing of Bosco because Meadows had been a close associate of Civello for many years. Like the Stone brothers, Meadows had a detailed understanding of Mafia operations in Dallas.

On October 21, the grand jury reconvened. Later that day, they returned a "16-count indictment for violation of federal gaming statutes" against John and James Stone and Isadore Miller.[13] They also indicted Meadows.[14] The four defendants were scheduled for trial.

Being one of Stone's operatives, Jack Ruby panicked, understanding that he would be next. Isadore Miller referred him to a doctor, who prescribed Ruby a "drug for nervousness."[15] Ruby, although aware that JFK was going to be assassinated within a few weeks (the solution to Ruby's impending indictment by the task force), was close to breaking point. In addition to his criminal association with Stone and Bosco, he had been in regular communication with a key Marcello lieutenant in New Orleans, Nofio Pecora, an Anonymous/Zuroma Club guest.[16]

On November 12, the defendants' attorneys in the John Stone prosecution filed motions for suppression of evidence—the critical electronic surveillance. The task force had ten days to respond, knowing that without the misur evidence, the case would be all but lost.[17]

Meanwhile, in New Orleans, Marcello's attempts to defeat his old narcotics conviction had failed. The threat of deportation hung over his head. The IRS continued its efforts to seize assets. His pretrial motions exhausted, he was by then on trial for "conspiring to defraud the United States" and for illegal reentry.[18] Public sentiment was turning against the Marcello crime family. So great had the pressure become that on October 21, Marcello's attorney, Jack Wasserman, filed for a change of venue, an extreme tactic. Wasserman also petitioned the court to "delay the trial for ninety days." Both motions were denied.[19]

The week before the assassination, Wasserman motioned for a mistrial—denied.[20] There followed a motion for a directed verdict of not guilty—denied.[21] In a last-ditch effort, Wasserman himself took the stand in a bizarre attempt to criminalize the prosecutor by demanding that he "admit" wrongdoing in Marcello's case.[22] The hysterical attack was a face-saving gesture. Wasserman had served as a U.S. attorney with the INS in Washington DC, during Tom Clark's time.[23] Wasserman had observed firsthand as the Mob's ally, Clark, engineered the early parole of Joe Civello. And Clark had undoubtedly had a hand in arranging Truman's pardoning of Frank Ianni. Marcello's choice of Wasserman as his counsel had been made with the attorney's connections to the Justice Department in mind, thus explaining the mafioso's seemingly impossible success at avoiding deportation over the years. The umbrella of protection extended to the Pearl Street Mafia by Clark had extended to Marcello via Wasserman. It was a small wonder that Wasserman described Marcello's 1961 deportation as a "double cross."[24] But in the end, under the Kennedy administration, the attorney's machinations had accomplished little.

With President Kennedy's visit looming, the atmosphere in Dallas became supercharged. Adding to this, for over a year *The Dallas Morning News* had been delivering a barrage of insulting articles, editorials, letters, and political cartoons designed to denigrate the President. He was accused of "laxity and stupidity." His ideas were "radical." In his dealings with the Soviets, he was following a "crazy blueprint for surrender." Letters of denunciation from other states were printed. He was a "far-wrong extremist," his policies "suicidal."[25] If the young, impressionable, left-wing Lee Oswald was looking for a reason to assassinate the liberal president, he would not have found it in the pages of local newspapers. The same media machine had made it clear to Dallasites that Vice President Johnson was far more conservative than JFK and wanted to remove Oswald's idol, Fidel Castro, from power. As a leftist, Oswald had every reason not to assassinate John Kennedy.

It is true that during the late 1950s, Oswald had briefly defected to the Soviet Union. He returned to the United States in early 1962, married with a Russian wife. He became a vocal supporter of Fidel Castro. In the fall of 1963, he traveled to Mexico City in an unsuccessful attempt to get a visa to Cuba. Upon his return, with the responsibilities of married life and children to support, he sought what work he could find with his meager education.

Henry Wade, by then obsessed with his dream that LBJ become president and increasingly distracted with Johnson's worsening political situation, allowed his processing-plant system of plea bargain and parole to break down.[26] Police Chief Jesse Curry complained, "We've got to get these offenders tried and convicted and we can't do it with the tremendous backlog of cases."[27] A sense that the criminal justice system was collapsing under Wade's tenure was becoming widespread in the local population.

In early November, even Dallas Crime Commission president Jim McKee attacked Wade.[28] "We have reason to raise some serious questions relative to gambling and narcotics cases, some of which have not been tried since 1958. The longer a case remains untried, the more we play into the hands of the criminal," he said.[29] Wade had no comment.[30] McKee, as a conservative and fanatical ally of Lyndon Johnson (and one who hated the Kennedys), had only gone public because the situation had become so dire. But mindful of the situation in Wichita Falls, he was careful to add that Dallas was "free of syndicates."[31]

As Wade and LBJ's situation continued to deteriorate, the Kennedys' war against their cohort J. Edgar Hoover intensified, causing political forces in Dallas to rally around the embattled FBI director.[32] It was in many ways a conditioned response. In *The Dallas Morning News*, the steady procession of laudatory editorials about Hoover accelerated.[33] Stories out of Washington to the effect that he would resign shortly were met with assurances he would stay.[34] Hoover, in turn, thanked the paper for its support, terming it "deeply gratifying."[35]

Despite Hoover's lack of cooperation with Robert Kennedy in his efforts to destroy the Mafia, the administration's successes against the Canadian drug cartel were having the desired effect. By the fall of 1963, the Mafia was forced to rely almost solely on the southern end of the drug corridor. Results came quickly. In mid-October, "U.S. Customs officials . . . seized a . . . shipment of pure heroin, worth about [$56 million] . . . , in a car crossing the border from Mexico. A Montreal, Canada, gambler . . . was arrested," proclaimed the press.[36] The bust, the equivalent of a $397 million loss to the Mafia in today's dollars, was a spectacular success for RFK.

The arrest had come as a result of a tip-off to border officials by informants working with RFK's Organized Crime Task Force. The driver of the car, Joseph Caron, was no ordinary Canadian. Caron had worked directly with Lucien Rivard, Paul Mondolini, Antoine D'Agostino, and Michael Mertz, major players in the Mafia's international heroin trafficking operation. As reveled in *Ultimate Sacrifice: John and Robert Kennedy, the Plan for a Coup in Cuba, and the Murder of JFK* by Lamar Waldron and Thom Hartmann (Carroll & Graf, NY, 2005), "Two of Mertz's partners in this heroin network, Lucien Rivard and Paul Mondoloni, had ties to [Santo] Trafficante and to associates of Jack Ruby." The seizure proved once again to the Mafia that JFK had to be stopped on November 22.

Civello's and Marcello's rage over the heroin seizure in Laredo, Texas, was heightened by the growing rumors of LBJ's impending removal from the 1964 presidential ticket. *The Dallas Morning News* followed this closely. One letter to the editor said, "I think Mr. Kennedy will push Vice President Lyndon Johnson out of the convention."[37] Said another, "Johnson is . . . an astute politician and has not forgotten what Kennedy said about him when both were seeking the nomination three years ago. [T]hey will get another candidate; and Johnson knows it."[38] Publicly, JFK sought to dispel the rumors, but his words had a hollow ring.[39]

There were signs that LBJ was, in fact, developing a backup plan for 1964. In his correspondence with Henry Wade, he gave indications he was preparing for a run at his old Texas senate seat, then held by John Tower of Wichita Falls.[40] Johnson simply could not be sure the contract on Kennedy would succeed. If it failed, JFK's plan to find another running mate would go forward, and LBJ knew that waiting until 1964 to begin a Senate run would only ensure defeat.

Kennedy's fears over the damage done to the space program by his United Nations speech about cooperation with the Russians proved justified. In early October, the House Appropriations Committee voted to cut the space program by $265 million.[41] On October 7, Thomas explained to the press, "[I]t's time to . . . take a look at the situation."[42] A few days later, John Kennedy received the formal invitation to address the Houston honorarium for Thomas on November 21.[43] Ever more anxious to curry favor with Thomas, JFK quickly accepted.

On November 16, the Dallas press reported that the White House had "flashed the green light . . . for President Kennedy to ride in a motorcade through downtown Dallas. . . . The President is expected to travel over Lemmon Avenue or Cedar Springs Road to the downtown area, then west on Main Street before turning north after driving through the Triple Underpass. [H]e would pass through the downtown area about noon."[44] It was all the Mafia's foreign hit men needed.

By November 20, Johnson was in Dallas, ostensibly to attend a bottler's convention. While there, the press observed that the vice president appeared extremely keyed up. Riding in the backseat of a black Lincoln with Barefoot Sanders, as reported, "Johnson, the political master, held exclusive court. . . . [T]he senior statesman and the boyish-looking attorney joined in a highly animated discussion. Two or three times, Johnson leaned over to shake a finger in Sanders' face. Whatever the point, it seemed to bring appropriate political anguish to the younger man's face. . . . Sanders . . . discreetly stayed in the car until Johnson boarded his plane."[45] Johnson's time was at hand; all was in place.

On the night of the twenty-first, President Kennedy appeared in Houston to honor Albert Thomas. The importance of the event dictated nothing less than the most glowing remarks: "I personally called Al Thomas and asked him to give up his retirement for the good of the country. For this man is, in many ways, one of the most remarkable members of Congress. . . . He has helped steer our country to its present preeminence in outer space. . . . [Our] hopes . . . depend on the effort we are willing to mount now here in Houston. . . . That is why I salute Albert Thomas."[46]

JFK flew into Dallas Love Field the following morning, passing over the Zuroma Club's meeting house and the Dallas Mafia's cemetery of choice, Calvary Hill. Later, his motorcade, in winding its way toward downtown, passed near Civello's house and then through the Pearl Street Market district. The police department's scout car proceeded ahead, watching for "potential agitators."[47] In Houston the day before, there had been "pickets chanting 'Cuba.'"[48] In New Orleans, Marcello sat in a federal courtroom. In Dallas, U.S. attorney Arnold Stone was ready with his response to the Stone defense.

At half past noon, the motorcade crawled into Dealey Plaza, Sheriff Decker in the lead car, Mayor Cabell five cars back. Ruby watched nervously from the nearby *Dallas Morning News* building. Representative Thomas was in the procession. A smiling Vice President Johnson, two cars behind President Kennedy, waved to the crowd.[49]

The trap was sprung. Fire poured into the President's car from the rear and the right front. John Kennedy's head snapped backward and to the left, exploding in a halo of blood and brain tissue. The moment captured on film, the Lincoln with its dying occupant, flickered frame by frame into history and with it, the war on organized crime.

11

TEXAS JUSTICE

> Wade said preliminary reports indicated more than one person was involved in the shooting.
>
> —*Dallas Morning News*, early edition

> Everyone who participated in this crime . . . is guilty of murder under Texas law. They should all go to the electric chair.
>
> —Henry Wade, afternoon of November 22

> We have formally charged [Oswald]. . . . [I]t is this man and this man alone.
>
> —Henry Wade, evening of November 22

> I haven't done anything to be ashamed of. . . . The only thing I know about killing the President is from reporters in the hall.
>
> —Lee Oswald, November 22, 1963

FOR LYNDON JOHNSON, containment was the first priority. As soon as he was sure Kennedy was dead, he left for Love Field and *Air Force One*. There, he ordered Barefoot Sanders to bring Judge Sarah Hughes before him to administer the oath of office.[1] By doing this, he simultaneously demonstrated solidarity with the Dallas Mafia and contempt for Attorney General Robert Kennedy. At LBJ's directive through Sanders, an all-too-cooperative Judge Hughes stopped the

Stone prosecution that very day.[2] Sanders was put in control of the prosecution, and RFK's task force attorney Arnold Stone was marginalized.[3] Justice Department Criminal Division chief Herbert Miller, RFK's man in charge of the overall situation in Dallas, was clearly in over his head and told Sanders it was a "most welcome delay."[4] A relieved Sanders, understanding that Miller had no experience in the field of organized crime, quickly seized the opportunity presented.

The general public, unaware of the Stone prosecution and LBJ's, Hughes's, and Sanders's corruption at the hands of the Dallas mob, only learned that day that Sarah Hughes was "the first woman to swear in a president."[5] The behavior of Houston representative "*Albert Thomas on Air Force One*." was revealing. When LBJ completed the oath of office, he turned away from the cameras and toward his old ally. The moment captured on film, Thomas grinned and winked at Johnson.[6] Wary of the photographers and others crowded into the small cabin, LBJ was careful to contain himself. His "despised" vice presidential status successfully cast off, with Thomas's and the Mob's help, there would be time enough for celebration. His wife Lady Bird, however, grinned broadly at the critical moment.[7] A dazed and blood-splattered Jackie Kennedy said nothing.

Later, in a private phone conversation with Thomas (one LBJ ordered not to be released until fifty years after his own death), Johnson expressed both his gratitude and power. "I sent for Thomas . . . when I took the oath, and I plan to stay with you when we go to the graveyard together," adding, "you've been the best soldier I've had."[8]

As Johnson and his allies flew east to take over the country, the reality of conspiracy swept through the streets of Dallas. The media swarmed over the scene and quickly began reporting what had occurred.

> A single shot through the right temple took the life of the 46-year-old Chief Executive.

[A] rifle slug ripped a gaping wound in the back of his head.

> [M]ost [people] ran to the west side of the [school book] building thinking the shots came from behind bushes and a fence dividing the street from a railroad yard.

> [N]ewspapermen scrambled to . . . see a policeman vaulting over a marble barricade . . . in pursuit of the gunman. . . . Dallas police stationed near the underpass rushed to the shooting scene, led by a motorcycle officer who had abandoned his vehicle to join in pursuit of the gunman. [Witnesses] glanced up to see a man run up the [grassy knoll] across the street from them. . . . Both women . . . were directly in the path of the bullet.

> This reporter . . . saw bystanders ducking for cover, and policemen, with drawn pistols running up the [grassy knoll], hunting the sniper.

> Guns drawn, police raced first toward a railroad embankment where they thought the rifle-wielder was hiding.

> The witness . . . seemed to think the shots came from in front of or beside the President. He explained the President did not slump forward as if he would have been shot from the rear. The book depository building stands in the rear of the President's location.[9]

ABC television affiliate WFAA had two reporters stationed near Dealey Plaza as the motorcade passed by. Jay Watson and Jerry Haynes heard gunfire and ran into the plaza. There, they observed Bill Newman and his wife as they lay on the ground between Elm Street and the grassy knoll.[10] Standing at curbside to JFK's right front as the motorcade was about to pass them, they were the quintessential eyewitnesses. Realizing the opportunity, Watson brought them to the ABC station located nearby. Within ten minutes, they were on the air. He read an initial dispatch from UPI: "President Kennedy and Governor John Connally have been cut down by assassins' bullets in downtown Dallas."[11]

Newman. [A] gunshot, apparently from behind us, hit the President in the side of the temple.

Watson. Do you think the first gun shot came from behind you too?

Newman. I think it came from . . . up on top of the hill. . . .
Watson. I saw across the street that you were . . . on the ground, to keep out of the line of fire.
Newman. . . . I feel that both [shots] were coming from directly behind where we were standing. [T]he mall behind us, . . . that's where he was.
Watson. I know that the police were taking off in that direction . . . toward the railroad cars.[12]

A few minutes later, Watson was joined on camera by Haynes, who said, "Some of the Secret Service agents thought the gunfire was from a . . . weapon fired . . . from a grassy knoll to which the police rushed," and added, "In other words, they fired into the car as it came down the hill."[13] "And these people were in the line of fire," concluded Watson.[14]

Approximately twenty minutes later, the affiliate set up a large chart of the plaza. Aided by the drawing, Watson pointed to a clump of trees at the top of the grassy knoll. "And from our eyewitness that you saw earlier, [the President] was shot from up in here."[15] Moments later, he again pinpointed the same spot, stating Kennedy "was shot from here."[16] Nowhere in the initial report, virtually a scoop, was there any mention of the school book depository.

Law enforcement focused entirely on the terrain to the President's right front. Dallas County sheriff Bill Decker issued an order via radio to his nearby department overlooking the plaza. "Take every man available from the jail and the office and go to the railroad yards off Elm near the triple underpass," he commanded, hoping to seal off the knoll area and trap the assassins.[17] Henry Wade, still waiting at the local trade mart for the presidential luncheon, was briefed on the situation. "The electric chair is too good for the killers," proclaimed the district attorney.[18]

The local press was already talking of prosecution that afternoon. "Ironically, the killers may stand trial in a courtroom within a stone's throw of the spot where the shooting took place. . . . Wade said Governor Connally and the President's widow would likely give testimony at the trials of the killers."[19]

Initial local reporting on both Kennedy's and Connally's wounds made obvious the fact that Kennedy had been caught in a crossfire.

Referring to JFK,

> In the back of the President's head was a gaping hole. . . . When Dr. Clark first looked at the stricken President, he saw "a large gaping wound in the back of the head. There was loss of tissue." Kennedy had two wounds, one in the throat just below the Adam's apple and another in the back of his head, "a large gaping wound with considerable loss of tissue." . . . "He was a dead man when he came in here. Oh, he was breathing, and we got some heart beat but that bullet shattered the back of his skull. . . . Even if we had kept the body alive the President would have had no sight. . . . The brain centers for sight seemed to be gone. . . . The bullet did . . . massive damage at the right rear of Kennedy's head. . . . It tore through . . . part of the "occipital lobe" at the back of the head.[20]

Reporters and the emergency room doctors referenced the occipital lobe to give the public a clear understanding of the area from which the head shot to the right temple had exited—at and below the bony protuberance at the back and base of the President's head.

Referring to Connally,

> Governor Connally . . . had whirled in the limousine . . . to see the President shot a moment before he himself was hit. . . . According to doctors attending the Governor, the bullet which hit him . . . fragmented, smashed through the ribs, punctured the lung, shattered the right wrist and then struck his thigh. One doctor said that if . . . Connally had not whirled to look at the President, the bullet might have gone through the middle of his back and into his heart. . . . The bullet that hit Connally in the back went through his chest, taking out a part of the fifth rib and collapsed the lung. The bullet then went into his right wrist, causing a compound fracture, and then buried itself in his left thigh. . . . Doctor's applied a cast to . . . Connally's right wrist . . . since the bullet splintered the right wrist bone.[21]

Based on the wounds, eyewitness accounts, and the Zapruder film, Dallas law enforcement officials and the local media initiated a conspiracy investigation. The fact that the presidential limousine had been hit almost simultaneously by multidirectional fire was never in dispute.

The foreign hit men who assassinated President Kennedy, French Corsicans (including possibly Lucien Sarti) or Canadians, escaped. Later that day, Lee Oswald, an employee of the nearby Texas School Book Depository, was arrested in the unrelated shooting of a Dallas police officer. Although Oswald had nothing to do with the police officer's death, he was taken into custody as part of the overall frenzy that had seized local law enforcement in the aftermath of JFK's death.

The naive Oswald had been led to believe by those who used him that he was going to be part of public demonstration in favor of Castro's Cuba. In that regard, on the morning of the assassination, he had taken a rolled-up pro-Cuba protest poster or flag into the depository when he came to work. At the instruction of his handler, he had left it at a prearranged place on the sixth floor, assuming it would be prominently displayed in one of several large windows when Kennedy's motorcade approached the building.

At the moment Kennedy was assassinated, Oswald was finishing his lunch in the book depository employee break room on the second floor of the building. Believing that a political demonstration had just taken place, he went out to observe, only to learn that the President had been shot. Oswald had no idea that he had been set up and that a rifle he owned had been stolen from his garage and planted in the depository to frame him after the fact. He panicked and was subsequently arrested in a case of mistaken identity. Later that day, when his rifle was discovered, he was already in custody. Near midnight, he was wrongly charged with the shooting.

Oswald was also charged with killing Dallas PD officer J. D. Tippit. The policeman was gunned down shortly after JFK was murdered. Although Oswald was charged with the crime, there has never been any reliable evidence to connect him with the murder. An excellent source on this subject is Mark Lane's classic work, *Rush to Judgment*. That book makes clear the facts that Oswald's pistol was not the murder weapon; the scanty eyewitness testimony was at best unreliable, and his police lineup was grossly biased in favor of a frame-up. So weak was the case that it became necessary after-the-fact for the Warren Commission to fabricate ballistics evidence via Hoover's FBI to imply that Oswald was responsible.

The same would be done by the Warren Commission to make it appear that in April 1963 Oswald had attempted to murder a local retired U.S. Army general, Edwin Walker. But as in the Tippit case, the ballistics evidence never supported the accusation. According to news reports, the weapon used was a .30-06, which used very different ammunition than Oswald's Italian-made 6.5 Carcano. I discuss the Walker case at length in my first book on the JFK assassination, *Act of Treason*.

Meanwhile, Lyndon Johnson had seized power in Washington. One of his first acts was to use the office of the presidency to prevent any conspiracy investigation by Dallas officials. Such an investigation would have led to close examination of the local power structure, the ongoing Stone prosecution, the Zuroma Club, and Mob arrests. To accomplish this, he exerted his control over Texas attorney general Waggoner Carr and DA Henry Wade. As prosecutor of Oswald, it was Wade's job to prepare and submit the indictment. Carr's position was almost totally civil versus criminal, but the attorney generalship was a proven means for exposure of corruption in public office via a court of inquiry.

To implement his plan, LBJ turned to federal officials under his authority: Hoover, Sanders, and personal aide Cliff Carter. Calls were made from the late afternoon into the evening hours by Carter and Sanders to Henry Wade and Waggoner Carr (and by Hoover's aides to Dallas FBI SAC Gordon Shanklin) to prevent a conspiracy-based indictment of Oswald from being filed in Kennedy's murder.[22]

The strong-arming of Carr and Wade the evening of November 22, 1963, was the primary subject of their questioning some months later by the Warren Commission. But by then, they were well aware that Johnson was firmly in control of both the commission and the Stone prosecution. Confident that their own political futures were secure, they testified candidly. Their testimony, in part:

Cooper. Do you desire a lawyer?

Wade. No, sir . . .

Dulles. In your talks . . . with Mr. Carter at the White House . . . did any questions come up . . . about not raising the issue that . . . there might be a conspiracy?

Wade. . . . I'm rather sure sometime Friday afternoon . . . he called me and said, "Are they making any progress on the case?" You see, Cliff Carter and I are close personal friends. [A]nd they were all upset, and I said, "I don't know. I have heard they have got some pretty good evidence." I think that is the only conversation I had with him.[23] . . . I . . . saw it come on the radio that they are going to file on Oswald as part of an international conspiracy in murdering the U.S. President, and I think I talked to Barefoot Sanders. He called me or I called him. . . .

Rankin. Well, did [Sanders] say anything to you about that point?

Wade. [H]e said he had heard it on the radio and didn't know whether it would be . . . he did not think it ought to be done, . . . so I went down there to be sure they didn't . . . I talked to . . . Carr that night. . . .

Rankin. Mr. Carr didn't try to tell you in any way how to handle [the] case?

Wade. Not that I know of.

Carr. Off the record. (Discussion off the record.) . . .

Wade. [H]e did mention that the rumor was out that we were getting ready to file a charge of Oswald being part of an international conspiracy, and I told him that that was not going to be done. [A]nd then . . . I talked to . . . my first assistant who had talked to, somebody had called him. . . . [T]hey . . . were concerned about . . . having received calls from Washington. . . . [A]nd that is what prompted me to go down and take the complaint. . . .

Rankin. Why did you not include . . . a charge of an international conspiracy?

Wade. The U.S. attorney and the [Texas] attorney general had called me and said that if it wasn't absolutely necessary they thought it shouldn't be done. . . .

Cooper. [C]onspiracy is a crime in Texas, isn't it, conspiracy to commit a crime?

Wade. Yes, sir . . .

Rankin. Have you ever had any evidence that Oswald was involved with anyone else in actually shooting the President?

Wade. I have always felt that [at] the minimum [there] was an inspiration from some cause, and [at] the maximum was actual pay [to Oswald]. . . .

Rankin. Was there anyone either from the State or Federal Government that urged you not to state . . . international conspiracy if you found one was present?

Wade. It is like I mentioned to you what Mr. Carr and Mr. Sanders both inquired, . . . and I told them right off that whether it was so or not doesn't make any difference. It wouldn't be alleged.

Rankin. Now going back to this telephone conversation with Mr. Carr. . . .

Wade. [H]e said that he had had a call from Washington. . . . I remember he said . . . 'This would be a bad situation, if you allege it as part of a . . . conspiracy, and it may affect your international relations, a lot of things of the country,' . . .

Dulles. You have testified as to a telephone call that [Carr] received from Washington, what he told you about that. Did you have anything further to add to that?

Wade. [D]uring all this investigation, I have talked to Cliff Carter in the White House. . . . [R]ight after they got back to Washington, I got a call from Cliff Carter.[24]

Texas AG Carr was an expert on the Dallas Mafia and knew of Wade's failure to effectively prosecute Stone, Miller, and Ferrantello in 1951. Carr, evidently in the room throughout Wade's five hours of testimony (a fundamental breach of standard interrogation procedure allowing Carr to taylor his responses to fit Wade's version of events), mirrored his statement later on.

Carr. As I recall, it was around 8 or 9 o'clock at night . . . when I received a long-distance call from Washington from someone in the White House. I can't for the life of me remember who it was. . . . So the request was made of me to contact Mr. Wade to find out if that allegation was in the indictment. . . . So I did call Mr. Wade. . . . And then I called back, and . . . informed the White House participant in the conversation of what Mr. Wade had said, and that was all of it.

Dulles. Was there any indication in the call . . . as to whether this was a leftist, rightist, or any other type of conspiracy or . . . was just the word conspiracy used?

Carr. As far as I recall, it was an international conspiracy.[25]

The failure of the commission to follow up on Wade's admission (that he had been manipulated into not filing a conspiracy-based murder complaint) exposes the questioning of both men as a transparent fraud, an eviscerating betrayal of the American people. JFK *had* been killed by an international conspiracy—the Marcello-Civello crime family acting in concert with the Mondoloni-D'Agostino drug cartel. Wade's testimony proved that it was LBJ's intervention the evening of the assassination that caused the lengthy delay in the filing of the Oswald indictment, which did not occur until around midnight.[26]

Late that Friday evening of the twenty-second, with the FBI already taking over, Wade met with the press after sanitizing the Oswald murder complaint. "I believe we have enough evidence to convict him," he announced. When asked about whether JFK had died as the result of an "international conspiracy," Wade answered as he had been instructed to: "No, it is this man and this man alone."[27] And as later reported, "squelching reports that the shooting was part of a well-organized plot, devised by a group of people, [Wade] said: 'As far as I know, there was no one else involved.'"[28]

Over the course of the next thirty-six hours, former FBI agent Henry Wade reiterated LBJ's no-conspiracy directive to reporters. "We, we're just interested in proving that he did it. . . . I can't describe him any other than—the murderer of the President," he stated, though he knew it to be a lie.[29]

12

A PAVLOVIAN RESPONSE

FBI DIRECTOR J. Edgar Hoover, briefed in the fall of 1962 about the Trafficante and Marcello conversations, which had revealed the existence of the contract on JFK, knew Kennedy had been the victim of a Mafia hit. Accordingly, on the afternoon of the twenty-second, he issued the directive to "get everyone involved in shooting the President and get them fast."[1] But at LBJ's directive, Hoover reversed course, seized the primary physical evidence in the case, and began narrowing the scope of the investigation to support a lone-gunman conclusion.[2]

Hoover had, by then, also been briefed by his agents on the colossal heroin seizure in Laredo in October and had followed the trail that led back to Marcello and Civello. The FBI director was all too aware of LBJ's and Price Daniel's efforts in the mid-1950s to hide the existence of Antoine D'Agostino (and probably Mondoloni) and his connection to the Mafia's heroin importation and distribution network in Texas. Understanding the implications of that connection, he moved quickly to contain the fact that one of D'Agostino's close associates, Michael Mertz, was evidently in Dallas on November 22.

Dallas researcher Jim Marrs, in his landmark work *Crossfire: The Plot That Killed Kennedy* (Carroll and Graf, NY, 1989), revealed that Hoover knew that "Jean SOUTRE aka . . . Michael Mertz . . . had been expelled from the U.S. at Fort Worth or Dallas 18 hours after the assassination. He was in Fort Worth on the morning of 22 November and in Dallas in the afternoon. The French believe that he was expelled to either Mexico or Canada." In a possible connection, an individual named "John Mertz . . . flew from Houston to Mexico City on November 23, 1963." Not surprisingly, Hoover provided "no further identifying data regarding [Mertz]." Why was Mertz in Dallas on the day Kennedy was killed? To simply observe the assassination, or was he one of the hit men? To this day, portions of the government's file on Mertz (Soutre) remain secret, exempt from disclosure by executive order on grounds of national security. The fact that Mertz had been expelled by the State Department under LBJ's watch was not lost on the FBI director, especially when considered in light of Johnson's swift actions to prevent the filing of an international conspiracy indictment against Oswald only hours after the assassination.

However, there was a problem with pinning the murder on the hapless Oswald. Through interrogation sessions on Friday night, the Dallas Police Department had discovered that the Dallas FBI had been monitoring the young leftist in the months prior to the murder. After thorough investigation, they had concluded, quite accurately, that Oswald was harmless. And it turned out the FBI had known of his job at the school book depository and his presence on the presidential parade route.[3] They understood that Oswald was just another nonviolent, politically active leftist.

Police Chief Jesse Curry's newly discovered knowledge that the FBI knew about Oswald prior to the assassination prompted him to make a public statement early Saturday afternoon. "I understand the FBI did know that he was in Dallas."[4] Within minutes, either Hoover or Dallas FBI SAC Gordon Shanklin called him and told him to minimize the damage caused by his disclosure.[5] Curry, an FBI Academy graduate, hurriedly arranged another press conference. Clearly intimidated, he told the press, "I'm certainly not saying that the FBI knew something that we should have known and didn't tell us."[6] But Curry's efforts only enraged the FBI director.

Chief Curry served at the pleasure of Dallas mayor Earle Cabell who was an ally to both Johnson and the Civello mob. Like Wade, the police chief denied there had been a conspiracy.[7] When asked by reporters, "Is there any doubt in your mind, Chief, that Oswald is the man . . . ?" He replied, "I think this is the man who killed the President."[8] But like Wade, Curry had by then viewed the Zapruder film, spoken to eyewitnesses, and read initial press coverage. Like Wade, he knew he was subverting justice.

Chief Curry held another press conference Sunday morning, shortly before Lee Oswald was forever silenced by Jack Ruby. The press had learned about anonymous death threats on Oswald's life earlier that morning. Their skepticism about Wade's and Curry's claim of no conspiracy was beginning to grow. "Sir, could you tell us whether or not there is a possibility of other people being involved?" asked one reporter. An increasingly nervous Curry responded, "I'm not making no more comments."[9] Pressure from LBJ and Hoover was apparently having its effect.

The media's growing skepticism of the official line had been exacerbated by police captain Will Fritz, who controlled Oswald's interrogation. Driven by loyalty to the PD and obsession with perfection, he said to reporters, "I can tell you that this case is cinched—that this man killed the President. There's no question in my mind about it."[10]

Shortly after Curry's press conference, Jack Ruby shot Lee Oswald to death at point-blank range as he was being transferred from the city to the county jail. The injection of Ruby into the crisis paralyzed local law enforcement. Ruby was a man known by authorities to be under federal investigation as an operative in the Civello mob's bookmaking operation and a man well acquainted with many officials in both the police department's and district attorney's offices. Curry issued a sketchy statement and stopped talking. Fritz, who was well acquainted with the thug, appeared shaken before reporters. Asked one, "Captain, was anyone else connected with Oswald in the matter? . . . 'Well, now, not that *I* know of,'" he managed.[11]

The killing of the only suspect in custody, by a known operative of the Dallas Mafia in the PD's own basement, gave FBI Director Hoover a legitimate civil rights action against the police department. He pursued it in a memo to Johnson only hours after the slaying. "Since we now think it involves the Criminal Code on a conspiracy charge under Section 2-11 [*sic*], we want them to shut up."[12] Hoover was referring to 18 U.S.C. 241, Civil Rights, Conspiracy against Rights of Citizens. His subsequent threat to Curry to investigate the Dallas PD, in combination with Ruby's Mob ties, had the desired effect. A profound silence fell over the Dallas Police Department.

That Sunday evening, Henry Wade prepared to go before the press and deliver the case against Oswald, also serving as judge and jury in the process. Wade knew Jack Ruby before the assassination, had previously dismissed a complaint against him, and knew of his gambling activity and association with the Miller brothers through the Enquire Shine and Press shop.[13] RFK's prosecution of the Stone defendants had previously made local headlines. Wade, as an experienced district attorney, now uncomfortably familiar with the Dallas Mafia, had quickly perceived Ruby's motive for participation in the assassination plot. Stop Kennedy and you stop the prosecution of the Mob's gambling operation, which was leading toward Ruby's own indictment.

As LBJ's close ally, Wade knew of Johnson's and Hoover's growing hatred toward the Kennedys. And it was common knowledge that LBJ had become a liability to the President. Through Wade's involvement with the Zuroma Club, he knew that Johnson was very popular with the local Sicilians. He had seen the FBI scrambling that weekend—seen them lie about their prior knowledge of Oswald. He had seen Hoover and Shanklin put Curry to the wall. Most seriously, Wade had already cooperated with LBJ by preventing the filing of a conspiracy-based murder complaint against Oswald. Lastly, LBJ was now president—a dream come true for Wade. There was only one possible course of action—convict Oswald and Oswald alone.

The most appalling aspect of Henry Wade's statement to the press was the huge void between the evidence he presented and his repeated conviction that Oswald was guilty of homicide. He spoke of the presence of Oswald's palm prints on packing boxes on the sixth floor of the Texas School Book Depository. Oswald worked in the building, however, and it was his job to fill orders and handle the boxes. He spoke of the rifle as if Oswald had attempted to conceal his ownership of it. But it had been left at the scene and within a few hours traced (via the intact serial number) to a PO box rented in Oswald's name.

The DA stated "his finger prints were found on the . . . rifle." But the police department's own report, prepared prior to Oswald's murder, concluded there were none.[14] Wade went on to claim that "the bullet from this gun killed the President."[15] The DA had known for days about overwhelming eyewitness statements pointing to a shooter in front of JFK. He knew about and had viewed the Zapruder film, with its verification of that fact. His conclusion that a rifle found in a building behind the assassination scene was the murder weapon was, then, legally baseless. Whenever pressed about the evidence held by the FBI, ex-FBI agent Wade's answer was the same. "I can't go into anything from the FBI. I'm not at liberty to."[16] He did not intend to repeat Curry's mistakes.

The press knew, however, that Jack Ruby had been seen repeatedly in and around police headquarters from Friday night on. One reporter said to Wade, "He looked to be like your good friend."[17] Under the pressure of questioning from so many, Wade began to stumble and make admissions which pointed to the ex-marine Oswald's innocence. When asked whether Oswald had expressed any "animosity toward the President," he avoided the question.[18] When asked what Oswald's motive was, Wade responded, "Don't—can't answer that."[19] When asked whether Oswald had been placed in the sixth-floor window by any eyewitnesses, he responded, "People cannot positively identify him from the ground."[20] Realizing his admission, he quickly added, "He fits their general description."[21] It became apparent to the journalists present that Wade's conference was a sham.

An increasingly uneasy press perceived a cover-up. When one member asked, "Why did you call us tonight and why did you go over this evidence?"[22] Wade, lying through his teeth, said, "Well, there's a lot of reasons. . . . I have heard nothing from any of the—from Washington or any of the officials in this country on this matter. . . . I thought in my own mind . . . that it's a good idea."[23] Another asked, "Are you investigating the possibility that Ruby might have killed Oswald because he feared Oswald might implicate him in some plot?"[24] Wade responded, "I'm not investigating anything."[25] The DA had done his best but knew that he had only heightened suspicions that JFK had died at the hands of a conspiracy.

Wade was clearly in over his head. The injection of local mobster Jack Ruby into the unfolding drama had unnerved him and made him realize that the only hope he had of saving himself was to simply cave in to the demands of Johnson. Within twenty-four hours, the Dallas DA relinquished his jurisdiction and turned the entire Kennedy case over to Hoover's FBI.[26]

13

THE PROSECUTION OF RUBY

JACK RUBY, CONFIDENT of his power over local law enforcement and the FBI, believed he could avoid the death penalty or long-term imprisonment for the murder of Oswald. As a longtime Dallas local, he knew prosecution for murder was a joke. Once arrested, his lawyer promptly stated that he would plead temporary insanity. The year before the assassination, the Texas legislature had passed a law making "it mandatory for a judge to grant freedom to anyone who appeal[ed] a commitment to a mental hospital, pending disposition of the appeal." One Texas official warned at the time, "This is a dangerous law."[1] In a pretrial sanity hearing for Ruby, the press pointed that out. "If the hearing ended with a jury ruling Ruby was temporarily insane when he shot Oswald, the night-club owner would never stand trial on the murder charges."[2] The Dallas mob did its part. When Ruby's confidant Sam Campisi was questioned by the FBI, he quickly volunteered that Ruby was "crazy."[3]

One of Ruby's defense attorneys in the Oswald murder prosecution was Tom Howard, a longtime Mob attorney. Like Ruby, he had an extensive record with the IRS, which included a conviction for income tax evasion.[4] Under Kennedy, Howard's circumstances had gone from bad to worse. The IRS's criminal intelligence division was closing in on him. Like Ruby, he owed huge sums of money to the government.[5] The IRS was the driving wedge in RFK's war on organized crime. It was the failure to pay gambling taxes that had brought the indictment of John Eli Stone and Isadore Miller.[6] During that time, the IRS was also turning up the pressure on Ruby with tax liens.[7] The combined pressure of Howard's own tax woes and the complex demands of Ruby's case proved too much. The attorney died suddenly while working in Ruby's defense.[8]

Like other mobsters before him, Ruby knew the value of lawyers associated with the district attorney's office. When arrested, he requested Fred Bruner as counsel. A former assistant DA, Bruner was close to Wade—literally. As the press reported, "Fred Bruner, a leading defense lawyer, was seated near Wade when the district attorney learned of the shooting."[9] A member of Ruby's defense team practically from the outset was former assistant DA Phil Burleson. An appeals expert in Wade's office, he had gone into private practice in September 1962.[10] He stayed on Ruby's defense team into the appellate process. During the appeal, Wade would "offer to reduce Ruby's death sentence . . . to life imprisonment."[11] One of Joe Civello's attorneys also joined Ruby's defensive team.[12]

Ruby's family had sought additional defense counsel. As Ruby's brother revealed while testifying before the Warren Commission, "Charlie Tessmer . . . turned it down. Why he never told us."[13] The commissioners did not address his bewilderment because they knew that Tessmer was at that moment representing the Stone defendants. Despite the absence of Tessmer, Ruby ultimately received a classic high-dollar defense, orchestrated by a seasoned group of attorneys. Even Wade was impressed, telling a reporter, "[S]omebody with lots of money wants Jack Ruby found innocent of a murder charge."[14] Understanding Ruby's role in the Mafia's elimination of JFK, Wade knew that the mobster had access to unlimited funds.

Defense counsel was quick to exploit Ruby's associations. Early on, Howard reminded the local press that "district attorney [Wade] has known Jack Ruby on a first name basis for many years."[15] Revealed by one reporter was the fact that Ruby "knew most of the officers who questioned him. . . . When Assistant Dist. Atty . . . Alexander entered the room . . . , Rubenstein [Ruby] looked up and said, 'Hi Bill.'"[16] As another reporter, who had seen Ruby in and out of the Dallas police station over the course of the weekend after the assassination, put it, "He could have killed [Oswald] five times."[17] Wade had no rebuttal for the scathing revelations.

When the realities of all that had occurred since November 22, 1963, began to sink in with Dallas authorities, it was also realized that the city's image had to be protected from scandal. The ugly exposé that would have followed if the American people learned that JFK had been the victim of a Mob hit—with the cooperation of the Pearl Street Mafia and acquiescence of a corrupt DA—would have irreparably damaged the city's image. So in the weeks, months, and years to come, the Dallas media repeatedly relied on the "lone nut" explanation. To this day, to many Dallasites, Oswald and Ruby were just two "crazy" individuals acting independently of each other.[18]

Assistant Dallas DA William Alexander had correctly perceived from the beginning that Oswald was merely a fall guy. Alexander was to handle much of the Ruby prosecution. But from prior confrontations with the FBI, he was also very fearful of Hoover's power.[19] Alexander had not missed the fact that one month before the assassination, one of his own assistants, Emmett Colvin, left the DA's office to work for Dallas mob attorney Charles Tessmer—as defense co-counsel in the Stone prosecution.[20]

When Alexander was interviewed by the FBI in latter December 1963, he discounted any connection between Oswald's murder and the Mafia.[21] However, immediately after Ruby's arrest, police had searched the mobster's cars and found Carousel Club membership cards in the names of mobsters Sam Campisi and John Grizzaffi—and William Alexander. Alexander had seen the police inventory report on the Ruby evidence before his interview with the FBI. And Campisi, in his first statement to investigators on December 13, had admitted knowing Ruby "for approximately ten years." One of the first people Ruby had called from the Dallas County jail after being arrested was Sam Campisi's brother Joe.[22]

The judge in Ruby's case, Joe Brown (a popular guest of the Zuroma Club), who had been in the local judiciary since the 1930s, bent over backward to aid Ruby's defense and prevent disclosures about the Dallas Mafia. Ruby was allowed public "courtroom press conferences" *before* jury selection to allow promotion of the insanity defense. Brown repeatedly granted defense motions over the issue. But the crucial support would come when he failed to grant a change of venue from Dallas to another more objective locale—a fundamental judicial error which he knew would trigger a reversal of Ruby's death sentence on appeal.[23] Brown's selection to preside over Ruby's trial, with his detailed knowledge of the Mob and its influence over local officialdom, had been the only recourse available to Dallas.

FBI director Hoover, already caught lying to the American people about his agency's knowledge and surveillance of Oswald before the assassination, had the Dallas field office destroy critical evidence after Ruby killed Oswald.[24] Field office SAC Shanklin ordered Ruby's files sanitized, hiding the fact that Ruby had served as an FBI informant in 1959.[25] LBJ then formalized Hoover's control of the investigation.[26] As police chief Curry explained it to a by then very disbelieving press, "Wade requested that we turn it over to the FBI."[27] The derailment of criminal justice was complete.

The American people were transfixed by the slaughter of President John F. Kennedy in the streets of Dallas on November 22, 1963. The horrific event had been compounded by the obvious silencing of the supposed assassin by a local mafioso—a man well known to authorities. The American people, conditioned by their respect for the office of president by Kennedy's predecessor Dwight Eisenhower and JFK's charisma, assumed the new president would be forthright in his handling of the matter. In the days that followed the double homicide, they waited—waited for answers, waited for truth. But Lyndon Johnson was now in control. It was a new day. He and his minions, motivated only by power and all that it offered, discarded the truth—discarded the American people.

14

A REPUBLICAN STAMP OF APPROVAL

Several Commission members, Senator Russell especially, are apparently disgusted by the conduct of the investigation.

—*National Review*, April 21, 1964

Russell: "They are trying to prove that the same bullet that hit Kennedy first was the one that hit Connally. . . . Well, I don't believe it."

Johnson: "I don't either."

—September 1964 telephone conversation

A U.S. CONGRESSIONAL MOVE to start its own investigation of President Kennedy's death forced Lyndon Johnson's hand one week after the assassination. That day he issued Executive Order 11130 and announced the formation of the Warren Commission.[1]

LBJ relied on FBI Director J. Edgar Hoover to supply dossiers on all members of the commission to ensure he only chose people he could control. He knew that in order to achieve the appearance of credibility with a commission of his own making, membership would have to be both conservative and bipartisan. He made sure that the voting majority of the commissioners were Republicans. Chosen were Supreme Court Chief Justice Earl Warren, Senator

John Cooper, Representative Gerald Ford, former CIA director Allen Dulles, and John McCloy. The other two were conservative Southern Democrats Senator Dick Russell of Georgia and Representative Hale Boggs of Louisiana.[2]

By using conservatives, Johnson also ensured cooperation with Hoover. Dick Russell was LBJ's closest ally in the Senate and was chosen for that reason. Hale Boggs was put on the commission to derail his previous call in the House for a congressional investigation. Mafia boss Carlos Marcello, who influenced Louisiana politics, in all likelihood had made campaign contributions to Boggs over the years. Boggs's district included New Orleans, the seat of Marcello's illegal operations. LBJ chose cohort Abe Fortas to coordinate the commission investigation.[3] Fortas had helped LBJ steal the 1948 Senate election and was a longtime political confidant—subject to Johnson's control.[4]

LBJ wanted the commission to be led by a member of the Supreme Court—Tom Clark. But Senator Russell was deeply opposed because he knew of Clark's reputation for corrupt dealings with the Dallas and Chicago Mafia. In a telephone conversation with Johnson, Russell said, "I don't know . . . you wouldn't want Clark, hardly."[5] The situation turned ugly.

> **LBJ.** I told you . . . I was going to name the Chief Justice. . . .
>
> **Russell.** You did not . . . you talked about getting somebody from the Supreme Court.
>
> **LBJ.** I told you I was going to name Warren and you said it would be better to name Clark.
>
> **Russell.** Oh . . . no . . . I said Clark *wouldn't* do.[6]

Convinced the commission was being designed to do LBJ's and Hoover's bidding, Russell refused to serve. Johnson exploded. "I can't arrest you and I'm not going to put the FBI on you but you're goddamned sure going to serve. . . . [Y]ou're going to be at my command as long as I'm here."[7] Russell served.

Earl Warren also had to be forced into service. LBJ said at one point to Russell, "They talked to him and he said he wouldn't serve under any circumstances . . . I called him down here and I spent an hour with him."[8] There were good reasons Earl Warren did all he could to avoid the appointment. An associate from his time as a district attorney in California had attempted to expose Johnson's theft of the 1948 U.S. Texas Senate election, only to be executed gangland style.[9] The man's son had attempted to continue the exposé but was attacked and nearly beaten to death.[10] Warren knew that Johnson and his cohorts were capable of anything when it came to holding on to power.

Earl Warren was also quite knowledgeable about the Mafia. He had observed JFK's attempt to destroy the organization—and the Civello mob along with it. Years before, during Warren's time as California's attorney general, he had investigated the West Coast Mafia extensively. That included the Los Angeles mob, which had ties to Dallas. Joe Civello had an associate in L.A. through whom he coordinated operations with the West Coast mob.[11] After his arrest at Apalachin, Civello was called to California to testify about his knowledge of the West Coast Mafia but took the Fifth against self-incrimination.[12] Warren's experience investigating the Mafia gave him a clear understanding of their murderous capabilities. In the case of JFK, he knew a Mob hit when he saw one.

Earl Warren had also been Republican Thomas Dewey's vice presidential running mate in the 1948 presidential election, in opposition to Harry Truman. They were the anti-Mob candidates. He knew firsthand of Truman's ties to the Mafia. Like many Americans, he had been appalled by Truman's appointment of LBJ's crony Tom Clark, first as U.S. attorney general, and later as a U.S. Supreme Court justice.[13] The chief justice knew then that any investigation of organized crime in Dallas would have to be handled with the utmost care in order to avoid scandal for the Supreme Court.

Before Warren could serve on the Supreme Court, he had to undergo an FBI background investigation. When he was nominated, damaging allegations surfaced. "Among other things, [he] was accused . . . of following the 'Marxist line,' of appointing dishonest judges when he was governor of California, and of having been under the control of a liquor lobbyist."[14] Hoover maintained a political dossier on Warren and shared it with LBJ.[15] There was at the time of the assassination a good deal of public sentiment calling for Warren's impeachment. So in the end, Warren also served out of fear—fear for the Supreme Court and fear that his career might be destroyed by some allegation of wrongdoing in his own past, whether true or not. Ardent Hooverites and political conservatives, Dulles, Ford, McCloy, and Cooper were, by contrast, eager to serve.[16]

Once the commission was created, it chose a general counsel. Not surprisingly, it rejected Mafia expert Warren Olney, who had told a Texas AG's conference on organized crime, "The toleration of gamblers and other parasites leads directly to consequences such as this."[17] Picked instead was conservative Republican J. Lee Rankin, a man unknowledgeable about the Mafia. He was also a former U.S. attorney who, as solicitor general, had worked closely with Hoover and the Supreme Court.[18]

Barefoot Sanders did his part in Dallas. It became his job to monitor the Ruby trial and control local questioning of the Warren Commission's witnesses. After a journalist spotted him at hearings, he reported, "Sanders is known to be a close political friend of . . . Johnson, whose interest in the Dallas hearings are apparent. 'Let's just say that we are working through the Justice Department,' Sanders said, smiling."[19] It was also his job to see to it that FBI "agents . . . testify only to the facts of their interviews with Ruby, not to venture any opinions nor touch on any other subject."[20] Sanders also made trips to Washington DC, and soon became omnipresent in the Johnson White House.[21]

Prosecuting Jack Ruby while simultaneously keeping Ruby's ties to the Dallas Mafia (and local officials) hidden from the public proved nearly impossible for the DA's office. Early in Ruby's trial, the press announced that his defense team wanted to place him on the stand. It was what authorities feared most—Jack Ruby having the opportunity to publicly discuss his close association with law enforcement. One such individual was Justice of the Peace Glenn Byrd. A Zuroma Club guest and confidant to both Ruby and Henry Wade, he was terrified by the prospect and died of a massive heart attack.[22]

The Dallas FBI understood that local people that were not compromised by the Dallas Mafia would have to be controlled. SAC Gordon Shanklin employed Gestapo tactics in the hope that locals would, in Hoover's words, "shut up." Just a few days after the formation of the Warren Commission, Shanklin made the Dallas press aware of the arrest of a New York man for giving false information in the investigation.[23] And when a Dallas woman accurately reported that she had seen Ruby at Parkland Hospital the afternoon of the assassination, Shanklin ordered her not to talk to the press.[24] The mobster's presence at the hospital proved to be of critical importance because many came to suspect that a nearly pristine bullet slug from Oswald's rifle had been planted on Connally's gurney that afternoon.[25] Just before her Warren Commission appearance, the woman received anonymous phone calls which "warned her to keep her 'mouth shut.'"[26] The effort to sell Johnson's "no conspiracy" conclusion to the public would require help from all levels of government if it were to succeed.

LBJ received critical support from Dallas mayor Earl Cabell (also a Zuroma Club guest), who from the beginning had tried to label the President's murder the work of a lone nut.[27] When three members of the Dallas city council attempted to launch an investigation into Oswald's murder, Cabell intervened.[28] In response, one councilman angrily warned, "The whole nation and world is watching us. They will judge us if we do not judge ourselves."[29] But Cabell was a powerful ally, and in his own testimony before the Warren Commission, he unhesitatingly endorsed the cover-up. In exchange for his critical cooperation, Johnson handed him the Democratic Party nomination for U.S. representative from Texas. LBJ would later tell him privately, "The years have been richer for me because of our friendship."[30] Cabell and LBJ also had friends at the state level who rallied to the cause.

Johnson's ally and a powerful state senator from the Dallas area George Parkhouse could have demanded formal investigation of the Kennedy assassination by the state legislature's General Investigating Committee or the formulation of a state-level commission. He did neither. In a letter to LBJ, he said, "I want you to know that I have been on your side from that tragic day in Dallas."[31] Critical to the selling of the "lone nut" deception was the notion that both Oswald and Ruby were insane at the time of the murders. Parkhouse was at that time chairman of a highly publicized state legislative study group on mental illness and the criminally insane. In an attempt to sell the temporary insanity defense for Ruby (as well as Oswald's act as that of a lone gunman), Parkhouse's committee publicly labeled the mobster, *before his trial*, a "sociopath who has boiled over and exploded in rage." And Oswald was a "schizophrenic . . . with terrific hostility and grudges—withdrawn, with eccentricities."[32]

The day after Ruby killed Oswald, Dallas Crime Commission director John McKee made the Dallas FBI aware that he understood the nature of the threat Ruby posed to investigators. He supplied Shanklin with a copy of the crime commission's file on the thug—a long rap sheet consisting of failed prosecutions and dismissals.[33] McKee knew that authorities were shielding Ruby and the Stone defendants but chose to remain silent because he was a strong supporter of Johnson and was ecstatic over his new status as president. McKee told him privately in a letter, "I am prepared to do anything that you think I am qualified to do in working on your behalf for the convention. . . . I have talked to Cliff Carter several times, but I am awaiting your direction."[34] McKee called no meeting of the Dallas Crime Commission until late January 1964 and made no investigation of JFK's assassination or Ruby's slaying of Oswald.[35] Aware of Johnson's loathing of the Kennedys, McKee called LBJ later on and expressed his hatred of Robert Kennedy.[36] Though McKee was initially motivated by the desire to gain opportunity from JFK's murder, he had (like local law enforcement) ignored the Dallas Mafia over the years and ultimately realized that cooperation with Johnson's cover-up was now mandatory.

When Bill Decker, a one-eyed chain-smoking ex-bootlegger turned sheriff, testified before Warren Commission counsel, he made three things very clear. One, beyond the briefest summation, he had nothing to say about his own past—a past which included his presence at the Zuroma Club and testimony before a federal parole board two decades earlier as a character witness *for* Joe Civello. Two, as the county jailer, he controlled all access to Ruby. And three, he had no desire to discuss Oswald's murder under oath.[37] He proved to be a man of his word.

It was not surprising that Lyndon Johnson, with the enthusiastic support of FBI Director Hoover, had been able to create a commission which would do his bidding. It was not surprising that Johnson's political flunkies in Dallas had leapt at the chance to gain opportunity by President Kennedy's slaughter. But what mystified the country was the seemingly inexplicable lack of action on the part of Attorney General Robert Kennedy in the weeks and months after his brother's murder.

15

RFK IS SILENCED

CONSPICUOUSLY ABSENT FROM practically all of the Warren Commission proceedings, both in Dallas and Washington DC, was Attorney General Robert Kennedy. Instead, he allowed his unqualified assistant AG, Herbert Miller, to be used in his stead. Compounding the problem, J. Edgar Hoover had ceased cooperation with Kennedy immediately after the murder of his brother. Ellis Campbell, who was the regional director for the Dallas district of the IRS and coordinated with the Justice Department in the *Stone* case, colluded with Johnson to hide Ruby's connection to the defendants. Ellis and Johnson also hid critical data on Oswald's growing interaction with the Dallas office of the IRS in the weeks before the assassination (over withholding on his paychecks).[1] The young leftist's effort to work within the system to resolve his need for more money to support his family only pointed to his innocence and orientation toward the future.

Although RFK logically concluded that Ruby had acted at the direction of the Mafia to silence Oswald, he was reportedly too overwhelmed with grief in the weeks after the murder of his brother to react. And when he was ready to return to work, Johnson was ready too. In mid-January, LBJ sent Kennedy to Indonesia to "get the facts" on the border dispute between that country and Malaysia over the island of Borneo.[2] By the time RFK returned, news editorials were circulating in Washington DC, which revealed that Hoover's report to Johnson, containing his own conclusions about the assassination, had been "leaked all over town."[3] The Warren Commission's ultimate conclusions would prove embarrassingly close to Hoover's. Robert Kennedy realized that he had lost the initiative—lost his opportunity to stop LBJ.

Not long after Kennedy's return from Borneo, LBJ let it be known that he intended to waive FBI Director Hoover's impending compulsory retirement.[4] The FBI director held the files on John Kennedy's adulterous sex life. RFK knew this and lived with the reality that LBJ would leak them if he were challenged about Hoover's remaining at his post. On the day of Johnson's announcement, Robert Kennedy informed the press, "I'm not going to remain as attorney general after November."[5] Officially a lame duck, his course was now set.

In an effort to demonstrate their loyalty to all things Italian, LBJ and his wife staged an extravagant and highly ritualized ball in honor of Italy's visiting head of state. To the Johnsons' delight, it was learned that the Italian leader planned to present them with a Tiberian marble. An ecstatic Lady Bird Johnson arranged to appear at the acceptance ceremony in classical Roman garb and hairstyle.[6] As in the case of their goodwill visit to Italy in 1963, the Johnsons left no doubt about their allegiances.

In May 1964, Johnson publicly demonstrated his gratitude to Hoover for containing the truth about JFK's murder by issuing an executive order waiving the director's impending retirement under federal law. A startling editorial in *The Dallas Morning News* only weeks before had focused on the power struggle between JFK and Johnson. "[T]he Kennedy team was out to seize the vice-presidency . . . after 1964 and the campaign to undermine . . . Johnson was doing fine until the assassination of President Kennedy changed the whole picture."[7] Kennedy's murder had saved Dallas from an explosive scandal that would have been triggered by a Mob exposé, and for that they were grateful. In keeping Hoover as FBI director, LBJ assured himself a place in the hearts of Texas Republicans.

Shortly after Johnson issued the executive order waiving Hoover's retirement, Henry Wade was assailed in the New York press for his obvious collusion with Johnson in the days after Kennedy's gangland slaying. However, the Dallas media was quick to support the district attorney, giving Wade an opportunity to counterattack. "The denials came from . . . Wade . . . and . . . Sanders after a newspaper inferred that

'Washington pressure' stopped prosecutors from filing a conspiracy charge against . . . Oswald."[8] The Dallas press knew that the New York story was accurate, but stonewalling was their only option.

Over the course of the Warren Commission's deliberations, Wade made a number of trips to Washington DC, hoping for tangible gain from President Kennedy's murder. Later, Johnson placed Wade's name in consideration for a vacancy on the federal bench in the Northern District of Texas (Dallas).[9] But public outcry over LBJ's handling of the assassination investigation prevented the nomination. In an attempt to soothe Wade, a Johnson aide told the embittered DA in writing that "the greatness of our Nation is . . . the result of the dedicated work of people such as you whose continued faithfulness to its principles and purposes have made it so."[10] Realizing that it was now his role to contain the truth indefinitely, Wade would stay on as DA. To the end of his days, he steadfastly refused to admit that the Dallas Mafia ever existed.

In the aftermath of the killings, the American people's perception that LBJ was somehow involved was widespread. One Warren Commission witness who knew Ruby well said, "I had even heard this comment made in the coffee shops and down in [South Texas], that the assassination was set up by Johnson."[11] LBJ could control what officials said in public, but he could not change public opinion.

But he did very well in controlling the actions of the Warren Commission. Almost none of the knowledgeable officials in Dallas and New Orleans were called to testify before the commission. This included the New Orleans FBI SAC and Marcello's case officer. The assistant special agent in charge (ASAC) in Dallas for much of the 1950s John Quigley probably knew as much about the Pearl Street Mafia and the corruption of local law enforcement as any bureau official. By decade's end, he was stationed in the New Orleans office. It was Quigley who interviewed Lee Oswald in the New Orleans jail in August 1963 regarding his pro-Castro demonstrations. Although he did testify, his prior service in Dallas was not mentioned—nor was he asked any questions about the Mob.[12] Gordon Shanklin, because the commission knew he had publicly lied about prior knowledge of Oswald, was not called to testify. Barefoot Sanders, by then lead counsel in the *Stone* case, wasn't either. It was the same for the PD's vice squad chief and Dallas FBI special agents Barrett and Gemberling. The commission's job had disintegrated into simply preventing those who knew the truth from having the opportunity to speak out.

Even though the Warren Report Name Index states that Johnson testified, he did not. He simply dictated a letter to Earl Warren, recounting the events of November 22, 1963—far too wary to allow himself to be placed under oath and questioned in a legal proceeding.[13]

The Campisi brothers were not called even though the commission knew both had been in contact with Ruby in the days after his arrest. Joe Civello's FBI interview was suppressed. And of course, Ianni, Bosco, and Grizzaffi were not called—nor were the Stone defendants.

The commission knew that in the weeks leading up to the assassination, someone acting in furtherance of the Dallas Mafia's plan to kill the President had represented himself as Oswald and staged incriminating acts in the Dallas area that would be used to wrongly implicate him after-the-fact. As it turned out, the commission was also aware that the same individual had been seen earlier in Montreal, Canada. A customs officer had reported shortly after Kennedy's murder that someone bearing a striking resemblance to the ex-marine had been seen handing out pro-Castroite leaflets in August 1963.[14] The real Oswald was known to have been in New Orleans at that time, doing the same thing. The commission, through narcotics and gambling reports, knew of Mob operations in Montreal and saw to it that the data was suppressed.[15]

In early December 1963, Texas attorney general Waggoner Carr held a press conference, stating that the convening of a court of inquiry to investigate the Dallas slayings (though expected of him by the state legislature) would be delayed.[16] Carr explained away his decision by saying it "might be more harmful than helpful."[17] But by the end of the year, he had become concerned about the public's reaction to his decision. He needed evidentiary documents in order to interface with Wade. Carr began privately complaining in memos to Warren Commission counselor J. Lee Rankin. In one, he said, "[T]he District Attorney is presently handicapped by the fact that all records . . . are in the possession of the FBI. Would you please see what can be done?"[18] But his pleas were ignored.

Soon after that, the commission interviewed Oswald's widow without notifying Carr beforehand. To his constituents, the Texas AG appeared uninvolved. Infuriated, he wrote to Rankin within hours. "I cannot . . . understand why you have apparently broken your commitment to have Texas represented. . . . If this development represents what Texas may expect in the future then we will feel relieved of our agreement to postpone further our own individual hearing."[19] Rankin, aware that Carr was quite knowledgeable about the Dallas Mafia and the Stone prosecution, realized that the Texas official had to be neutralized. Rankin demanded that Carr provide him with a position statement on the powers of the Texas AG. Carr complied and was forced to admit that he had no power to prosecute criminal cases such as murder.[20] With no legal basis to demand evidence, he was powerless. In the end, Carr and his staff were allowed merely to examine records and galley proofs of the impending Warren Report at commission offices in DC.[21] None of Carr's letters of complaint to Rankin and Warren were published in the Warren Commission's findings, and Carr himself was not even cited in the report.[22] The Texas court of inquiry simply rubber-stamped the commission's final report.[23]

Despite his humiliation at the hands of Johnson and Hoover, Carr was quick to defend the Warren Commission's collusive cover-up of the multigenerational Mafia-orchestrated corruption in Dallas in 1964. In a public address to the people of that city designed to trivialize their silence in response to Oswald's murder while in police custody, he proclaimed, "You can hold your heads higher today. . . . Your accusers have folded up their tents and quietly slipped away into the night. The shame is on their houses. The hate was in their hearts."[24] In an attempt to dehumanize Oswald, he said, "He wanted to be represented by a lawyer who had represented Communists."[25] Like Wade, Waggoner Carr had realized that to prosper politically under the heel of Johnson, he had to remain silent about the Dallas Mafia and cooperate with the Warren Commission.

Although Phil Bosco was not called before the Warren Commission, in February of 1964, the Dallas FBI interviewed him. He was, by then, conducting his bookmaking operation as usual. Realizing that Johnson, Sanders, and Wade were in Joe Civello's pocket, he defiantly refused to discuss the assassination, Jack Ruby, or the Stone bookmaking operation.[26]

In April, with the Democratic National Convention looming, LBJ moved to shut down the Warren Commission. Critical to containment of the truth was party nomination. With that accomplished, he would have at least four years to control the facts, probably eight. Without the nomination, he faced potential exposure and prosecution for his role in JFK's murder. His old Senate seat would have been the only option left. Even there, his opponent would have been Senator John Tower, who had monitored the Stone proceedings in Wichita Falls. Feeling LBJ's pressure to conclude the Warren Commission investigation, Rankin announced to reporters "his staff [was] working as fast as possible . . . ," adding, "there are only 24 hours in a day."[27] Suppression of so grave a historical truth had proven to be no easy matter.

After the Hoover retirement waiver by Johnson, the commission's final conclusions were leaked to the press. Oswald had been a "hater of authority," an "embittered introvert," a Marxist, and an "unstable ne'er-do-well" who acted alone. Ruby was a "crazy" nightclub owner who also acted alone and did not know Oswald.[28] To bolster that image of Ruby, the Dallas press said he was still, even in his cell, "occasionally exploding in wild outbursts."[29] The report claimed there had been no grassy knoll shooter, no conspiracy. The report would, it was said, "substantiate overwhelmingly the original findings of the FBI."[30] J. Edgar Hoover, in his determination to remain in power, had kept his part of the bargain.

There followed between June 2 and 10, a political confluence profound in nature. RFK spoke to the press about his brother's administration and the goals that they had pursued. He said, "Certain things [were] started by President Kennedy. I am trying to work out my future so as to assure that his efforts will be continued."[31] Two days later he met privately with Johnson to promote what remained of JFK's plans and position himself for a run at the upcoming U.S. Senate election in New York. Later, Kennedy publicly pronounced that Oswald had acted alone, although he knew it to be a lie. In the fall, he was rewarded with the Senate seat in New York. Johnson loathed Robert Kennedy, but had grudgingly accepted the fact that the family name was still a force to be reckoned with.

16

TRUTH DERAILED—THE WARREN REPORT

Anyone who has proclaimed violence his method, inexorably must choose lying as his principle.

—Aleksandr Solzhenitsyn

LYNDON JOHNSON HAD satisfied himself that Robert Kennedy was no longer a threat. With FBI Director J. Edgar Hoover's enthusiastic support, LBJ then set about the business of ensuring that the Warren Commission produced the results he needed to hide the fact that President Kennedy had died at the hands of the Mafia.

In Texas, the press leaked the fact that on Sunday morning, June 7, the Warren Commission would personally interview Jack Ruby in the Dallas County jail. The night before the jailhouse interview, Guy Banister, an ex-FBI SAC from Chicago and a key employee of Carlos Marcello's, was found dead in his New Orleans apartment of a heart attack.[1] Banister knew that Oswald was merely a "nut" whom Marcello had used to mislead authorities after the assassination and feared Ruby was about to tell all. When the interview came, Ruby pleaded with the commissioners to take him from Dallas to Washington, where he could speak freely:

> Gentlemen, my life is in danger here. . . . I may not live tomorrow to give any further testimony. [T]he only thing I want to get out . . . and I can't say it here, is . . . the truth of everything and why my act was committed. . . . [It's] got to be said amongst people of the highest authority that would give me the benefit of doubt. . . . I tell you gentlemen, my whole family is in jeopardy. . . . At this moment, Lee Harvey Oswald isn't guilty of committing the crime of assassinating President Kennedy. Jack Ruby is. [A] whole new form of government is going to take over our country, and I know I won't live to see you another time.[2]

Ruby did not understand that the interview had only been granted because the Warren Commission had perceived that the public would expect it. It would give their report more credibility. The commissioners knew about Ruby's status as a bookmaker in the Stone operation and understood his role in silencing Oswald. The Dallas mobster's pleas were ignored, and he was left in his cell. There would be no more interviews with the commission.

By then, the John Eli Stone prosecution had resumed in Dallas. U.S. Attorney Arnold Stone, although he had lost control of the prosecution to Barefoot Sanders, still managed to fight off an intense eleventh-hour attempt by Sanders's dedicated assistant, Robert Ward, to trigger a complete dismissal of the case.[3]

However, U.S. Attorney Stone could not outmaneuver Judge Sarah Hughes. On the morning of the eighth, she eviscerated the government's primary case by ruling the wiretap evidence (misur) inadmissible.[4] That same day, Henry Wade and Waggoner Carr made their only appearance before the Warren Commission in Washington DC, and did not challenge its "lone nut" premise. On June 9, Wade met with LBJ at the White House.[5] Like Judge Hughes, Wade had done his part to stifle the truth. It was a moment of triumph for LBJ and his allies.

On June 10, Hoover issued a fraudulent position statement to the Warren Commission, categorically denying the existence of the Stone prosecution and any connection between Ruby and Isadore Miller. The commission, although knowing the statement to be false, published it to prop up their conclusion of "no conspiracy."[6] In doing so, they simply ignored the fact that Dallas FBI agents Barrett and Gemberling were under subpoena to testify in the *Stone* case.[7] Both had also been extremely active in the context of the field office's handling of the assassination. Gemberling, who prepared many reports, was attacked in testimony by various assassination witnesses. They had learned that he had falsified their affidavits to make it appear that Oswald had been on the sixth floor of the Texas School Book Depository at the time of the murder.[8] Despite the witnesses' testimony, the commission used Gemberling's documents to wrongly implicate Oswald and hide the fact that JFK had been the victim of a conspiracy.[9]

Gemberling was also the agent who, in a report on the contents of Oswald's address book, hid the fact that it contained the name of the former marine's Dallas FBI case officer who had contacted him and his wife in the weeks leading up to the assassination. The commission learned of it, but allowed Hoover to avoid the issue. He had Gemberling swear out an affidavit explaining the omission, which Hoover then referred to, but excluded from his response to the commission. The affidavit itself, proof that Gemberling had committed obstruction of justice, was suppressed in total.[10]

Robert Barrett, the Dallas field office's organized crime section chief, had interviewed Joe Campisi after Oswald's murder. Campisi claimed that "he had never heard of RUBY ever gambling or engaging in bookmaking either as a bookie or a person placing bets."[11] But a Dallas FBI Crime Condition report had flatly stated that "the primary bookmaking operation in Dallas was directed by John Eli Stone [and] Albert Meadows" in "close association" with gambler James Dolan. And the office knew that Dolan was "engaged in 'booking' with John . . . Patrono."[12] Under questioning, Campisi did admit that "RUBY was acquainted with . . . Patrono."[13] In a meeting with the Dallas PD's vice squad chief after interviewing Campisi, Barrett received further confirmation of the Patrono connection.[14] He knew then that Campisi was lying about Ruby's status as a bookmaker in the Dallas Mafia. Barrett had direct proof of a conspiratorial relationship between the man who had silenced the supposed assassin and individuals then under prosecution by the President's brother. He had Ruby's motive for participating in the plot and killing Oswald.

Because the *Stone* case was primarily an IRS action, that bureau had to be controlled. Herbert Miller, as head of the criminal division at the Justice Department, had (either at Johnson's or RFK's directive) instructed the IRS's Dallas field office Intelligence Division "not to initiate any investigations of . . . Ruby, or any of [his] associates, without prior . . . approval."[15] In January 1964, Chief Justice Warren had obtained the IRS file on Jack Ruby, which revealed that the agency began closing in on the gambler in the spring of 1963 as part of the intensification of the Stone investigation.[16] To the commission, the picture became clear. As a target of RFK's task force investigation of Stone, Ruby had murdered Oswald to prevent investigators from discovering that someone other than the former marine had assassinated the President.

In furtherance of LBJ's overall plan to control the actions and conclusions of the Warren Commission, Hoover launched an assault on a low-level staff member by claiming that he was a communist. Through Commissioner Ford, an attempt was made to terminate his employment. It failed, but Hoover's ability to intimidate commission staffers was made clear.[17] Hoover also had help from the House Un-American Activities Committee (HUAC), which in its July 1964 report labeled Oswald a "fanatical Marxist."[18] The HUAC's chairman was a staunch Hooverite and U.S. representative from Louisiana.[19] Another committeeman was Zuroma Club guest Joe Pool of Dallas.[20] From decades of experience, Hoover knew that he could use the threat of un-Americanism to ensure that Warren Commission staffers, as well as fellow "patriots," would rally to his cause. The commission would do Johnson's bidding.

Former FBI agent Henry Wade needed no Persuasion. By then, the DA had become desperate for LBJ's election as president in the fall of 1964. His hope was that it would give his idol legitimacy in the eyes of an increasingly skeptical public. Hoping the end was near for the Warren Commission, Wade expressed the fears of all his cohorts when he told a reporter, "There has already been too damned much said about Jack Ruby."[21] But Johnson was not worried. He had successfully defused the investigation of his hated predecessor's murder. There remained only formalities.

The Stone trial came to a close on September 21, 1964, with the conviction of the Stone brothers on only minor charges. Isadore Miller's trial was avoided until after the presidential election. The Stone brothers were sentenced on September 24 to nominal fines and probation. A Mob-corrupted Judge Hughes told the defendants, "I don't think you have injured anybody else. . . . You didn't make anybody gamble. They gambled of their own accord. [But] Congress has seen fit to pass a law making the things you have engaged in a crime."[22] Something else happened that day. The members of the Warren Commission signed and submitted their final report to Lyndon Johnson.

Dallas Mafia boss Joe Civello's big gamble had paid off. Allowing the use of his city by Carlos Marcello as the location to have JFK murdered had been the right decision. Kennedy's war on the Mafia had been stopped. Local authorities had scrambled to aid Johnson's cover up in an effort to protect, and promote, their interests. For Stone, Miller, and Bosco, it was again business as usual. Revenues were flowing. The federal government was with them—the Warren Report a reality. At least for a while.

17

THE BIG LIE IS CHALLENGED

> Justice consists in giving every man what he deserves. Revenge is a kind of wild justice.
>
> —Francis Bacon

IN JULY OF 1966, legal and historical reality began to catch up with Lyndon Johnson and the Pearl Street Mafia. Public skepticism over the Warren Report and its "lone nut" thesis was growing. More and more people were coming to the conclusion that Lee Oswald had been nothing more than a simple dupe. The government's case had too many loose ends. Suspicion about complicity on the part of LBJ was spreading.

Harold Weisberg's *Whitewash: The Report on the Warren Report* revealed that LBJ's confidant Cliff Carter had taken possession of Texas governor John Connally's bullet-riddled, bloodstained clothes at Parkland Hospital just after the assassination and at Johnson's directive had them laundered, obliterating critical forensic evidence. LBJ then had the interior of Kennedy's death car stripped out and destroyed. After President Kennedy was autopsied, and the results falsified, Johnson had the coffin in which the President's body had been transported back to Washington DC flown out to sea off the east coast of the United States and dumped in deep water.[1] Johnson had studied law in his earlier years and knew exactly what he was doing. A former member of JFK's inner circle reviewed Edward Epstein's *Inquest: The Warren Commission and the Establishment of Truth* and publicly called for a new investigation of Kennedy's murder, the first to do so.[2]

Late that month, Pearl Street mobster Russell Mathews, a convicted cocaine trafficker and bookmaker, was arrested in Dallas on gambling tax charges.[3] The government had had Mathews, a gambling associate of the Stone and Miller brothers, under surveillance from October 1962 onward.[4] The first week in August 1966, a U.S. commissioner ordered the bookmaker "bound over for grand jury action."[5] Dallas Mafia defense attorney Charles Tessmer served as his defense counsel.

The very day the grand jury recommended Mathew's indictment, Cliff Carter resigned as "executive director of the Democratic National Committee," a position created by LBJ. [6] Carter's startling departure sent shock waves through the party. The Democratic Party chairman, a JFK appointee who had "never been considered close to . . . Johnson," eliminated Carter's position immediately.[7] LBJ, clearly unnerved, flew to his ranch for the weekend to collect his thoughts.[8]

With the release of several books undermining the credibility of the Warren Report, Mathews's arrest, and Carter's sudden resignation came renewed fear for Joe Civello. In October, he began seeing a doctor for heart problems.[9] It was in October that New Orleans district attorney Jim Garrison began his conspiracy investigation into JFK's assassination.[10]

In December, the U.S. Justice Department again moved against Philip Bosco.[11] Both he and Dallas police detective Charles Sansone were arrested for running a bookmaking operation out of Bosco's service station and police headquarters.[12] Though Sansone was fired, neither he nor Bosco were convicted—the pair saved by a ruling from the Warren Court.[13]

In the first week of January 1967—to the relief of Phil Bosco and all other members of the Dallas Mafia (as well as Henry Wade, LBJ, Sarah Hughes, and Barefoot Sanders)—Jack Ruby died of cancer in the Dallas County jail while awaiting a new trial for the murder of Oswald.[14] All knew that had he been given a second chance with the press, he would have disclosed facts about the Mob's contract on Kennedy and his role in it.

On February 17, New Orleans DA Jim Garrison went public with allegations of conspiracy in the murder of President Kennedy.[15] Two days later, a frightened former Warren commissioner Gerald Ford demanded that any evidence Garrison had be immediately turned over to the U.S. Justice Department.[16] Ford had secretly served as an FBI informant for J. Edgar Hoover throughout the course of the commission's deliberations and had real reason to panic. He had regularly smuggled documents and findings out of the commission's secret executive sessions, delivering them to Hoover via courier.[17] Were he to be found out, he would face serious felony prosecution under federal criminal law.

Garrison's investigation began to gain momentum. On the last day of the month, the DA subpoenaed his first witness.[18] That very day, Henry Luce, owner of *Life* magazine and the Zapruder film, which recorded JFK's murder, died of a heart attack.[19] Luce, an ardent Hooverite, had purchased the film at an exorbitant price, only to suppress it in collusion with Johnson to hide the truth about Kennedy's slaying. The film was clear, legal proof of conspiracy, and Luce had realized when Garrison's investigation began that it would be subpoenaed as evidence. Luce's motivation to suppress the Zapruder film lay, in part, with his personal background. Like Johnson's wife, he was fixated with Italian history. In the end, like in some Machiavellian tale, his devious mind and assistance to the Mafia had proved his undoing.

A few hours after Luce's death, the press reported that "President Johnson [had] named . . . Ramsey Clark . . . Attorney General."[20] Two hours after that, Clark's father, Tom (LBJ's longtime partner in crime and ally of the Pearl Street Mafia), announced his retirement from the U.S. Supreme Court.[21]

In Dallas, mafioso John Stone and his attorneys appealed his 1964 conviction. Via lead counsel Charles Tessmer, he fought the case all the way to the U.S. Supreme Court. On March 4, 1968, the Warren Court threw out his conviction.[22] That same day, Earl Warren, who was also chairman of the Federal Judicial Center, appointed Tom Clark its director. Disgusted by the turn of events, within twenty-four hours RFK made up his mind to seek the Democratic Party nomination for president.[23] He had decided to take matters into his own hands. Once elected, he would finish the job in Dallas.

In the days that followed, public condemnation of LBJ grew. French President Charles De Gaulle labeled him a "cowboy . . . a sergeant who's been crowned, and [a] man without any style."[24] JFK's secretary Evelyn Lincoln's just-published memoirs revealed that shortly before his murder, Kennedy had told her that his 1964 running mate "[would] not be Lyndon."[25]

On March 28, Dallasite and *Texas Tribune* publisher Joe Gennaro, like a ghost from the past, paid a visit to the White House. He had been one of LBJ's connections with the Zuroma Club and the man who had sought Johnson's help against the INS on behalf of Dallas murderer Sam Savalli during the 1950s.[26] And Gennaro had hosted the Zuroma Club the night Barefoot Sanders appeared with Phil Bosco. The day after Gennaro's White House visit, former Warren Commission member Allen Dulles was scheduled to testify in New Orleans as a result of DA Garrison's subpoena.[27] Shaken by Gennaro's visit and terrified by what Dulles could disclose, within forty-eight hours Lyndon Johnson publicly announced that he would not seek reelection in 1968.[28]

When RFK made the decision to run for president, he knew what had happened in Dallas. He had watched the Stone prosecution collapse because of Johnson, felt the bitter sting of defeat at the hands of Warren. The Civello mob knew that RFK would try again. Were he to win the presidency, they faced certain oblivion. If they had any doubts, they were eliminated when Kennedy said publicly that if elected, the government would "stop talking about crime and begin doing something about it."[29]

But just as RFK did not grasp the degree of Johnson's involvement with the Pearl Street mob prior to his brother's assassination, so too he failed to understand the complexities of the Civello mob's relationship to the Los Angeles Mafia—and what Hoover knew about them. Robert Kennedy knew that Joe Civello was a cousin to Frank De Simone, who ran the Los Angeles organization until his death in January 1968.[30] But he knew little of the man who followed him, Nick Licata—a close criminal associate of Civello's.[31]

FBI Director Hoover had learned as early as November 1963 that Jack Ruby had a direct connection to the Licata mob via criminal associates Dave Yaras and Leonard Patrick.[32] That information was part of an internal post-assassination report which RFK never saw. From the death of John Kennedy onward, Hoover was briefed almost weekly by the Dallas SAC regarding the daily activities of Civello, Joe Ianni, and Ross Musso. As early as July 1966, he knew that Dallas mafioso Johnny Ross Patrono, a close associate of both Joe Ianni and Jack Ruby, frequented Los Angeles's Santa Anita racetrack—Sirhan Sirhan's place of employment in the spring of 1968.[33] In late April of that year, RFK's presidential candidacy came up during a weekly FBI briefing presided over by Hoover's longtime fanatically loyal number-two man, Clyde Tolson. Enraged by the candidacy, Tolson told the group, "I hope someone shoots and kills the son of a bitch."[34] He got his wish.

Kennedy was executed in gangland fashion in Los Angeles in early June by Sirhan and another hit man whose identity remains unknown.[35] The man in charge of the Los Angeles FBI field office on the day RFK was assassinated was a former Miami, Florida, SAC named Wesley Grapp, a Hoover favorite. He had been in charge in Miami in 1962 when mobster Santo Trafficante's disclosure to an informant that JFK was going to be "hit" was reported to that office and Hoover—but not the Secret Service. [36] As in the death of President Kennedy, Hoover rode roughshod over underlings in an attempt to prevent the truth behind RFK's murder becoming known.

The Mob's killing of Robert Kennedy stunned the American people. With LBJ still in power and Hoover at his beck and call, many people became disillusioned with politics. But Johnson and his cronies had begun to realize that the truth would, in fact, catch up with them. They knew that one day the Warren Report would collapse like a house of cards.

18

RETRIBUTION

Every guilty person is his own hangman.

—Seneca

LYNDON JOHNSON'S WITHDRAWAL from the 1968 presidential race and the assassination of Robert Kennedy fundamentally altered the political landscape in Washington DC. Richard Nixon's time had arrived. And with it came the opportunity to enact federal legislation which would allow the government to crush the Mafia. Some of those who had allowed themselves to be corrupted and used by LBJ began a mad scramble to save themselves any way they could. Others sought to clear their consciences before being exposed and disgraced.

Supreme Court Chief Justice Earl Warren was unnerved by RFK's murder and the mishandling of the subsequent investigation. He tried to resign from the court, but LBJ, determined to maintain solidarity with all former Warren commissioners to the end, persuaded him to stay on.[1]

Thinking beyond his presidency, Johnson tried to place Barefoot Sanders on the U.S. Circuit Court of Appeals in Washington DC, just one step below the Supreme Court. With Tom Clark in retirement, a much needed replacement on the court would have proved invaluable in the event LBJ were prosecuted after he left office. But opponents, by then realizing that Sanders was nothing more than LBJ's bag man and a flunkie of the Dallas Mafia, blocked the appointment.[2]

In early 1969, despite J. Edgar Hoover's best efforts, a Mafia exposé entitled *The Grim Reapers* was released. A watershed event in the unraveling of the mystery behind President Kennedy's murder, for the first time Marcello was connected to the assassination in a mass market publication available nationwide. Joe Civello was named as a lieutenant in his machine.[3] Marcello's 1962 death threat against President Kennedy became public knowledge. The presence of Paul Mondoloni (a man with ties to Cuba) in Mexico City at the time of Oswald's trip there to get a Cuban visa was also made known. There were revelations about Lucchese and the southern end of the drug corridor. Author Ed Reid revealed that Los Angeles mob boss Nick Licata "share[d] the rule with Joe Civello . . . in Dallas."[4] Hoover was enraged by Reid's exposé, but with Johnson soon to leave office, he could no longer contain the truth.

The Pearl Street Mafia also felt the winds of change. Phil Bosco was again indicted on bookmaking charges. Though found guilty, he was given probation.[5] The press in Dallas finally began talking of the ties between the Dallas and New Orleans Mafia. Dallas was then in the throes of yet another gang war, with more executions, more car bombings. One article said of the Dallas Mafia, "They have what they refer to as their strong arm man and their payoff is a certain per cent to a group in New Orleans that is run by the Mafia."[6] A few weeks before LBJ left office, Joe Civello, terrified by the fact that his protection against prosecution was about to disappear, suffered a massive heart attack. He managed to survive but began to go downhill.[7]

With Johnson's departure from office on January 20, 1969, the Pearl Street Mafia's federal protection was gone. Over the course of the summer, momentum grew behind Reid's exposé. In mid-October, New Orleans DA Jim Garrison told the press, "It is not over by a long shot. You will find out what they did to John F. Kennedy."[8] He also asserted that "former President Lyndon Johnson . . . played [a] role" in the assassination.[9] In Washington DC, on October 24, 1969, it was announced that the FBN was initiating a new program, Operation Intercept, to again ramp up the war on the Mafia's "international illicit drug traffic." Targeted border cities included Laredo, Texas, scene of Attorney General Kennedy's spectacular heroin bust six years earlier.[10]

The snowballing developments proved too much for Joe Civello. He was struck down by yet another heart attack the same day and died in January 1970.[11] In April of that year, Bosco was convicted yet again on bookmaking charges.[12]

The beginning of the end for the Dallas Mafia came in August, with federal legislative hearings clearing the way for signing of the Organized Crime Control Act of 1970, along with its lethal Racketeer Influenced and Corrupt Organizations Act (RICO) provisions.[13] The act enabled, as the press put it, "total war against organized crime." President Richard Nixon made it clear to the press that he intended to use it to prevail against the Mafia, declaring, "We will end this war."[14] Most ominous were the Immunity of Witnesses provisions, the very weapon RFK had lobbied for in the months prior to his brother's murder. Criminals would soon be compelled to reveal the type of information needed to destroy the Mob.[15] The effective date was several months away, but federal authorities had already begun to move against the Dallas mob.[16]

Dallas County sheriff Bill Decker, realizing that RICO was the handwriting on the wall, died of a heart attack on August 29, 1970.[17] Later that day, Sanders's assistant in the Stone prosecution, Robert Ward, died of heart failure at age thirty-nine. The following day, Dallasite Abraham Zapruder, whose film of JFK's murder provided gut-wrenching proof of conspiracy, died as well.[18] Knowing the significance of the evidence he had captured that day in November 1963, Zapruder had perhaps realized that justice would, in fact, finally prevail. Perhaps the thought of reliving it all proved too much.

While waiting for the effective date of RICO, the Justice Department worked out the details of its plan for a large-scale investigation of organized crime in Dallas. Police Chief Frank Dyson confirmed the worst in a statement to the press. "There is a great deal of talk that one is coming. I'm sure you've heard it and I've heard it."[19] Tension ran high in the Pearl Street Mafia, now commanded by heir-apparent Joe Ianni.

Three days into the new law, at the direction of the Justice Department, the New York City FBI seized confidential membership and contribution lists of the Italian-American Civil Defense League, "purportedly belonging to [mafioso] Joseph Columbo."[20] The story made headlines. Within twenty-four hours Zuroma Club guest, Italian-American activist, and LBJ confidant Pete Tamburo was dead, felled by a massive stroke.[21] One week into the new law, Sam Campisi was dead at age fifty, reportedly of an intestinal hemorrhage.[22]

Over the course of 1971, the Justice Department strike force instituted intensive electronic surveillance on the Dallas Mafia's gambling operations, targeting among other things, the "Bosco Service Station . . . and Ianni's Italian Restaurant."[23] Ruby's former associate Johnny Ross Patrono, employee at Ianni's, was placed under investigation as well.[24]

Former Warren Commission member Richard Russell had followed the developing federal investigation in Dallas. In declining health and no longer willing to be constrained by LBJ's subversion of the truth, he decided to reveal his true beliefs about John Kennedy's murder. In a statement to the press, he declared, "I think someone else worked with Lee Harvey Oswald."[25] No longer burdened by a guilty conscience, he died a few weeks after RICO took effect.[26]

In the fall of 1971, the U.S. Senate Judiciary Committee learned that despite the enactment of RICO, Louisiana Mafia boss Carlos Marcello (by then successful in defeating RFK's 1963 effort to imprison him) was expanding operations across south and east Texas. On September 20, the Texas press headlined the contents of an American Bar Association report sent to the judiciary committee revealing the extent of his criminal operations.[27] Marcello had made "several trips to San Antonio over the past 18 months" and had become a "frequent traveler to . . . Houston and Dallas."[28] The mobster was aggressively seeking new "business investments," it was reported.[29] Business consultant Cliff Carter, who had long overseen machine politics for LBJ in that area, a man born and raised in the area between Austin, San Antonio, and Houston, died suddenly the following day, reportedly of a heart attack. LBJ, mindful that Carter had been instrumental in preventing a conspiracy investigation in the aftermath of JFK's murder, attended his funeral.[30]

In January 1972, the government's anti-Mob strike force staged simultaneous raids on "Bosco['s service station,] . . . Ianni's Italian Restaurant . . . and several homes in Dallas." It was disclosed that "Bosco ha[d] the biggest basketball book in Dallas."[31] Johnny Ross Patrono was booking from Ianni's. Joe Ianni was not arrested, but the U.S. attorney said the "investigation [was] continuing." He added, "All evidence obtained at the conclusion of the investigation will be presented to a federal grand jury."[32] Armed with RICO, the Justice Department was beginning to gain traction in its war against the Dallas Mafia.

From the January raids forward, persistent media reports stated that "Justice Department and intelligence agents for the Internal Revenue Service have been attempting to discover whether a link exists between some Dallas policemen and known gambling figures."[33] In federal raids, "police officials were caught by surprise."[34] At the end of March, in an unprecedented act, Dallas Police Chief Dyson "abolished the 165-man special investigations bureau" (vice squad), remodeling the department to conform to the federal model.[35] Dallas officials had realized that RICO had the power to destroy them as well, should they refuse to address the issues which had again brought federal investigation to Dallas.

On Tuesday, April 4, it was suddenly announced in Dallas that LBJ's ally Ellis Campbell, longtime District IRS director, would retire within ten days.[36] After the assassination, Campbell had met officially "off record" with Johnson at the White House on three separate occasions.[37] Because the Dallas IRS had spearheaded RFK's investigation of the Civello mob in the early 1960s, Campbell knew everything. He had undoubtedly kept Johnson abreast of developments and his ongoing efforts at keeping the public from finding out about the Stone prosecution. But now, with the renewed federal presence in Dallas and Johnson out of power, he realized that the day of reckoning was at hand.

Within forty-eight hours of Ellis's announcement, LBJ was in Virginia at his daughter's house, with plans to be in Washington on Saturday.[38] The federal strike force assault (utilizing wiretaps) on the Ianni mob, coupled with upheaval in the Dallas PD and Campbell's sudden retirement, had panicked him. Known during his administration to have strenuously "opposed wiretapping in the organized crime area," Johnson feared that the truth about JFK's death would become known—all was about to be lost.[39]

Lyndon Johnson awoke early Friday morning clutching his chest. In the grip of a crushing heart attack, he was rushed from his daughter's house to a nearby hospital.[40] Had he remained at his ranch in Texas during the breaking Dallas developments, he surely would have died. Stabilized in the East, a week later LBJ was flown to Brooke Army Hospital in San Antonio where he remained for some time. He returned to Texas a broken man. "Looking pale and worn," he said to the press, "it's mighty good to be this close to home."[41] In the days that followed, his fears would only continue to grow.

The strike force continued its work, exposing more of the relationship between the Dallas Mafia and local officials. It was reported that "at least a dozen and perhaps more voices on taped telephone conversations . . . have been identified as Dallas policemen."[42] The public's perception of Dallas had begun to change—a true picture was beginning to emerge. Reverberations were felt as far away as Washington DC.

The consequences of the Justice Department's assault on the Dallas Mafia and LBJ's nearly fatal heart attack weighed heavily on the mind of J. Edgar Hoover, by then infirm and out of favor with President Nixon. Hoover's agents closely monitored the strike force investigation in Dallas, but could only watch as the government continued to build its case against Mob boss Joe Ianni and his operatives. Back in Washington, Hoover had troubles of his own. On May 1, 1972, it was revealed in federal hearings that during the LBJ administration, Hoover had, via illegal wiretaps, "prepared secret memos" on the private lives of Johnson's political opponents. In turn, LBJ used them for "bedtime reading."[43] The media reacted quickly to the explosive news. Though pressed by reporters the same day, "Johnson and the FBI had no comment."[44] It was a career-ending scandal for the aging FBI director. Early the next morning, Hoover died of a heart attack in his bedroom.[45] His death sent shock waves through Dallas. The city sent Police Chief Frank Dyson to the funeral as its representative.[46]

There followed not long after Hoover's demise, the strike force's much-awaited federal grand jury hearings in Dallas, which "resulted in gambling conspiracy charges against 11 Dallas area men." The Justice Department pressed on with its investigation of Bosco and Patrono.[47]

Lyndon Johnson slowly went downhill. On November 22, 1972, former President Truman, who had watched the Dallas situation unravel and had seen LBJ's collapse, himself fell ill.[48] Because of his profoundly regretted appointment of Tom Clark, he felt a certain responsibility for the unfolding disaster. Prior to his death, Truman characterized his appointment of former Dallasite Tom Clark to the U.S. attorney generalship decades earlier as the "worst mistake" of his presidency.[49] The AG was, he said, a "damn fool from Texas."[50] By early December, Truman's heart and lungs were failing. The day after Christmas, he died.[51] Less than a month later, Lyndon Johnson suffered yet another, and this time fatal, heart attack.[52] At his ranch and far from any hospital, his last words were gasped over the phone from his bedroom in an attempt to reach his personal Secret Service agent. "Get me Mike Howard," he uttered.

The Nixon administration's war on the Mob under RICO had not concerned itself with political niceties. Though mafiosi like Joe Civello were its primary targets, their political cohorts were considered no better. Simply put, justice had been subverted under Johnson. And in the end, just as he had stood with the Mob, so too he fell. A traitor and moral coward, he had simply lacked the courage to confess his crimes. As LBJ liked to put it, "They say everything will come out in the long run, but in the long run we'll all be dead."

19

THE WHEELS OF JUSTICE

Justice is truth in action.

—Benjamin Disraeli

THE DEMOCRATIC NATIONAL Party, in an attempt to avoid being discredited by LBJ's criminal acts, implemented a damage control plan. Realizing they could not stop the government's plan to destroy the Pearl Street Mafia, they did their best to put people in place who could spin developments in Dallas to their advantage whenever possible.

Shortly before Truman's and Johnson's death, and realizing the end was near for both men, the Democratic National Party appointed a new chairman, Dallas attorney Robert Strauss.[1] No ordinary replacement, Strauss had gotten his start in politics "as a volunteer in Lyndon B. Johnson's first Congressional campaigns."[2] He had also formed a close relationship with Texas governor John Connally. Joining the FBI at the outbreak of World War II, during the critical rise of Tom Clark and early parole of Joe Civello from federal prison, Strauss became an agent in the Dallas field office. He left the bureau at war's end, practicing law (and presumably continuing to support LBJ) until long after the murder of JFK.[3]

In Dallas, the Justice Department continued its prosecution of the Mob's gambling operation into 1973.[4] However, its investigation of Joe

Ianni came to a sudden end in late May. Overwhelmed by an investigation that would have resulted in his imprisonment or exile, he died of a heart attack.[5] The local press reported the fact that his restaurant "was the site earlier this year of a . . . meeting [with] Mafia boss Carlos Marcello of New Orleans and several businessmen. Their discussion . . . centered on gambling operations in Dallas." Ianni's death had not deterred Carlos Marcello. In mid-July, an informant to the strike force scheduled to meet with authorities about Marcello's operations in the area "was found shot to death in a far northeast part of Dallas. . . . He was found shot three times beside a road," his body then dumped in a ditch. In reaction, the Dallas press revealed that "Marcello is believed to be heavily investing in land and business properties in Dallas and has long been linked to bookmaking operations here."[6] The strike force redoubled its efforts.

By January of 1974, yet another federal grand jury had been convened in the North Texas city.[7] More wiretap evidence was presented. In March, mobster Joe Campisi was "subpoenaed to testify before [a] federal grand jury investigating gambling links between Dallas and Las Vegas."[8] The following day, Jack Ruby's former associate Isadore Miller was also called before the hearings. Incredibly, Judge Sarah Hughes once again came to the aid of what was left of the Pearl Street Mafia. She had managed to become the judge in the grand jury hearings and gave Miller "immunity from prosecution . . . in exchange for his testimony."[9] And who was the prime target of investigation? None other than John Eli Stone.[10] It was October 1963 all over again. But this time the press, no longer in denial, reported that Stone had "strong connections with Carlos Marcello."[11] And this time Judge Hughes could not single-handedly save the Dallas mob.

Former Warren Commissioner Earl Warren followed the hearings in Dallas and feared the worst. The same month that the new Stone grand jury convened, the former Supreme Court justice began suffering heart problems. He died that summer—like Johnson, a coward to the end.[12]

On November 5, John Eli Stone and five others were indicted by the grand jury for "violating federal gambling and racketeering laws." Isadore "Miller was named as an unindicted co-conspirator." The following day, Phil Bosco, who had been drinking heavily since the enactment of RICO, died of kidney failure.[13]

With the new year, control of the Stone prosecution was formally transferred to Sarah Hughes.[14] It was a fundamental violation of judicial code and ethics. She had clearly demonstrated bias in Stone's first prosecution, and the new prosecution was on nearly identical charges—failure to pay gambling taxes. Hughes's grant of immunity to Miller, who had a 25 percent take of the action in one of the largest syndicate gambling operations in the Southwest, was a travesty of justice.[15] Hughes soon began granting delaying motions filed by Stone's counsel.[16] But the Pearl Street mob's legal woes were not limited to income tax evasion charges.

On January 30, 1975, news broke of the Drug Enforcement Administration's (DEA) arrest of key members of the Paul Mondoloni drug cartel in Canada, New York, Mexico, and Marseilles, France. The same story concluded with the ominous statement that "others are being sought."[17] Former number-two man to Joe Civello, Ross Musso, the man who had for decades been involved with the distribution of heroin via the Mondoloni cartel, died that day of a massive heart attack.[18]

Occurring simultaneously with the federal government's crushing assault against the Mafia were the Rockefeller Commission hearings on the CIA.[19] Convened under former Warren Commissioner Gerald Ford's presidency, the commission soon found itself reexamining the Warren Report in an attempt to neutralize the efforts of the U.S. House Judiciary and Senate Intelligence Committees, which had begun their own investigations into JFK's death.[20] But the government no longer had exclusive control over the most damning evidence of all—the Zapruder Film. With New Orleans DA Jim Garrision's investigation of Kennedy's death had come access to and copies of the original footage.

In the first week of March 1975, it was announced that ABC, through Geraldo Rivera's *Goodnight America*, would broadcast computer expert Robert Groden's enhanced version of the Zapruder film at midnight on the sixth.[21] Virtually the first national airing of the footage, word of the coming event reverberated throughout Dallas. Belo Broadcasting Corporation (owned by *The Dallas Morning News*), which in turn owned the local ABC affiliate planning to broadcast *Goodnight America*, intervened, announcing it would not air the Zapruder film.[22] A storm of public protest followed, in part because of Groden, who had just shown the film at a local press conference.

Dallas ABC affiliate manager Mike Shapiro revealed to reporters that on the afternoon of the assassination "he saw the Zapruder film . . . and thought then 'I wouldn't run it now or ever.' "[23] It was a damning admission. The affiliate had had Abraham Zapruder on its November 22, 1963, afternoon special report. It had viewed the film along with officials, but then chose to withhold it from the public at the critical moment in history when its release would have done the most good. But now, the public would not be denied. The film aired as scheduled. A desperate Shapiro ran a disclaimer prior to its broadcast: "[You] are not going to see, by looking at the film, any new version of the assassination. It just doesn't exist."[24] But the film made clear what everyone already suspected—crossfire, two shooters, conspiracy.

The event shocked the city and the nation. U.S. Attorney General Edward Levi, a Chicagoan who had worked at the Justice Department with Tom Clark throughout World War II, a man appointed by former Warren Commissioner Gerald Ford, tried to maintain control of the situation in Dallas. It was revealed that months earlier, a designated assistant U.S. attorney in Dallas named Kenneth Mighell had been placed in charge of "forward[ing] to Washington what he consider[d] 'new evidence' in the case."[25] And who was Mighell? An LBJ appointee who had been handpicked by Barefoot Sanders. He had been there since 1961 and was first assistant.[26]

In the days prior to the Zapruder film's airing, Mighell "refused to come to the Adolphus Hotel to view the Groden film."[27] His role, it was publicly claimed, "was merely to 'pacify' conspiracy theorists interested in the assassination."[28] He admitted to reporters, "I've personally seen the Zapruder film, when we had it before *Life* magazine got it. So what is he going to show me that's new?"[29] Mighell viewed the film on TV like others and publicly attacked its implications the following day. By 1977, he would be the U.S. attorney for the Northern District of Texas.[30]

A beleaguered Judge Hughes, struggling to contain the Stone prosecution, was asked about the Zapruder film by the press. She admitted that she did not watch the broadcast. Her course was set long ago, and she was unable to confront her collusion with LBJ in 1963 (and the trauma it had brought to the country). She said only, "Some people are always looking backward, but I believe in looking forward. Nothing can bring Jack Kennedy back to life."[31] Whether Hughes did or didn't believe JFK had been killed by conspiracy, the Dallas Mafia owned her. Not long thereafter, she again delayed the Stone prosecution.[32] Former U.S. Texas senator Ralph Yarborough, who had ridden with LBJ the morning of the assassination, said, "So many millions of people disbelieve [the Warren Report]. The only way to lay all questions to rest is to have a Congressional investigation. . . . No one in the whole world hardly believes that one man did it except in the United States."[33] He was not alone in this perception. Yarborough's reaction to the Zapruder film echoed the beliefs of the great majority of Americans.

Back in Washington, on May 5, renowned forensic pathologist Cyril Wecht denounced the members of the Rockefeller Commission as nothing more than a collection of "governmental sycophants" and publicly called for the reinvestigation not only of JFK's death but also RFK's.[34] The same day, Hughes issued an order delaying, until June 5, consideration of the all-important electronic surveillance evidence submitted by the federal strike force.[35] As if moving in tandem, the following day the Rockefeller Commission announced it would release its report on June 6.[36] The rising tension caused by the dual proceedings took its toll in Dallas.

Former Dallas Country deputy sheriff Roger Craig, the man who had seen an Oswald look-alike flee the Texas School Book Depository just after the assassination (when the real Oswald was known to be elsewhere), was found shot to death—reportedly a suicide.[37] Craig's sighting had been dismissed by the FBI. The day Craig died, it was announced in Washington that Dallas FBI SAC Gordon Shanklin would retire. Shanklin had broken under the strain of developments and, as he explained it to reporters, could no longer take "this 24-hour day."[38] Predictably, he was replaced by an agent who had worked in Washington DC in the FBI's organized crime division during the Kennedy administration.[39] He was an expert on Mob surveillance and was undoubtedly briefed on the 1963 Stone task force electronic surveillance which Judge Hughes had suppressed.[40]

In DC, government sources began leaking the findings of the Rockefeller Commission. To no one's surprise, the commission had decided to back the Warren Report. Its executive director was none other than David Belin, former legal counsel to the Warren Commission.[41] The vice chairman of the simultaneously running Senate Intelligence Committee, Texan John Tower, defended the Warren Report. With the aborted 1963 *Stone* case, as well as current prosecution in mind, he said, "We have to accept the conclusions of the Warren Commission since it would be virtually impossible to make a thorough and exhaustive investigation now."[42] A frightened Barefoot Sanders, by then in private practice, quickly sided with Tower, telling the press he held "the same conclusions as the Rockefeller Commission."[43] Its conclusions were denounced by Senator Ted Kennedy and soon dismissed by the public because it had contributed nothing to the truth behind JFK's death.[44]

The U.S. Senate Intelligence Committee, in mid-June, made a dramatic attempt to get answers from the Mafia. Chicago Mafia boss Sam Giancana was located—to call him to testify.[45] Meanwhile, the courtroom atmosphere in Dallas became explosive. Sarah Hughes again delayed the *Stone* case when a loud and bitter courtroom debate over the contents of the "wiretap tapes" brought jury selection to a halt.[46] The same day, Giancana flew to Houston, Texas, supposedly for "corrective surgery for a gall bladder operation." But he evidently met with members of the Marcello organization while there.[47] Shortly thereafter, the Chicago mobster, clearly unnerved by the meeting, fled the city. According to the press, "[P]olice said he slipped out of the hospital Wednesday dressed in a hospital gown, was whisked away on a stretcher and came home without being spotted [that night]."[48] Giancana was executed gangland fashion at his Chicago home the following night—shot in the mouth, as in the case of Johnny Carcelli.[49] Sam Giancana and Joe Civello were now gone. And gone with them was critical knowledge about the Mob contract that took down John Kennedy. A cryptic expression often used by Marcello in later years was "Three can keep a secret if two are dead."[50]

Tuesday the twenty-fourth, mafioso Johnny Roselli, who had obtained early parole from federal prison decades earlier with Tom

Clark's help, testified before the Senate Intelligence Committee.[51] That day in Dallas, the Stone defendants suddenly waived their rights to a jury trial, allowing Judge Sarah Hughes to become the sole arbiter of guilt or innocence. There would be no public airing of the contents of the government's Mob surveillance tapes.[52] On the last day of June, she pronounced John Eli Stone guilty on two lesser charges and handed him a minimal sentence and fine.[53] The Dallas Mafia had done its part as well. The exasperated U.S. attorney prosecuting the case told reporters that "witnesses had reported receiving threatening phone calls . . . after he complied with defense motions [approved by Hughes] to identify witnesses who testified before the grand jury."[54] The same day, Hughes ordered the surveillance tapes sealed and placed "in the custody of the FBI, Dallas, for 10 years."[55] The Mafia had won the day, but not the war.

Within days after her decision in the *Stone* case, Sarah Hughes decided to withdraw from active service, obviously broken by the case and unfolding events. She announced that in the future she would only take cases on a voluntary basis. She did not, however, relinquish control of the John Stone matter, because in latter July he appealed, taking his case once again all the way to the Supreme Court. But Warren and Clark were gone, and Stone's luck ran out in 1978 when the Court refused to hear his case.[56] But even then, after he began serving his abbreviated sentence, Hughes reduced one of the two minor charges on which he had been convicted.[57]

Though Joe Ianni and Phil Bosco were now dead, the Dallas Mafia's troubles were far from over. Federal investigators continued their war on the Mob. The old guard in the Democratic Party now gone and elements within that organization came to the realization that only by addressing the past could they put it behind them.

20

THE DAWN OF TRUTH

Half a truth is often a great lie.

—Benjamin Franklin

THE INAUGURATION OF Jimmy Carter as president in January 1977 brought the resignation of Lyndon Johnson's ally Robert Strauss as Democratic Party chairman.[1] Carter was all about change and wasted no time. The first real congressional probe of JFK's murder began in earnest. The House Select Committee on Assassinations appointed Robert Blakey as its chief counsel. Blakey had formerly served as a U.S. attorney under RFK and was on Kennedy's Organized Crime Task Force. Blakey had been the driving force behind the design and enactment of RICO. On the day of his appointment, Tom Clark died of a heart attack.[2]

What the democratically controlled HSCA gave the American people was the long-awaited admission that President Kennedy had been killed by conspiracy. But much of what they uncovered during the most intensive investigation in congressional history was sealed from public view. Classification rulings used to suppress some findings were extended into the next century.[3]

In all probability the HSCA secretly interviewed John Stone and his brother Jim during committee hearings. As revealed in the depositions of those whose testimony was ultimately released—Joe Campisi,

Russell Mathews, and others—John Stone was "in town" during the Dallas hearings.[4] But the HSCA did not make public what they had learned from the Stone brothers.

The only time Phil Bosco's name came up in hearings before the HSCA was during the May 16, 1978, executive session testimony of Chicagoan Irwin Weiner, a key Mafia bail bondsman. Testimony turned on his refusal to discuss the subject of a twelve-minute phone call a panicked Jack Ruby had made to him on October 26, 1963.[5] Indictments in the *Stone* case were handed down on October 21. In contacting the bondsman, Ruby was reacting to the indictments in anticipation of his and Bosco's own arrests. The day after Weiner's testimony, Isadore Miller died of a massive heart attack.[6]

In August 1978, the HSCA privately deposed Nicholas Katzenbach, U.S. attorney general under LBJ.[7] He revealed that on the day of the assassination, he "had a number of conversations that evening . . . until sometime after midnight, primarily with Barefoot Sanders."[8] But when Katzenbach testified publicly in late September, Sanders was not mentioned. Katzenbach's earlier deposition was merely "made a permanent part of the record."[9] Shortly after that, Texas senator Lloyd Bentsen, a longtime crony of John Connally's, submitted Sanders's name to President Carter for appointment to the federal bench—in Dallas.[10] With Sarah Hughes in declining health, political forces in Texas needed a new keeper of the keys.

On March 29, 1979, Senator Ted Kennedy chaired the Senate Committee on the Judiciary, which controlled nominations to federal judgeships. That day, Bentsen appeared with Sanders for his nomination hearing. He revealed that Sanders's nomination had actually been the result of a "2-year selection process."[11] In truth, the scheme to place him on the bench corresponded almost to the day with the U.S. House Resolution that had created the HSCA. In making its decision, the Judiciary Committee relied in large part on an FBI investigation into Sanders's background. As one senator put it, "We know more about you . . . than is necessary to know."[12] But did they? Did Kennedy and his committee know about Sanders's manipulation of the *Stone* case to save himself in 1963 and his involvement with Bosco and the Zuroma Club?

Despite those issues, Sanders was approved by Kennedy's committee the same day of his appearance.[13] Also that day, the HSCA filed its report finding probable conspiracy in the death of JFK.[14] The report had also provided "recommendations for further investigation" by the Department of Justice.[15]

But nothing of substance would be done by the department even though the truth was now at their doorstep. They would not tell the public that they had known from the beginning what the HSCA had discovered about Kennedy's death. They did, however, take one positive, and very important, step in the right direction. Carlos Marcello, the driving force behind JFK's murder, was taken down in a post-HSCA FBI sting operation after he appeared in executive session before that committee. He was then prosecuted, convicted, and kept in prison until he was broken—a shell of his former self.[16]

Following the HSCA's overturning of the Warren Report's conclusions, an anguished former Warren Commission member Senator John Cooper went public with his belief in conspiracy, telling the press, "I heard Governor Connally testify very strongly that he was not struck by the same bullet, and I could not convince myself that the same bullet struck both of them."[17] Cooper knew, as did the other commissioners, that separate bullets meant two shooters and conspiracy. Now there remained only Gerald Ford and John McCloy to continue the big lie that had been the Warren Report. In Dallas, the forces of reckoning were about to catch up with Sarah Hughes.

On a morning in early May 1982, the Dallas press reported on three events occurring the day before, events of critical interest to Sarah Hughes. U.S. Judge William Sessions (soon to become FBI director) sealed aspects of a court record concerning the prosecution of Joseph Chagra, coconspirator in the 1979 Mob assassination of federal judge John Wood in Houston, a colleague of Hughes. It had been alleged that Wood's assassin, Charles Harrelson, had been seen in Dallas, in Dealey Plaza, on November 22, 1963.[18] In another story, former Dallasite John Hinckley, who attempted to assassinate President Ronald Reagan in 1981, finally came to trial. The paper ridiculed the federal judicial system for the long delay.[19] In California, Robert Kennedy's assassin, Sirhan Sirhan, was also in the news. At his parole hearing, a convict testified that "Sirhan once told [him] he was paid to assassinate Kennedy." That hearing had been immediately closed.[20] At the time, Sirhan was scheduled for release under state law. Hughes was an intensely political personality and no doubt read that morning's paper. The full impact of her collusion with Johnson came home. Had she not blocked effective prosecution of the Pearl Street Mafia in 1963, would RFK have died? Would Judge Wood have been murdered? The truth in 1963 would have spared the country the agony of protracted government betrayal. She drove to her doctor's office where she collapsed and was rushed to a hospital. Over the next forty-eight hours she suffered a near-fatal stroke.[21] Hughes died in 1985, but before doing so, she confided to an aide, "You know . . . [the oath to Johnson] is not really what I consider to be the brightest point of my career."[22] Indeed.

District Attorney Wade relinquished his post two years later, still denying the Pearl Street mob ever existed. His time had come and gone. Dallas, soon to be overtaken by scandal because of his reckless mismanagement of so many criminal cases, could no longer afford Henry Menasco Wade. Only federal judge Barefoot Sanders remained to hide the truth.

Jack Ruby, in a brief jailhouse interview, once said, "The same people who want me to get the electric chair are ones who wanted President Kennedy killed."[23]

Ruby. The only thing I can say . . . Everything pertaining to what's happening has never come to the surface. The world will never know the true facts of what occurred, my motive.

Q. Do you think it will ever come out?

Ruby. No, because, unfortunately the, the people . . . that had so much to gain, and had such a material motive for putting me in the position I'm in, will never let the true facts come above board to the, the world.

Q. Are these people in very high positions, Jack?

Ruby. Yes.[24]

The U.S. Department of Justice, although it would not tell the American people the truth about President Kennedy's murder, realized that the masterminds behind his death had to be punished. And punished they were. It had taken time, but the Dallas and New Orleans Mafia had been destroyed and their leaders taken down. The Democratic Party, to the best of its ability, had only scrambled to protect its own interests. The forces of corruption had prevailed that day in Dallas in 1963—the truth crushed by LBJ and his fellow traitors. Had they not been in power, the facts would have become known. What should have been would have been.

21

AMERICAN TRAITORS

You got gangsters in power and lawbreakers making rules.

When you gonna wake up?

—Bob Dylan, 1979

HAD DISTRICT ATTORNEY Henry Wade cared about the people of Dallas, had he cared about exercising the legal responsibilities of his office, had he followed through with his exclusive jurisdictional obligation to investigate the murder of President John F. Kennedy (in the face of opposition from LBJ), the conspirators responsible for JFK's death would have been apprehended and brought to justice.

In the initial hours after President Kennedy's murder, DA Henry Wade had it right. He started to pursue a conspiracy-based investigation, only to allow his effort to be stopped by Lyndon Johnson and his co-conspirators.

In the critical hours after John Kennedy's murder, Wade should have moved to close down ingress and egress to the city of Dallas. Area airports should have been closed. The Texas Department of Public Safety and state guard should have been brought in to meet the manpower needs of the moment. Wade could easily have coordinated with the mayor to declare a curfew and clear the streets of ordinary traffic and commerce. Police agencies of surrounding municipalities should have been brought into play. In 1963, Dallas was a relatively isolated medium-sized city located in the open plains. Mafia hit men trying to escape the city did not have many options. A concerted sustained manhunt could have trapped Kennedy's murderers in the immediate area. Critical evidence of conspiracy would have been gathered, ensuring the filing of a conspiracy-based indictment on November 22, 1963. Wade had what few prosecutors ever have, an actual film of the victim's murder—absolute proof of conspiracy. He could have seized the film as evidence, had it aired on television to make clear the gravity of the situation, and mobilized public support. Henry Wade knew the U.S. Department of Justice, via its Organized Crime Task Force, was about to put the Dallas Mafia (including well-known Mob bookmaker Jack Ruby) to the wall. Wade knew RFK was planning to deport Joe Ianni and Phil Bosco. The Stone defendants and their associates should have been the first people detained and interrogated. While they did not participate in Kennedy's killing (and very likely knew little more than the fact it was to occur), incriminating information about Joe Civello could have been obtained. That, in turn, would have established probable cause to arrest him. Once in custody, his indictment could have been expanded to ensure his prosecution as a coconspirator in the murder of John Kennedy. His involvement in the planned silencing of Oswald by Ruby would have become known.

As members of the media (most of whom did not know Jack Ruby) had observed the evening of November 22, Ruby could have killed Oswald "five times." Wade knew Ruby personally, knew he was an object of RFK's investigation of the Pearl Street Mafia. The mobster's presence in the Dallas police station, at Wade's press conferences, should have brought the nature of the conspiracy clearly into focus for the seasoned prosecutor. Federal criminal indictments had been handed down on October 21. Ruby's own indictment was imminent. The Dallas DA, upon seeing Ruby in the police station in close proximity to the only suspect in custody, should have had him arrested on the spot and questioned. Simultaneously, the prosecutors in the *Stone* case should have been alerted.

Had Wade done that, he could have quickly arranged, via his close ally Barefoot Sanders, access to the evidence the task force was accumulating. That, combined with Wade's personal knowledge of the workings of the Civello mob, would have given him the information necessary to ask the right questions of all suspects arrested. One of the first things he could have asked of the Stone defendants, Joe Ianni, and Phil Bosco, was their whereabouts at the time of the assassination. Wade knew these men, both from their arrest records and his presence at the Zuroma Club over the years.

When U.S. Attorney Arnold Stone arrived in Dallas months earlier to launch an investigation of the Civello mob, Henry Wade knew that he had a serious problem on his hands. But he also knew that the people of Dallas loved gambling, loved his acquiescence in the status quo. Although arrest and prosecution of JFK's killers would have exposed Wade's association with the Civello mob through the Zuroma Club's weekly poker game, it would not have resulted in the district attorney's arrest. At worst, he would have failed to win reelection to office.

Wade should have put the duties of his office ahead of his concerns over losing his job. But he did not. Euphoric over LBJ's sudden seizure of power, he soon turned a blind eye to his responsibilities. He knew that what Lyndon Johnson's cohorts Cliff Carter, Barefoot Sanders, and Texas attorney general Waggoner Carr wanted him to do—forego a conspiracy investigation–was fundamentally wrong and an illegal attempt to derail a homicide investigation. At that point, Wade should have expanded his investigation to include the three officials. Instead, he allowed them to reduce him to the status of a lackey.

Texas attorney general Waggoner Carr could have come to Wade's aid, could have brought state resources and manpower into play in the critical hours after President Kennedy's murder. Instead, he sought only to hinder the investigation. Carr was an authority on the Dallas Mafia. Like Wade, he knew about the Stone prosecution and Ruby's ties to it. Carr maintained detailed files on Dallas mafiosi and had classified reports compiled by the FBN about the Civello mob.[1] In all likelihood the AG knew about Johnson's efforts in the 1950s to help Dallas mafiosi escape deportation.

When Waggoner Carr was contacted by Cliff Carter (and possibly Johnson) in the hours after the assassination and told to stop any potential conspiracy-based investigation by Wade, he should have refused. Carr should have alerted Wade to LBJ's attempt to interfere in his prosecution. It was clearly a red flag to a man of Carr's experience and knowledge. He should have immediately called a joint press conference with Wade and alerted the media to the fact that federal officials were attempting to subvert the homicide investigation of JFK's death. At the time, the murder of a president was not a federal crime. Federal officials had no legal standing to intervene. Carr, as a former assistant DA and county attorney, was well aware of that fact.

Understanding the gravity of the situation, Carr should then have used his office to establish a court of inquiry under Texas law. He should also have coordinated with the state legislature to establish an investigative committee which then would have exposed the Civello mob's operations in Dallas. But he did none of these things. Instead, he allowed himself (and the office of the Texas attorney general) to be used, trivialized, and ultimately discarded by the federal government. Like Henry Wade, he betrayed the American people, betrayed his Texas constituency, and betrayed the citizens of Dallas.

Dallas Crime Commission president John McKee, though he loathed the Kennedys, could have, even with his limited resources, exposed Wade's corruption. He could easily have provided the media with copies of *The Texas Tribune*, detailing Wade's, Sanders's, Sheriff Decker's, and a host of other local officials' long-term relationship with (and tolerance of) the Pearl Street Mafia. With his criminal files, he could have alerted the media to the fact that Wade had allowed Joe Ianni to get away with murder and had ignored the repeated arrests of Jack Ruby by the Dallas Police Department. However, McKee wanted what Wade and Sanders wanted—political gain under the new Johnson administration. Therefore, he did nothing to expose Wade. The credibility of the Dallas Crime Commission evaporated almost overnight.

But unlike Wade and the others, McKee had a personal reason to fear Johnson and Hoover. McKee was actually a navy deserter who was then living under an assumed name.[2] FBI director J. Edgar Hoover undoubtedly knew this, but did nothing because he knew that McKee was a fanatical supporter of Johnson. Through Hoover, Johnson knew McKee's real identity and used the knowledge to ensure his continued loyalty. McKee's cooperation in the hours and days after the assassination, like Wade's, Carr's, and Sanders's, was something LBJ needed in order to escape prosecution as a coconspirator in the President's murder.

Once the Organized Crime Task Force began its investigation of Stone and Bosco, Barefoot Sanders should have gone to his superiors, explained his presence at the Zuroma Club, and requested his removal from the investigation. At most, Sanders would have been reprimanded for frequenting a gambling house with known criminals. Had that been done, he would not have been subject to leverage by Johnson once Kennedy had been killed.

Barefoot Sanders should have simply refused Johnson's demand to intervene in Wade's original plan to pursue a conspiracy investigation. Sanders knew as much about Jack Ruby's ties to the Stone prosecution as anyone. When approached by LBJ, he should have immediately contacted his superiors at the Justice Department in Washington DC. He should have called Criminal Division Chief Herbert Miller and Attorney General Robert Kennedy. They knew of Johnson's corruption and could have used the intervention as evidence against him. They could have gone to Congress and initiated impeachment proceedings against LBJ.

But Sanders was ambitious and saw only opportunity in Kennedy's death. In doing Johnson's bidding that Friday evening, he protected himself from exposure for incompetence and at the same time furthered his career. From his work with Judge Hughes, Sanders knew that Lyndon Johnson rewarded those who protected him.

U.S. District Court Judge Sarah Hughes had the power to stop Lyndon Johnson and his minions in their tracks. She understood the conspiratorial significance of Jack Ruby's murder of Lee Oswald, how it tied in with the Stone prosecution. She understood that JFK had been killed, in part, to stop the Stone investigation. As soon as Ruby was identified as Oswald's murderer, she should have immediately called a press conference, identified Ruby as a subject of the ongoing prosecution of the Dallas Mafia, and requested assistance from the Department of Justice.

But she had allowed herself to be compromised by Johnson. She knew that he had the FBI file on her gambling arrest years before. He had manipulated her into acting as the presiding judge in the Stone prosecution because he knew she could be controlled in the event problems arose. It didn't have to be that way. With her well-known support of illegal gambling, she could easily have recused herself from service as trial judge in the *Stone* case at the outset. Having been appointed as a federal judge, she could only have been removed by Congress and had nothing to fear from Johnson. He had no legal authority over her.

Sarah Hughes's decision to do nothing to make the public aware of the obvious tie between the Kennedy and Oswald murders and the Stone prosecution stands as a fundamental betrayal of her oath of office. Had her gambling arrest in the 1940s been made public, she would have survived the ensuing scandal. She could have dismissed it as something the U.S. Senate Judiciary Committee was aware of when it approved her appointment to the federal bench in Dallas. The Texas State Bar Association knew of the 1943 event and did not oppose her appointment. Public disclosure in 1963 would not have resulted in her removal from the bench.

We will probably never entirely understand Sarah Hughes's motivation for conspiring with LBJ to subvert the truth in the matter of John Kennedy's murder. She had been on the Dallas scene for many years and was a longtime friend of Johnson's. There may have been other skeletons in her closet. She may have simply been drawn to LBJ, grateful to him for her appointment to the federal bench. Whatever it was, it was incentive enough for her to bring disgrace to her court and throw away any semblance of personal integrity. Clearly, her decision to protect rather than expose Johnson for the corrupt official she knew him to be was something that haunted her for the rest of her days. In the end, she suffered from the same lack of courage as other officials who were in a position to do the right thing but failed to act.

Regional IRS director Ellis Campbell could have made the press aware of Oswald's growing interaction with the Dallas office regarding the issue of excess withholding on his Texas School Book Depository paychecks in the weeks leading up to Kennedy's murder. Would anyone have seriously believed that someone intensely concerned about a few extra dollars in his paycheck would simultaneously be planning to assassinate the President of the United States? Campbell could have told them about Ruby's connection to the Stone prosecution, publicly establishing motive in the mobster's murder of Oswald. In doing so, he would have forced Wade's hand, forced him to tie his investigation of the assassination to the Stone prosecution.

Instead, like Henry Wade, Campbell cooperated with Johnson and met off the record with him after the fact. And what would Campbell be talking with Lyndon Johnson about in the context of JFK's assassination? Over withholding on Lee Harvey Oswald's paychecks? Perhaps a refund to his widow? Campbell and LBJ were talking containment, how to keep the *Stone* case under wraps. LBJ was making sure that the IRS did not allow the public to find out about Jack Ruby's ties to Stone and Miller.

Ellis Campbell, as regional director of the IRS, should have pressed the government's tax evasion cases against the Stone defendants through other means. Through the Criminal Investigative Division (CID) of the IRS, he could have investigated and successfully prosecuted the Dallas mobsters without the help of the Organized Crime Task Force or state officials. He had his own machinery for taking down Mob gamblers and did not need investigative agencies like J. Edgar Hoover's FBI.

I contacted Campbell in writing, with details of what I had uncovered, in an effort to get him to talk about the Stone investigation, but he had suffered a stroke and could not communicate. His wife, however, having seen the letter I sent, said to me, "Please believe me, he would help you if he could."[3]

J. Edgar Hoover should have been assisting District Attorney Henry Wade by providing evidence against the Civello mob. Instead, he had agents like Robert Gemberling and Gordon Shanklin obstruct justice in order to promote the director's own interests. In many ways it was so typical of Hoover, always turning official responsibilities into opportunity for political gain at the expense of the U.S. Constitution and the American people. Hoover could have prevented JFK's death by telling the U.S. Secret Service about the Mafia's contract on the President's life, which he had learned about in September 1962 via FBI field offices' informants. But he chose to remain silent because it served his interests and because he knew he would have no trouble controlling Dallas officials once JFK had been murdered.

A decade earlier, there had been a dry run of sorts involving a homicide committed in downtown Dallas, in broad daylight, in front of numerous witnesses. The murderer was a former FBI agent of considerable fame (and a favorite of Hoover's) named Robert Jones, who had become the local chief of police. Jones's daughter had married a Dallas man whom the police chief suspected of infidelity. As his suspicions grew, he became enraged. One day, Jones decided to take matters into his own hands and began stalking his son-in-law. He followed him into a downtown jewelry store, confronted him, pulled a handgun, and shot him to death in front of witnesses.[4]

It was a clear case of premeditated first-degree murder, sure to bring scandal to the FBI. But Jones had no intentions of paying for his actions and brought his close association with Hoover to bear. Local officials who should have prosecuted Jones instead came to his aid out of respect for, and fear of, J. Edgar Hoover. The Dallas district attorney coordinated with the local judiciary to obtain a change of venue and get Jones's case transferred out of Dallas to a distant much smaller Texas town. Dallas County sheriff Bill Decker; Will Fritz, Oswald's future interrogator; Joe Brown, Jack Ruby's future trial judge; and others testified as character witnesses for Jones.[5] That did the trick, and Jones was acquitted. The stellar reputation of a Hoover favorite was cleared, and the bureau's image was saved from tarnish. Hoover's G-men could do no wrong. Years later, when Hoover took control of JFK's murder investigation at LBJ's directive, he knew there would be only cooperation from Dallas officialdom.

In the years prior to the Kennedy administration, Hoover could easily have exposed the corrupt Lyndon Johnson, exposed his efforts at protecting mafiosi like Frank Ianni and Sam Savalli from deportation by the INS. The FBI director could also have stopped LBJ in 1948 by forcing the Justice Department and the Texas state legislature to investigate his theft of the U.S. Senate election through vote fraud. But Hoover did nothing because he feared that Johnson would reveal his homosexuality to the press, thereby disgracing him and ensuring his loss of federal employment.

In the hours after John Kennedy's death, Hoover should have told Johnson he had no jurisdiction to intervene in the case. It was purely a local matter. The FBI director had more than enough evidence on LBJ to implicate him in wrongdoing on any number of ongoing federal investigations: the Billy Sol Estes case, the Bobby Baker scandal, his misuse of Federal Communication Commission (FCC) regulations to gain a monopoly on regional television broadcasting through his wife's media corporation, to name a few.

Hoover had known for years about the Zuroma Club and its weekly "heavy game of poker" orchestrated by Dallas Mafia boss Joe Civello. Through the Dallas FBI field office and their criminal informants (CIs), he knew about Wade's and the other officials' ongoing presence there.[6] He knew that the proceeds from Civello's large-scale bookmaking operation were being used by the Mafia to buy hundreds of pounds of heroin to be resold on the streets of U.S. cities, destroying whole generations of American youth. But he did nothing to assist the INS in their efforts to deport Mob narcotics traffickers.

Hoover simply stood by and watched Lyndon Johnson's power grow and his corruption erode the integrity of the political system. In 1961, Hoover should have thrown the weight of his agency behind Attorney General Kennedy. Understanding Kennedy's youth and naïveté, the older, experienced law enforcement official would have proved invaluable at breaking the Mafia—and the officials who had been corrupted by it.

When the identification of Jack Ruby as Oswald's killer became known to Robert Kennedy, he should have taken personal charge of the Stone prosecution. He should have flown to Dallas under proper security and held a press conference to explain the connection between the two cases. At that point, he knew that Sheriff Bill Decker (a Zuroma Club guest) had appeared as a character witness in behalf of Joe Civello years earlier and couldn't be trusted.[7] Kennedy should have authorized U.S. Marshals to seize Ruby, remove him from the Dallas County jail, and place him in federal custody. What would Lyndon Johnson have done to stop him? Had he fired RFK, it would only have brought full-scale congressional investigation and ultimately, impeachment for high crimes and misdemeanors under the Constitution. Congress was aware of Johnson's corruption and knew he couldn't possibly have a legitimate reason to stop the attorney general had RFK chosen to act. Once the public knew about the Stone prosecution's connection to the assassination, they would have expected, even demanded, Justice Department intervention.

By the time JFK was murdered, Robert Kennedy had a clear understanding of the degree to which Dallas officials had been compromised by the Pearl Street Mafia. He knew about the Zuroma Club and knew about Barefoot Sanders and Sarah Hughes's bias in favor of Mob gambling in Dallas. Robert Kennedy had surely opposed JFK giving Johnson control over federal appointments in Texas in 1961. In truth, given the realities on the ground, John Kennedy should never have gone to Dallas in November 1963. Robert Kennedy demonstrated extremely poor judgment in allowing the trip. Permitting his brother to ride in a top-down motorcade tour of downtown Dallas with a full-blown Mob investigation bringing indictments at that very moment was inviting disaster. JFK, fully aware of his brother's efforts to destroy the Civello mob, was a fool to expose himself. At most, he should have limited his appearance in Dallas to the planned indoor Trade Mart luncheon—nothing more.

Had Robert Kennedy taken charge in Dallas, he could easily have expanded the *Stone* case to encompass investigation of his brother's murder. Through prosecution of Ruby and interrogation of the Stone defendants, Joe Civello, who backed the Stone and Bosco operations, could have been brought into the case. Before pursuing that course, Kennedy could have had Judge Sarah Hughes removed as presiding judge in the Stone prosecution.

But Robert Kennedy did nothing to bring his brother's killers to justice. He allowed the knowledge of his brother's philandering and the fear of its discovery to come before his duties as attorney general. In effect, he simply walked away, allowing LBJ and Sanders to throttle the truth. When Robert Kennedy took the job of attorney general, when he set out to destroy the Mafia, when he allowed his brother to go to Dallas, he assumed certain responsibilities. He had an obligation to the American people. In the end, he betrayed that trust. Had he chosen to lead that November 22, 1963, others would have followed. There were honest, capable people in positions of power.

Dallas police chief Jesse Curry knew Henry Wade was corrupt long before JFK was cut down in Dallas. He had also seen the Zapruder film and knew what it meant. Like Wade, he knew of Ruby's status as a mobster. Oswald was held at police headquarters and was under Curry's control. Once Ruby was spotted in the building, Curry should have had him detained and questioned. Curry had exclusive control over the situation. Had RFK acted promptly, Oswald would have been transferred directly from Curry's control to federal marshals.

Curry was an FBI Academy graduate and had a good understanding of Hoover's jurisdiction. He should never have allowed Dallas FBI SAC Gordon Shanklin to dictate what he said in press conferences. Curry had spoken the truth about the FBI's prior knowledge of Oswald's job at the Texas School Book Depository. The reality was that the Dallas FBI had done nothing wrong. They had a file on Oswald well before the assassination and knew he posed no threat to President Kennedy.

Had Oswald not been killed, Curry's people would have soon discovered that the young leftist had an unbeatable alibi—being seen by competent witnesses finishing his lunch in the depository's second-floor lunchroom at the moment JFK was killed. Following that, Oswald had stopped to explain to a reporter who dashed into the building only seconds after the assassination where to find a telephone. Having interrogated Oswald for hours on Friday and Saturday, Curry's people had already learned that he had no motive to assassinate the President (in fact, he admired Kennedy) and would admit no part in the killing. He was, as his wife had described him, nothing more than a "brave rabbit." In police custody, he began to behave and react much like any other wrongly accused citizen. At first indignant, he then became very angry. Sooner or later, Chief Curry would have realized that he had the wrong man.

There were many missteps made in the aftermath of JFK's and Oswald's murders, some accidental, some deliberate. The latter were made by people willing to violate state and federal law to protect their own interests and seize political opportunity. Those people are all long dead, never having faced justice for their betrayal of the American people. And so they will be judged in absentia. Their crimes will become known, made forever a part of the legal and historical record. Their crimes will become their epitaphs. And when they have been exposed for what they were, the American people will have justice.

Every crime demands payment.

22

PROSECUTION—UNITED STATES V. LYNDON BAINES JOHNSON, ET AL

> In my mind, and by the direction of the, of the blood and brain from the President from one of the shots, it, it would just seem that it would have to be fired from the front, rather than behind. . . . I think . . . there could have been another man.
>
> —Dallas Police Chief Jesse Curry

VICE PRESIDENT LYNDON Johnson committed criminal acts, at both the federal and state level, in conspiring with the Mafia to assassinate John Kennedy and prevent investigation of the crime after the fact. The evidence has proven that he lured JFK to Dallas, Texas, on November 22, 1963, for the purpose of putting him at a location where he would be killed. In doing this, under federal law he became a party to *Treason* (18 U.S.C. 2381) and *Conspiracy* (18 U.S.C. 371, 372). Once JFK was pronounced dead, as president, Johnson violated additional federal and Texas criminal statutes, including *Obstruction of Justice* (18 U.S.C. 1510, 1511, 1519) and *Accessory* (18 U.S.C. 3) (Texas Penal Code, Articles 77–79). In agreeing to help Johnson hide the facts behind the crime, U.S. Attorney Barefoot Sanders, Texas Attorney General Waggoner Carr, District Attorney Henry Wade, and federal judge Sarah Hughes became coconspirators. In remaining silent about LBJ's betrayal, they became guilty of *Misprision of Treason* (18 U.S.C. 2382).

The legal components of the criminal statutes Johnson and his cohorts violated are as follows:

> Treason: Whoever, owing allegiance to the United States . . . adheres to their enemies, giving them aid or comfort . . . is guilty of treason and shall suffer death or shall be imprisoned not less than five years . . . and shall be incapable of holding any office under the United States.
>
> Misprision of Treason: Whoever, owing allegiance to the United States and having knowledge of the commission of any treason against them, conceals and does not . . . disclose . . . to some judge . . . or . . . governor . . . of a particular State, is guilty of misprision of treason and shall be . . . imprisoned not more than seven years.
>
> Conspiracy to Commit Offense: If two or more persons conspire . . . to commit any offense against the United States . . . and one or more . . . do any act to effect the object of the conspiracy . . . each shall be imprisoned not more than five years.
>
> Conspiracy to Impede Officer: If two or more persons . . . conspire to prevent, by . . . intimidation . . . any person from . . . discharging . . . the duties of his office . . . each of such persons shall be . . . imprisoned not more than six years.
>
> Obstruction of Justice: Whoever knowingly alters, destroys, . . . conceals, covers up, falsifies . . . any records . . . with the intent to impede, obstruct, or influence the investigation . . . of any matter . . . shall be . . . imprisoned not more than 20 years.
>
> Accessory after the Fact: Whoever, knowing that an offense against the United States has been committed, . . . assists the offender in order to hinder or prevent his apprehension, trial, or punishment, is an accessory after the fact. . . . An accessory after the fact shall be imprisoned. . . . If the principal is punishable by life imprisonment or death, the accessory shall be imprisoned not more than 15 years.

When Lyndon Johnson prevented DA Henry Wade from filing a conspiracy-based murder indictment against Lee Oswald the evening of November 22, 1963, and then engaged in the destruction of evidence in JFK's murder, he violated the *Obstruction of Justice* and *Accessory* statutes. Cliff Carter and Barefoot Sanders, in conspiring with Johnson that day, became parties to his criminal acts. Like LBJ, they aided and abetted the escape of those responsible for President Kennedy's murder.

The U.S. attorney to the Northern District of Texas (Dallas), Barefoot Sanders, violated his oath of office when he worked to prevent the successful prosecution of the Stone defendants by Robert Kennedy's Organized Crime Task Force in the months leading up to (and after) the assassination of President Kennedy. Under 39 *U.S.C.A 1011 (Oath of Office)*, he agreed to the following:

> I do solemnly swear that I will support and defend the Constitution of the United States against all enemies, foreign and domestic; that I will bear true faith and allegiance to the same . . . and that I will . . . faithfully discharge the duties of the office on which I am about to enter. So help me God.

In knowingly making a false public statement (that the Dallas Mafia did not exist), he violated the *Obstruction of Justice* statute. After JFK was killed, Sanders's attempt to derail the Stone prosecution and hide Jack Ruby's connection to the group, constituted *Misprision of Treason* and *Obstruction of Justice* under federal statute. At the state level, he violated the *Accessory* statute in aiding LBJ in preventing the filing of a conspiracy-based indictment against Oswald.

During the course of the Warren Commission proceedings, Sanders, in assisting the Dallas FBI with the falsification of witness affidavits and the alteration of evidence (which were submitted to both the commissioners and the Texas prosecutors of Jack Ruby), he violated the *Obstruction of Justice* statute.

I confronted Judge Barefoot Sanders on September 3, 1996, with thirty questions and supporting documentation via certified mail (P-300 972 018), which detailed his actions while U.S. attorney to Dallas. But he refused to address the issues, lacking the courage to respond.

I confronted Barefoot Sanders about his presence at the Zuroma Club with Phil Bosco, Joe Civello, and Lyndon Johnson's ally Pete Tamburo. But he lacked the courage to respond. Under *Texas Penal*

Code, Offenses Against Public Policy and Economy (Articles 615–42), the Zuroma Club, with its weekly poker games orchestrated by Joe Civello, constituted a gaming house. Sanders and Wade, in appearing as guests, violated *Article 631—Going in Gaming House*. And during the course of the Stone prosecution in 1963, did Sanders meet again with Phil Bosco and other mobsters at the club? Did he express his outrage at the presence of Kennedy's Organized Crime Task Force in Dallas? Did he convey his and LBJ's hatred of John Kennedy to Joe Civello? Did he talk of his desire to see Lyndon Johnson become president?

Dallas district attorney Henry Wade, in allowing Barefoot Sanders and Cliff Carter to override his decision to pursue a conspiracy investigation and prosecute JFK's killers, violated his oath of office. Under the Texas constitution, Wade agreed to the following:

> I do solemnly swear that I will faithfully execute the duties of the office of District Attorney, of the City of Dallas, State of Texas, and will to the best of my ability preserve, protect and defend the Constitution and Laws of the United States and of this state and the Charter and ordinances of this city . . . So help me God.

Wade's collusion with Johnson rendered him guilty of the charges of *Misprision of Treason, Conspiracy*, and *Obstruction of Justice*. He became an *Accessory* to murder, guilty of aiding and abetting the escape of President Kennedy's real killers. In telling obvious lies to the media during press conferences, he sent a clear message to the Mafia that they had nothing to worry about. He was on board with Joe Civello and Lyndon Johnson.

As in the case of Barefoot Sanders, I confronted Henry Wade the same day in writing via certified letter (P 300 972 019) with twenty-three questions, detailing his malfeasance in office and actions in the aftermath of the President's slaying. But like Sanders, he refused to respond. Wade simply lacked the moral fiber and personal integrity to address his actions. In truth, he had been ecstatic over Johnson's seizure of power and didn't give a damn about doing his job, didn't give a damn about the American people.

I confronted Wade about his repeated presence at the Zuroma Club with convicted killers and heroin traffickers—about why he had not raided and closed the club for operating a gambling house, a violation of state law. He had no comment. I confronted him about his cowardly inability to successfully prosecute and imprison Mob killer Joe Ianni, but he had no answer. I confronted him about using his position as Dallas district attorney to conduct surveillance on political opponents of Lyndon Johnson during his senate years. There was no answer.

Prior to confronting Wade in writing, I called him and arranged an interview. He took pride in claiming to be able to get a jury to convict anybody of "anything," as he put it. He spoke of Lyndon Johnson in glowing terms. But when the interview turned to the Mafia's narcotics trafficking during the 1950s (and its use of social clubs as fronts), Wade quickly became a defensive, then angry man who had no desire to engage in further conversation. When I pressed about contacting him for a second interview, he said, "You can try." Clearly, Henry Wade had no intention of discussing his presence at the Anonymous/Zuroma Club.

Texas attorney general Waggoner Carr, Wade's coconspirator that Friday evening of November 22, 1963, proved equally unwilling to discuss his knowledge of the Dallas Mafia. In a taped interview, he prided himself on being the Mob expert and lead interrogator when he served on the Texas state investigative committee examining organized crime activity during the 1950s. But when the interview turned to Jack Ruby's close bookmaking associate, a man named Louie Ferrantello, Carr suddenly developed selective memory loss. Carr knew that Ruby's ties to Ferrantello provided yet another clear link to the Pearl Street Mafia. And when it came to his questioning of witnesses in Dallas, he again seemed to remember little.

When Waggoner Carr allowed himself to be used by Johnson to put pressure on Henry Wade to forego a conspiracy investigation, Carr himself became party to *Obstruction of Justice*. When he agreed to forego a court of inquiry, he failed in his oath of office and in his responsibilities to the people of Texas. As the Warren Commission hearings proceeded and began to take on the look of a whitewash, Carr began to look like a fool for not acting. Like Wade, he became an *Accessory after the Fact*, aiding and abetting the escape of the President's killers. With his knowledge of the Stone prosecution, the Dallas Mafia, and the obvious evidence of conspiracy in the aftermath of the assassination, Carr had a clear picture of what had happened that day in Dallas. He knew treason when he saw it. In failing to act as Texas

AG, he was in clear violation of the *Misprision of Treason* statute. In the end, Carr lost all credibility with the Warren Commission and Lyndon Johnson. He had served his purpose and was discarded when it was concluded he posed no threat.

Judge Sarah Hughes, like Carr, suffered from a similar paralysis when it came to acting upon the obvious. Prior to the assassination, she had no doubt been made aware of Jack Ruby's bookmaking role in the Stone prosecution. Ruby would have been in the next round of indictments and prosecution by the task force had JFK not been killed. And yet she allowed LBJ, Sanders, and Herbert Miller to simply stop the Stone prosecution. Like Sanders and Carr, she could well have been prosecuted for *Misprision of Treason*.

When Hughes finally resumed the Stone trial, her obvious bias in the case became readily apparent to the task force. Her collusion with Sanders to gut the government's case amounted to extreme judicial misconduct. She had taken the same oath of office as Sanders. She had also taken a second judicial oath.

> I Sarah Hughes do solemnly swear that I will administer justice without respect to persons, and do equal right to the poor and to the rich, and that I will faithfully and impartially discharge and perform all the duties incumbent upon me as District Court Judge under the Constitution and laws of the United States. So help me God.

A decade later, when she presided over yet another prosecution of John Eli Stone, her bias again came into play. Again she worked to subvert judicial process. Had the code of judicial conduct been applied to her actions, she would have been taken off the case, censured by her peers, impeached by the U.S. Congress, and removed from the federal bench. From there, she would have been disbarred from the practice of law.

These, then, are the crimes of Lyndon Johnson and his co-conspirators. In life, they avoided legal responsibility and prosecution for what they did. They are not here to defend themselves, but their failure to follow the law, failure to execute the oath of office, and failure as American citizens is now historical fact.

Guilty as charged.

23

THE STONE SUPPRESSION

UNDER THE REQUIREMENTS of the President John F. Kennedy Assassination Records Collection Act of 1992, the FBI and all other investigative agencies were required to turn over to the National Archives and Records Administration (NARA) in Washington DC, the originals of all documents they held, which pertained to the murder of JFK. Over a period of years, those documents were reviewed. Some were declassified and made available to the public, some remain sealed. The FBI files I obtained on the Dallas mobsters exposed in this book contained numerous notices of documents withheld from release. The reason used was always as follows:

These documents were provided to the National Archives and Records Administration (NARA) under the JFK Assassination Records Collection Act of 1992.

Additionally, I was told that "Provision of the JFK Act allowed for certain information to be postponed from public release until the year 2017."

Among the files that remain at least partially sealed are those of Joe Civello, his brother Charles Civello, Ross Musso, Joe Ianni, Philip Bosco, Johnny Ross Patrono, Isadore and David Miller, Russell Mathews, and John Eli Stone and his brother James Stone. The data suppressed is considerable. In the case of Bosco, eighty-two documents were withheld from me when the FBI responded to my demand for his file. In Joe Ianni's case, twenty-four documents were suppressed. Patrono's file contains sixty-five suppressed documents. Civello's lieutenant and brother-in-law, Ross Musso, was subjected to intense surveillance and warranted personal scrutiny by J. Edgar Hoover. At least fifty-one documents in Hoover's headquarters (HQ) file on the mobster were turned over to NARA. The FBI HQ file on Joe Civello's brother, Charles, contained thirty-nine documents which were withheld and turned over to NARA. John Eli Stone's FBI HQ file was handled in the same manner. In the case of Joe Civello and Ruby's confidant David Miller, their FBI files were turned over to NARA in their entirety. And that was just what the FBI had. Clearly, portions of these mobsters' FBI files have been suppressed by the government because the facts contained therein reveal the truth behind JFK's assassination.

The Stone prosecution also involved the IRS and the Bureau of Alcohol, Tobacco Firearms and Explosives. As I discovered, the relevant portions of their files on the same individuals were suppressed by the government as well. Not surprisingly, the IRS and the ATF denied my FOIA request for their files on the 1963 Stone prosecution.

In all, NARA is holding hundreds of assassination documents—on individuals we were told had nothing to do with John Kennedy's death because Oswald was just a "lone nut." NARA and the investigative agencies involved in the suppression of the Stone prosecution have acted in concert with the courts.

The U.S. District Court for the Northern District of Texas denied that the 1963 Stone prosecution ever took place. I obtained a "twenty year search" of their court docket for the 1960 to 1980 time period regarding all prosecutions of John Eli Stone. In 1996, at the height of Sanders's power in that court, they responded with a certified court document listing only Stone's RICO prosecution in the early 1970s. According to their certification, Stone was not prosecuted and convicted by RFK's task force. With Sarah Hughes serving as chief judge in the Northern District Court and later Barefoot Sanders, it is small wonder that the Stone prosecution disappeared from the court record. In 2010, not long after Sanders's death (while still on the bench), I repeated my request for a "twenty year search." Now, Stone's 1963 prosecution is once again part of the official record. Clearly, in an effort to protect himself, Johnson's cohort had seen to it that Robert Kennedy's attempt to break the Civello mob in 1963 was not part of the public record during the time he controlled the Dallas court.

But the case file was not destroyed. I know that because I traveled to the Fort Worth, Texas, branch of NARA and was allowed access to the court record, even though it had not been made a part of the official record (accessioned). Why after over thirty years it was not part of the official record, I don't know. When I questioned Robert Blakey about the Stone file, his only response was, "Does it exist?" Why I was allowed to make copies of the key court documents, I don't know. It was most likely an honest mistake on the part of the archivist present at the time.

Just as there is a pattern to the suppression of documents surrounding the Stone prosecution, there is also suppression with regard to the portions of the Dallas mobster's FBI files. Almost without exception, the documents seized and withheld by NARA relate to the 1963 through mid-1964 time period. That coincides with the Stone prosecution, JFK assassination, and activity of the Warren Commission.

Clearly, the remaining NARA documents withheld from the public until 2017 (at least) are at the heart of the matter with regard to the solution to President Kennedy's murder. What I have uncovered about the Civello mob and RFK's attempt to destroy it are a large part of what remains classified.

A search today of NARA's online JFK Assassination database with regard to the Dallas Mafia reveals almost no information. And yet, the FBI has indicated to me that substantial portions of the files on individual members of the Civello mob were sent to NARA at their request under the JFK Act in 1992. Why aren't they listed as a part of NARA's holdings, even if still classified? And why, in the few instances when a series of documents for a given mobster (e.g., Phil Bosco or Isadore Miller) are listed, is there a gap between 1963 and mid-1964?

In the context of the Civello mob and the murder of President Kennedy, what NARA says it has and what we now know to be the case are two different things. In the world of classified documents, what the public doesn't know about, the public can't ask about. But now, with the evidence contained in this book, the government can no longer hide the truth.

The big lie is finished.

24

ARNOLD STONE NOVEMBER 22, 1930–DECEMBER 3, 2012

The marvel of all history is the patience with which men and women submit to burdens unnecessarily laid upon them by their governments.

—George Washington

ARNOLD STONE, THE man U.S. Attorny General Robert F. Kennedy had handpicked to investigate and ultimately prosecute the Pearl Street Mafia, died on December 3, 2012. He served his country with great courage in his prosecution of East Coast heroin traffickers and in his attempt to bring down the Dallas Mafia via the John Eli Stone prosecution. Had President Kennedy not been assassinated, U.S. Attorney Stone would have succeeded, and the course of American history from November 22, 1963, forward would have been very different. As the man who knew the truth about the conspiracy behind JFK's murder from the beginning, but who could not relay that information to the American people, he carried an extraordinary burden to his dying day. I know this because on August 21, 1995, after considerable negotiation, he granted me an off-record interview about the Stone prosecution, who was responsible for JFK's murder, and why he was killed.

With Arnold Stone's death, I am now free to reveal what he told me in that interview. By 1995, Stone was retired from the Department of Justice and in private practice on the East Coast. From the outset of the interview, by phone, it was obvious to me that he understood the importance of what he was doing. By then, my first book on the JFK assassination, *Act of Treason: The Role of J. Edgar Hoover in the Assassination of President Kennedy*, had been in circulation for four years. In connection with that book, I had made appearances on national television news programs such as Larry King Live and Geraldo, as well as numerous talk radio programs around the country. Stone knew that, ultimately, what he said to me would be made public.

I began the interview by asking him about the John Eli Stone, et al prosecution that he had spearheaded in 1963. Arnold responded by saying, "Have you read my report?" I had not, and to my knowledge, its existence was unknown to the research community. He went on to explain that a few weeks prior to the President's scheduled arrival in Dallas, he had become so fearful about the situation surrounding the Stone prosecution that he had prepared and sent a report to his superiors at the Department of Justice. In that report, he had made it clear that John Kennedy should not come to Dallas because it would simply be too dangerous. Presumably, RFK saw that report. Despite this warning, Stone was ignored. I gathered from this that he was still angry over the fact that his advice was not taken. Based upon the information revealed in this book, who could blame him?

When I asked him about his superior, Robert Kennedy, he became agitated. "That man . . ." his voice trailed off. "November 22 is my birthday," he went on. "My father was a bookie," he said, indicating that it was because of that and his experience prosecuting mob heroin traffickers that Kennedy had picked him to take down the Dallas Mafia.

The interview turned to Stone's first trip to Dallas and his meeting with local U.S. Attorney Barefoot Sanders. Stone made it clear to me that he had nothing but contempt for Johnson's crony. Undoubtedly, Stone had been briefed on Sanders prior to the trip because the latter had done his best to keep the mob prosecution from ever getting off the ground. In reality, Barefoot Sanders was nothing more than a corrupt, criminal associate of an even more corrupt Lyndon Johnson. Stone told me that within an hour of his arrival in Dallas, Sanders had learned of it and came to the hotel where Stone was staying. Pounding on the door until Stone let him in, Sanders wasted no time. Obviously enraged, he said to Stone, "Your presence in Dallas is no longer welcome. . . ."

From the beginning of Stone's investigation, Sanders had kept LBJ informed of Robert Kennedy's plan to take down the Pearl Street Mob. The Dallas attorney had failed in his attempt to stop the investigation and knew he would have to answer to LBJ. Lyndon Johnson was not a man who tolerated failure in his underlings. That aside, Sanders knew too that his own presence at the Anonymous Club with Phil Bosco and other Dallas Mafiosi could easily become a matter of public record. In his mind, if the investigation ran its course, it would only be a matter of time before his corruption would be exposed and his position as U.S. Attorney to Dallas lost.

I turned the interview to the subject of Frank and Joe Ianni and what Stone knew of them. By 1961, Joe had been placed in control of the Civello Mob's bookmaking operation. Mafiosos John Eli Stone, Phil Bosco, Isadore Miller, and Jack Ruby answered to him and coordinated closely in their day-to-day operations. And by the time the Stone investigation began, RFK had also set in motion plans to deport both Joe Ianni and Phil Bosco. Arnold Stone, from his experience prosecuting heroin traffickers, knew about Joe Ianni's direct ties to the vicious and ruthless John Ormento.

My question about what he knew of Frank and Joe Ianni seemed to stun Stone. He hesitated a moment, choosing his words carefully, and then said, "There are people in this world I would not write about. Don't write about the Iannis." By 1963, former U.S. Attorney General Tom Clark's corrupt assistance to Frank Ianni in preventing his deportation for heroin trafficking was common knowledge at the Department of Justice. Whether Stone was also aware of Ianni's close ties to Lyndon and Claudia Johnson during LBJ's senate years will never be known. But my question had clearly disturbed him. Perhaps Stone said what he did in an attempt to intimidate me; perhaps he said it out of fear.

Because of what I had already learned about the Dallas Mafia, their involvement with Marcello in bookmaking and heroin trafficking, and their corruption of Henry Wade and LBJ, I knew going into the interview that it was RFK's attempt to destroy those operations that had led to President Kennedy's murder. And through the Mafia's use of disassociation, I also knew that they would have used imported contract killers to carry out the assassination, not local thugs.

Not surprisingly then, when I asked Stone about the John Eli Stone prosecution in the context of the JFK assassination, he was quick to say that the defendants in the case "had nothing to do with that." True enough, they were bookmakers, not hit men. And given the tremendous pressure they were under by the fall of 1963, they were in no position to attempt a crime of such magnitude. But their prosecution was the reason Joe Civello cooperated with Carlos Marcello in allowing Dallas to be used as the killing ground.

Stone went on, focusing on RFK's spectacular heroin bust, via the Federal Bureau of Narcotics, in Laredo, Texas, on the border with Mexico in October 1963. That, he revealed, was what the JFK assassination "was all about." I replied that I knew of the bust and its relationship to the Mondoloni heroin cartel as well as that entity's role as the supplier to Marcello and Civello. He provided no further details, but his admission was incredibly important in and of itself. A former U.S. Attorney, who had been operating at ground zero on November 22, with all that he knew about the Mafia's heroin trafficking operations in the United States, had just revealed the fact that the Justice Department had known from the beginning that JFK had been the victim of a Mob conspiracy.

The former prosecutor shifted the conversation back to the Stone investigation. He said that after the President's murder, the Stone "case was taken away from me. Barefoot decided it was his case." He added, "Sanders was never going to let us prosecute it."

In that context, I asked about Mafioso Phil Bosco, who had "taken the Fifth" so many times during the fall of 1963 rather than tell federal prosecutors what he knew about the criminal operations of the Civello Mob. Did he ever talk? Oddly, Stone said he "couldn't remember." I talked about the Anonymous Club and Sanders's presence there with Bosco. Stone was noncommittal on the subject of the club. I couldn't tell if he understood that aspect of the situation in Dallas, but I was struck by his silence on the subject.

We ran out of time, and the interview came to an end. Shocked by all that Stone had revealed, I pressed him for a second interview—on the record. But clearly wary of going public, he said only that he would consider it, adding that I should send him copies of the documents I had uncovered regarding the Anonymous Club and the LBJ–Wade relationship. Once he had those, he said, he would decide whether to grant the interview. I sent the documents the following day, by registered mail, return receipt. He received them, but in the end refused to allow a second interview.

Arnold Stone was a good man who served his country with great courage in his attempt to bring down the Pearl Street Mafia. But he was also loyal to the Department of Justice. And the non-disclosure agreement he had signed when he left Justice undoubtedly provided added incentive not to grant "on record" interviews or publish anything about the Stone case. I kept to the terms of our agreement until he died. In retrospect, it is my conclusion that he was deeply conflicted about his obligations as a federal prosecutor and what he knew the American people ultimately had the right to know. Perhaps that is why he gave me the opportunity to speak for him.

Former U.S. Attorney and House Select Committee on Assassinations general counsel G. Robert Blakey is like Arnold Stone in many ways. I interviewed him after Stone, on September 13, 1996. By then, Blakey was a law professor at Notre Dame and was known for his refusal to discuss details of what the HSCA had not made public when it issued its report in 1979. Of course, constrained by secrecy laws governing the disclosure of evidence uncovered through federal investigative hearings, he can hardly do otherwise.

Still, armed with the facts that I had uncovered, I felt compelled to see what he might disclose about the John Eli Stone prosecution and the Dallas Mafia. I sent a letter of inquiry to him, laying out questions based upon what I was convinced the HSCA had to have known. He did not respond, so I called him by phone. I began the interview by going to the most important issue. Did the HSCA follow Arnold Stone's lead and further investigate the Stone bookmaking operation as it related to the JFK assassination? I knew the HSCA had examined the case because bookmakers Stone's and Miller's names (but little more) appeared in documents that the HSCA released in 1979. Predictably, Blakey would not reveal anything and deflected my question by saying he "couldn't remember" whether they had or not. Nor did he address the subject in his own book on the assassination, *The Plot to Kill the President*, which was released not long after the HSCA's report was made public in 1979. Despite that, I again pressed him for answers. His patience finally exhausted, he became angry and said, "Look, I did not want to be general counsel to the HSCA. I was drafted. I have moved on. You should too."

In heated tones, he spoke of his frustration with the New Orleans end of their investigation and their inability to get important data. The interview went nowhere and ended shortly thereafter. Blakey has remained resolute in his adherence to U.S. secrecy laws, but I have no doubt that what you have read in this book makes up the bulk of what the HSCA placed under seal in 1979.

Prior to the Stone and Blakey interviews, a talk radio interview I granted on December 5, 1991, in connection with the release of my first book on the JFK assassination, *Act of Treason*, triggered a response from a listener which may shed critically important light on Jack Ruby's motivation for murdering Lee Oswald. The interview took place by phone with KLAV radio in Las Vegas, Nevada, late at night. The following morning, the host of the show called me. He said he had received a call after we went off the air from an individual who had information but wished to remain anonymous.

The caller had told the following story. He said he had once been close to a woman who had previously been married to a big-time bookmaker in Dallas, Texas, back in the 1960's. The woman, whom he did not name, had confided to him that very soon after President Kennedy had been murdered and Oswald arrested, her then husband and several other gamblers had met in private with Jack Ruby. In that meeting they had told, in effect ordered, Ruby to kill Oswald. The caller had indicated to my host that he would be willing to discuss it further under the right circumstances.

But at that time, I knew nothing of the Pearl Street Mafia and the Stone prosecution. I was in the middle of a very busy publicity tour and had heard numerous stories about the "truth" behind the assassination. I did not attempt to meet or talk with the caller, but made note of his story.

It was only after the research I conducted in connection with this book that I realized the caller that December evening years before could very well have been recounting the truth about Ruby's role in the JFK murder mystery. Here's why. By the time of my interview, John Eli Stone had died while living in Las Vegas. His wife, however, had lived on, dying in the same city in 1997. Val Stone had been with her husband in Dallas from the 1950's onward and moved with him to Las Vegas in the latter 1980's. The fact that she had remained married to him despite his long criminal record and violent reputation during their years together, makes it clear that she knew as much about him as anyone. Was she was the caller's source?

Now, the caller's story made sense. Had Val confided in the anonymous caller after her husband's death? The group closest to Jack Ruby at the time of the JFK assassination consisted of Isadore Miller, his brother David, and John and Jim Stone, all bookmakers and gamblers for whom Ruby "ran book." John Stone was considered armed and extremely dangerous by Dallas police officials, as were his cohorts. If anyone could have leveraged Ruby to kill Oswald, it would have been the Stone group.

But why would Stone and the others want Oswald dead? The answer may lie with Oswald's family ties in New Orleans. As discovered by the HSCA, Oswald had an uncle in the Marcello bookmaking operation named Dutz Murret. In that time, Mob bookmakers often used young men as "runners" to help facilitate operations. It is very possible that Oswald was such an individual. As late as mid-August 1963, Uncle Dutz had been in close contact with Oswald in New Orleans. When the former Marine moved back to Dallas on November 3 of that year, he was unemployed and had little money. Through Murret, Oswald could easily have been put in contact with the Stone bookmakers for the purpose of earning some quick cash. At that point, the Stone group had not yet been indicted.

If this scenario is accurate, it would go a long way toward explaining Oswald's panic and flight from the School Book Depository after the assassination. Simply by reading the Dallas newspapers from October

21 onward, he would have learned about the Stone prosecution and about how dangerous his previous employers were. By mid-October, Oswald had obtained full-time employment at the Texas School Book Depository. With an income established and knowledge about the disaster about to befall the Stone bookmakers, he would have had good reason to distance himself from that group.

After JFK was murdered outside the depository, did Oswald then flee the building to get his revolver because he had concluded that the defendants in the Stone case, men he had interacted with and could identify, had been behind the President's murder? And now, because of that connection and his knowledge, was his own life in danger?

Clearly, something had gone terribly wrong with the Mafia's plan to eliminate Oswald immediately after the assassination. With his rifle planted in the depository, they had all that they needed to frame him. All that remained was to silence him—disassociation. But the erratic Oswald had somehow been arrested and was now in police custody. So, the Stone defendants had the same problem as their superiors, Civello and Marcello. How to get to Oswald and kill him before he revealed to investigators that he had worked for Stone and the others?

The obvious and only way was to recruit someone with inside access to the Dallas police station. Jack Ruby was that man. Close to numerous Dallas law enforcement figures, including D.A. Henry Wade, he had long had the run of the Dallas jail and criminal justice facilities. Accordingly, on Friday evening of November 22, Stone and his cohorts drew Ruby into the meeting that the anonymous caller in Las Vegas had spoken about. Ruby then did as he was instructed, confident in his belief that his ties to Dallas law enforcement would, in the end, save him from imprisonment or execution for killing Oswald.

From Friday evening onward, Ruby was repeatedly seen in the Dallas Police Department building, often in close proximity to Oswald. As one journalist put it, "He could have killed Oswald five times." At various points, Ruby went so far as to masquerade as a reporter in order to get close to the hapless ex-marine. Had Lee acted as a runner for the Stone bookmakers even briefly, he would have come in contact with Ruby. Even without knowing him, Oswald would have understood the mobster's criminal association with the Dallas Mafia, which was by November 1963 in the public spotlight because of RFK's Task Force investigation. Given that, it is entirely probable that Oswald recognized Ruby among the crowd of national reporters, seeing him move freely around law enforcement officials. Recall then Oswald's anguished cry to journalists not long before being murdered by Ruby, "I'm a patsy!" A desperate, young pro-Castroite realizing that he was being framed by local Mafiosi to take the fall for President Kennedy's murder.

Earlier in this book, I discussed the U.S. Senate Judiciary Committee's disgraceful approval of Barefoot Sanders's nomination to the federal bench in Northern Texas in 1979. During that hearing, the chairman that day said to Sanders, "We know more about you . . . than is necessary to know." Indeed. Having read the FBI's background report on Sanders, he knew, or at least should have known, that the Dallas lawyer was little more than a mobbed-up, white-collar criminal. And who was the senator who chaired the hearings that day and made that statement to Barefoot Sanders? It was Joe Biden, now Vice President of the United States.

It's been fifty years since JFK's murder. The time to address the entire, sordid cover up has now arrived. It is time for our leaders to live up to the ideals our founding fathers put forth in establishing our form of government. The whole world is waiting, Joe.

25

WHAT IS DUE

The past lies upon the present like a giant's dead body.

—Nathaniel Hawthorne

AND NOW WE know the truth. President Kennedy and Lee Oswald were murdered by Joe Civello's Pearl Street Mafia and the Carlos Marcello mob with the help of the Paul Mondoloni heroin cartel because of the Kennedy administration's efforts to destroy those organizations' illegal narcotics and gambling operations in the southwestern United States. President Lyndon Johnson participated in and covered up the plot via the Warren Commission to save himself from prosecution as a coconspirator by obtaining the presidency. After LBJ left office and FBI Director J. Edgar Hoover fell at his post, the U.S. government moved against Civello and Marcello. A protracted process, the wheels of justice finally began to turn in 1970 with the passage of RICO. The implementation of RICO resulted in the deaths of those primarily responsible for JFK's murder, the finding of conspiracy, and the imprisonment of Marcello.

But what about historical truth? What about restoring our government's credibility? This country and its people have paid a terrible price for Congress's and the Department of Justice's failure to publicly address and resolve these issues.

Over the years, the Democratic Party rolled with the punch because it feared the mortal wound that might well come with disclosure of the truth. The Republicans went along because of Hoover, because he had conspired with LBJ for personal gain, and because of his value as an American icon—the champion of right-wing thought. They also went along because of Gerald Ford's collusion with Johnson and Hoover to subvert the efforts of the Warren Commission. But in the final analysis, both parties acquiesced because they shared a common disease—collusion with the Sicilian-American Mafia—a disease which had evolved over four decades through contributions, private bills, and outright bribery. By November 22, 1963, the disease had become a national constituency. That day, the system of government created by our forefathers, a system we had thought was unshakeable, in fact imploded.

The presidential administration of Lyndon Johnson caused great hardship, here and abroad. Vietnam became a war under LBJ because it offered him the opportunity to hide the truth. By escalating the conflict, he was able to focus public attention away from JFK's murder and toward external threat—a classic method of corrupt leadership as old as Rome itself. And the Eastern Bloc knew it. They had observed the clueless Lee Oswald for years when he lived in Russia, subjecting him to intense surveillance. They knew he was no killer. From the beginning, they understood the nature of LBJ's presidency. When he escalated the Vietnam conflict, they knew what he was doing. As dissension over the Warren Report grew, so grew our involvement. Ultimately, it was a sham which destroyed Johnson and blackened his name.

The Sicilian-American Mafia has betrayed the Italian-American people just as it has betrayed Italy. We have all seen the press coverage of Mob-orchestrated carnage in that country. We have all seen the fall of governments, the endless prosecution of corrupt officials. Simultaneously, in the United States, narcotics trafficking and gambling operations are flourishing. Political corruption is commonplace. To borrow a phrase from the Italian experience, "It is corruption exercised by a few at the expense of many."

What is due is formal public apology to the American people by the U.S. Department of Justice for failing to apprehend JFK's killers. What is due is a public apology to the Marine Corps by the U.S. Congress for wrongly accusing former marine Lee Oswald of murder. What is due is public apology to the Oswald family. What is due is the removal of J.

Edgar Hoover's name from the FBI building in Washington DC. In its continuing defiance on this issue, the FBI effectively stands as a fourth branch of government answerable to no one.

What is needed is a blanket waiver of all nondisclosure agreements signed by former federal officials who were involved in the Stone prosecution, investigation of the Dallas Mafia, and participation in the activities of both the Warren Commission and the HSCA. These individuals need to be able to speak freely about what really happened and why the truth was suppressed.

What is long past due is a public apology by the city leaders of Dallas to the American people for its unwillingness to confront its past and take responsibility for creating the conditions which led to the murder of President John F. Kennedy.

Former president Bill Clinton, who likes to speak fondly of his childhood meeting with JFK, controlled the release of classified materials relating to the murder under the terms of the Assassination Materials Disclosure Act of 1992. In his eight years in office, he never took the substantive steps necessary to resolve this crisis.

What is due is the release of all government documents on the Mexican/Montreal heroin cartel that RFK tried to take down in 1963—files on men such as Paul Mondoloni, Antoine D'Agostino, Lucien Sarti, Michel Mertz, and Lucien Rivard. All electronic surveillance data recorded by RFK's Organized Crime Task Force operatives in the course of the Stone investigation, as well as the Dallas FBI's electronic surveillance (ELSUR) product on the Civello mob during the Kennedy administration, should be released in total. What is due is the release of all assassination documents held by NARA. Not in 2017, but now.

This book comes too late for the America we once knew. But it is never too late for the truth. In the words of John Kennedy the night before his murder,

Where there is no vision, the people perish.

ACKNOWLEDGMENTS

I ESPECIALLY THANK MY wife, Wendy, who has stood by me throughout the thousands of hours that went into the development of *Betrayal in Dallas*. With her editorial skills, I was able to bring focus and clarity to this work. My partner, she listened when others would not.

I thank my longtime agent, Bob Silverstein, of Quicksilver Books, for his belief in the importance of this work, unending support, and extraordinary effort to achieve its publication.

I thank my publishers, Tony Lyons and Herman Graf of Skyhorse Publishing. It is because of their courage and grasp of the importance of historical truth that this book has been published. Thanks to my editor, Jennifer McCartney.

I would like to thank the archival personnel at the following facilities: National Archives, SW Region, Fort Worth (esp. Barbara Rust); Texas History Center, Dallas Public Library; Lyndon B. Johnson Library, Austin, Texas; Texas State Archives (including genealogy), Austin, Texas; Center For American History, Austin, Texas; Austin History Center; Legislative Reference Library, Capitol Complex, Austin, Texas; State Bar of Texas, Governor Bill And Vara Daniel Center for Legal History (especially Angela Dorau), Austin, Texas; Perry-Castaneda Library (PCL), University of Texas at Austin (reference and government documents, especially Paul Rascoe and Bill Kopplin); University of Texas at Austin Law Library; Harry Ransom Humanities Research

Center, Austin, Texas; Texas Tech University Library (Southwest Collection), Lubbock, Texas; Louisiana State University Library, New Orleans, Louisiana; New Orleans Public Library; Center for Research Libraries, Chicago, Illinois.

I would also like to thank those current and former Dallasites and Austinites who were willing to provide their perceptions on the JFK assassination, the Dallas Mafia, and Lyndon Johnson. I thank my brother Richard North III, who brought insight and clarity to this work. Special thanks to James Gardner and Tom Johnson.

EXHIBITS

A Federal Documents (FBI Headquarters, Dallas Field Office), Department of Justice

B John Eli Stone Prosecution

C Author's Letters to Barefoot Sanders and Henry Wade

D Lyndon Johnson Correspondence (Dallas District Attorney Henry Wade, J. Edgar Hoover, others)

E Anonymous (Zuroma) Club Meetings

F Warren Commission Documents

EXHIBIT A

FBI Headquarters
Dallas Field Office
Department of Justice

OPTIONAL FORM NO. 10
MAY 1962 EDITION
GSA FPMR (41 CFR) 101-11.6
UNITED STATES GOVERNMENT

Memorandum

TO : SAC, DALLAS (92-331)

DATE: 2/16/68

FROM : CLERK [redacted] b7C

SUBJECT: PHILIP STEPHENS BOSCO, aka,
Philip S. Bosco, Phil Bosco,
P. S. Bosco, Philip Steve Bosco,
Phillip Stevens Boscoe
ANTI-RACKETEERING

CORRELATION MEMORANDUM

All References on index cards have been reviewed and the following summaries set set out:

Subject file 165-92: PHILIP STEPHENS BOSCO. Interstate Transmission of Wagering Information.

Serial 4, Dallas Weekly Summary airtel to Director, dated 6/10/63. Informant [redacted] furnished information that BOSCO operated as a bookmaker over the telephones at his Gulf Service Station, 2701 Ross Avenue, Dallas. Customers come to the station to pay off or collect under the pretext of purchasing gasoline.

b2
b7C
b7D

Serial 6, Memo from SA [redacted] dated 6/28/63. [redacted] Special Agent, Intelligence Section, Internal Revenue Service, advised on 6/27/63, that it had been ascertained through a recording device attached in a pay telephone booth used frequently by JOHN ELI STONE, a known bookmaker, that STONE was receiving the betting line from Las Vegas, Nevada, and immediately disseminating this information to BOSCO.

Serial 8, Dallas letter to Director, dated 7/24/63. [redacted] Vice Squad, Dallas Police Department, advised that on 7/17/63, BOSCO was arrested at his service station, and charged with vagrancy. They searched him with a search warrant and made a search of the service station looking for bookmaking paraphernalia. The Dallas police officers obtained a baseball schedule sheet from BOSCO, which contained the betting odds for each individual game and the scheduled pitchers for that date. Also obtained was a 2x3 piece of paper containing several telephone numbers

92-331-246
SEARCHED ___ INDEXED ___
SERIALIZED ak FILED ___
FEB 19 1968
FBI — DALLAS

b7C [redacted]

Buy U.S. Savings Bonds Regularly on the Payroll Savings Plan

5010-108-01

and a partial book of paper containing first names of individuals or abbreviations with amounts of money following the name or abbreviation.

BOSCO was interviewed 7/17/63 by Bureau Agents, at which time he admitted the baseball schedule line was made out in his handwriting; however, he either denied or refused to discuss the writing on the other two pieces of paper. BOSCO denied any bookmaking activities.

Serial 13, Memo from SA [redacted] dated 8/26/63. Informant [redacted] advised that BOSCO had been putting out the baseball line, and he had heard through his sources that BOSCO was going to put out the football line during the football season.

Serial 17, Newspaper Clipping, Dallas Morning News, dated 10/2/63. BOSCO appeared as a witness before a Federal Grand Jury, Wichita Falls, Texas, investigating Dallas gambling. BOSCO refused to answer several questions in the grand jury on the grounds that he might incriminate himself and by taking the Fifth Amendment. BOSCO was granted immunity by USDC Judge SARAH HUGHES, but still refused to answer questions by the grand jury on basis of the Fifth Amendment.

b2
b7C
b7D

Serial 21, Dallas Weekly Summary airtel to Director, dated 10/28/63. An article appearing in a Dallas newspaper on 10/20/63, stated that BOSCO was scheduled for a reappearance on 10/21/63 before a Federal Grand Jury at Wichita Falls, Texas, in connection with an inquiry into the bookmaking activities of JOHN ELI STONE. It was contemplated that BOSCO, who was granted immunity by the court, will be required by the court to answer questions put to him by the grand jury and if he refused, he would be held in contempt.

Serial 23, Report of SA [redacted] dated 11/20/63, at Dallas. Informant [redacted] advised that he had heard from other gamblers that BOSCO continued to operate as a bookmaker from his service station.

Serial 28, Dallas letter to Director, dated 2/11/64. BOSCO was interviewed by Bureau Agents in connection with his knowledge of JACK RUBY. BOSCO claimed he had never known RUBY and stated he did not care to discuss any matter with the FBI.

Serial 30, Dallas Weekly Summary airtel to Director, dated 10/19/64. Informant [redacted] advised that BOSCO was handling his booking operations at his Gulf Service Station, but that he only accepted wagers from reliable customers, and only on a person to person basis, nothing by phone.

2

Freedom of Information
and
Privacy Acts

SUBJECT Philip S. Bosco

FILE NUMBER 92-5666 Section 1.

DEPARTMENT OF JUSTICE
FEDERAL BUREAU OF INVESTIGATION
FIDELITY BRAVERY INTEGRITY

Federal Bureau of Investigation

6 Page(s) withheld for the following reason(s): These documents were provided to the National Archives and Records Administration (NARA) under the JFK Assassination Records Collection Act of 1992.

X The following number is to be used for reference regarding these pages:
92-5666-1 cover page A, E, F, 1, 4, 7

1 Page(s) withheld for the following reason(s): These documents were provided to the National Archives and Records Administration (NARA) under the JFK Assassination Records Collection Act of 1992.

X The following number is to be used for reference regarding these pages:
92-5666-2 page 1 (12-28-61)

28 Page(s) withheld for the following reason(s): These documents were provided to the National Archives and Records Administration (NARA) under the JFK Assassination Records Collection Act of 1992.

X The following number is to be used for reference regarding these pages:
92-5666-3

12 Page(s) withheld for the following reason(s): These documents were provided to the National Archives and Records Administration (NARA) under the JFK Assassination Records Collection Act of 1992.

X The following number is to be used for reference regarding these pages:
92-5666-5

5 Page(s) withheld for the following reason(s): These documents were provided to the National Archives and Records Administration (NARA) under the JFK Assassination Records Collection Act of 1992.

X The following number is to be used for reference regarding these pages:
92-5666-6 cover page A+B, 1, 2, 3

5 Page(s) withheld for the following reason(s): These documents were provided to the National Archives and Records Administration (NARA) under the JFK Assassination Records Collection Act of 1992.

☑ The following number is to be used for reference regarding these pages:
92-5666-9 pgs. A, 1, 5, 6 and 7

7 Page(s) withheld for the following reason(s): These documents were provided to the National Archives and Records Administration (NARA) under the JFK Assassination Records Collection Act of 1992.

☑ The following number is to be used for reference regarding these pages:
92-5666-10 pgs. A, B, C, 1, 3, 8 and 9

10 Page(s) withheld for the following reason(s): These documents were provided to the National Archives and Records Administration (NARA) under the JFK Assassination Records Collection Act of 1992.

☑ The following number is to be used for reference regarding these pages:
92-5666-14 pgs. cover page A - 8

3 Page(s) withheld for the following reason(s): These documents were provided to the National Archives and Records Administration (NARA) under the JFK Assassination Records Collection Act of 1992.

☑ The following number is to be used for reference regarding these pages:
92-5666-15 pgs. A, B, 4

5 Page(s) withheld for the following reason(s): These documents were provided to the National Archives and Records Administration (NARA) under the JFK Assassination Records Collection Act of 1992.

☑ The following number is to be used for reference regarding these pages:
92-5666-16 pg A, B, 1, 2, 3

Freedom of Information
and
Privacy Acts

SUBJECT ROSS MUSSO

FILE NUMBER HQ- 92-4213

Federal Bureau of Investigation

4 Page(s) withheld for the following reason(s): These documents were provided to the National Archives and Records Administration (NARA) under the JFK Assassination Records Collection Act of 1992.

☑ The following number is to be used for reference regarding these pages:
92-4213-3

2 Page(s) withheld for the following reason(s): These documents were provided to the National Archives and Records Administration (NARA) under the JFK Assassination Records Collection Act of 1992.

☑ The following number is to be used for reference regarding these pages:
92-4213-3 p. 4 & 5

5 Page(s) withheld for the following reason(s): These documents were provided to the National Archives and Records Administration (NARA) under the JFK Assassination Records Collection Act of 1992.

☑ The following number is to be used for reference regarding these pages:
92-4213-4

6 Page(s) withheld for the following reason(s): These documents were provided to the National Archives and Records Administration (NARA) under the JFK Assassination Records Collection Act of 1992.

☑ The following number is to be used for reference regarding these pages:
92-4213-7

4 Page(s) withheld for the following reason(s): These documents were provided to the National Archives and Records Administration (NARA) under the JFK Assassination Records Collection Act of 1992.

☑ The following number is to be used for reference regarding these pages:
92-4213-8

3 Page(s) withheld for the following reason(s): These documents were provided to the National Archives and Records Administration (NARA) under the JFK Assassination Records Collection Act of 1992.

The following number is to be used for reference regarding these pages:
92-4213-8

5 Page(s) withheld for the following reason(s): These documents were provided to the National Archives and Records Administration (NARA) under the JFK Assassination Records Collection Act of 1992.

The following number is to be used for reference regarding these pages:
92-4213-9

1 Page(s) withheld for the following reason(s): These documents were provided to the National Archives and Records Administration (NARA) under the JFK Assassination Records Collection Act of 1992.

The following number is to be used for reference regarding these pages:
92-4213-18

1 Page(s) withheld for the following reason(s): These documents were provided to the National Archives and Records Administration (NARA) under the JFK Assassination Records Collection Act of 1992.

The following number is to be used for reference regarding these pages:
92-4213-18

4 Page(s) withheld for the following reason(s): These documents were provided to the National Archives and Records Administration (NARA) under the JFK Assassination Records Collection Act of 1992.

The following number is to be used for reference regarding these pages:
92-4213-18

1 Page(s) withheld for the following reason(s): These documents were provided to the National Archives and Records Administration (NARA) under the JFK Assassination Records Collection Act of 1992.

☒ The following number is to be used for reference regarding these pages:
92-4213-19

3 Page(s) withheld for the following reason(s): These documents were provided to the National Archives and Records Administration (NARA) under the JFK Assassination Records Collection Act of 1992.

☒ The following number is to be used for reference regarding these pages:
92-4213-19

1 Page(s) withheld for the following reason(s): These documents were provided to the National Archives and Records Administration (NARA) under the JFK Assassination Records Collection Act of 1992.

☒ The following number is to be used for reference regarding these pages:
92-4213-20

2 Page(s) withheld for the following reason(s): These documents were provided to the National Archives and Records Administration (NARA) under the JFK Assassination Records Collection Act of 1992.

☒ The following number is to be used for reference regarding these pages:
92-4213-20

4 Page(s) withheld for the following reason(s): These documents were provided to the National Archives and Records Administration (NARA) under the JFK Assassination Records Collection Act of 1992.

☒ The following number is to be used for reference regarding these pages:
92-4213-24

2 Page(s) withheld for the following reason(s): These documents were provided to the National Archives and Records Administration (NARA) under the JFK Assassination Records Collection Act of 1992.

☑ The following number is to be used for reference regarding these pages:
92-4213-29

1 Page(s) withheld for the following reason(s): These documents were provided to the National Archives and Records Administration (NARA) under the JFK Assassination Records Collection Act of 1992.

☑ The following number is to be used for reference regarding these pages:
92-4213-27

2 Page(s) withheld for the following reason(s): These documents were provided to the National Archives and Records Administration (NARA) under the JFK Assassination Records Collection Act of 1992.

☑ The following number is to be used for reference regarding these pages:
92-4213-27

Freedom of Information and Privacy Acts

SUBJECT John Ross Patrono

FILE NUMBER 92 - 5693

Federal Bureau of Investigation

1 Page(s) withheld for the following reason(s): These documents were provided to the National Archives and Records Administration (NARA) under the JFK Assassination Records Collection Act of 1992.

☒ The following number is to be used for reference regarding these pages:
92-5693-1 page A. (cover page)

1 Page(s) withheld for the following reason(s): These documents were provided to the National Archives and Records Administration (NARA) under the JFK Assassination Records Collection Act of 1992.

☒ The following number is to be used for reference regarding these pages:
92-5693-1 page C. (cover page)

1 Page(s) withheld for the following reason(s): These documents were provided to the National Archives and Records Administration (NARA) under the JFK Assassination Records Collection Act of 1992.

☒ The following number is to be used for reference regarding these pages:
92-5693-1 page 2.

2 Page(s) withheld for the following reason(s): These documents were provided to the National Archives and Records Administration (NARA) under the JFK Assassination Records Collection Act of 1992.

☒ The following number is to be used for reference regarding these pages:
92-5693-1 pages 4 & 5

2 Page(s) withheld for the following reason(s): These documents were provided to the National Archives and Records Administration (NARA) under the JFK Assassination Records Collection Act of 1992.

☒ The following number is to be used for reference regarding these pages:
92-5693-1 pages 8 & 9

1 Page(s) withheld for the following reason(s): These documents were provided to the National Archives and Records Administration (NARA) under the JFK Assassination Records Collection Act of 1992.

☒ The following number is to be used for reference regarding these pages:
92-5693-3 page A (cover page)

2 Page(s) withheld for the following reason(s): These documents were provided to the National Archives and Records Administration (NARA) under the JFK Assassination Records Collection Act of 1992.

☒ The following number is to be used for reference regarding these pages:
92-5693-5 pages 2+3

5 Page(s) withheld for the following reason(s): These documents were provided to the National Archives and Records Administration (NARA) under the JFK Assassination Records Collection Act of 1992.

☒ The following number is to be used for reference regarding these pages:
92-5693-5 (pages A, B, 1, 2+3)

1 Page(s) withheld for the following reason(s): These documents were provided to the National Archives and Records Administration (NARA) under the JFK Assassination Records Collection Act of 1992.

☒ The following number is to be used for reference regarding these pages:
92-5693-6 cover page A.

3 Page(s) withheld for the following reason(s): These documents were provided to the National Archives and Records Administration (NARA) under the JFK Assassination Records Collection Act of 1992.

☒ The following number is to be used for reference regarding these pages:
92-5693-6 cover page C, and 1-4.

1 Page(s) withheld for the following reason(s): These documents were provided to the National Archives and Records Administration (NARA) under the JFK Assassination Records Collection Act of 1992.

☒ The following number is to be used for reference regarding these pages:
92-5693-8 cover page A.

1 Page(s) withheld for the following reason(s): These documents were provided to the National Archives and Records Administration (NARA) under the JFK Assassination Records Collection Act of 1992.

☒ The following number is to be used for reference regarding these pages:
92-5693-8 cover page C.

2 Page(s) withheld for the following reason(s): These documents were provided to the National Archives and Records Administration (NARA) under the JFK Assassination Records Collection Act of 1992.

☒ The following number is to be used for reference regarding these pages:
92-5693-8 pgs. 3 & 4

9 Page(s) withheld for the following reason(s): These documents were provided to the National Archives and Records Administration (NARA) under the JFK Assassination Records Collection Act of 1992.

☒ The following number is to be used for reference regarding these pages:
92-5693-13 A-D, 1-5

6 Page(s) withheld for the following reason(s): These documents were provided to the National Archives and Records Administration (NARA) under the JFK Assassination Records Collection Act of 1992.

☒ The following number is to be used for reference regarding these pages:
92-5693-13 pages 7 thru 12

5 Page(s) withheld for the following reason(s): These documents were provided to the National Archives and Records Administration (NARA) under the JFK Assassination Records Collection Act of 1992.

☒ The following number is to be used for reference regarding these pages:
92-5693-13 pages 17 thru 21

5 Page(s) withheld for the following reason(s): These documents were provided to the National Archives and Records Administration (NARA) under the JFK Assassination Records Collection Act of 1992.

☒ The following number is to be used for reference regarding these pages:
92-5693-13 pages 25-29

9 Page(s) withheld for the following reason(s): These documents were provided to the National Archives and Records Administration (NARA) under the JFK Assassination Records Collection Act of 1992.

☒ The following number is to be used for reference regarding these pages:
92-5693-14

3 Page(s) withheld for the following reason(s): These documents were provided to the National Archives and Records Administration (NARA) under the JFK Assassination Records Collection Act of 1992.

☒ The following number is to be used for reference regarding these pages:
92-5693-15 pgs. A-C.

3 Page(s) withheld for the following reason(s): These documents were provided to the National Archives and Records Administration (NARA) under the JFK Assassination Records Collection Act of 1992.

☒ The following number is to be used for reference regarding these pages:
92-5693-18 pgs. A, B, 1

Freedom of Information
and
Privacy Acts

SUBJECT Charles Cirello

FILE NUMBER 92-4204 (Headquarters file)

DEPARTMENT OF JUSTICE
FEDERAL BUREAU OF INVESTIGATION
FIDELITY BRAVERY INTEGRITY

Federal Bureau of Investigation

5 Page(s) withheld for the following reason(s): documents were provided to the National Archives and Records Administration (NARA) under the JFK Assassination Records Collection Act of 1992.

☒ The following number is to be used for reference regarding these pages:
92-4204-19 pages A, 1, 3, 4+5

7 Page(s) withheld for the following reason(s): documents were provided to National Archives Records Administration (NARA) under the JFK Assassination Records Collection Act of 1992.

☒ The following number is to be used for reference regarding these pages:
92-4204-3 pages A, B, 1, 2, 3, 4 and 5

5 Page(s) withheld for the following reason(s): documents were provided to the National Archives and Records Administration (NARA) under the JFK Assassination Records Collection Act of 1992.

☒ The following number is to be used for reference regarding these pages:
92-4204-17 pages A, B, 1, 2, and 3

6 Page(s) withheld for the following reason(s): documents were provided to National Archives and Records Administration (NARA) under the JFK Assassination Records Collection Act of 1992

☒ The following number is to be used for reference regarding these pages:
92-4204-20 (pages A, 1, 2, 3, 4 and 5)

For Informational Purposes Only

The originals removed from this file and replaced with duplicate copies of the original were accessioned to the National Archives and Records Administration (NARA) pursuant to the JFK Records Collection Act of 1992. Provision of the JFK Act allowed for certain information to be postponed from public release until the year 2017; therefore, the pages have NOT necessarily been released for public review in their entirety.

Under the JFK Act, originals to all material deemed assassination records must be accesssioned to NARA regardless of whether the material is open in full or released with information postponed. Therefore, any documents or pages from FBI files accessioned to NARA pursuant to the JFK Act are no longer considered the possession of the FBI. The duplicate pages have been inserted strictly for research purposes.

The copies contained herein do not necessarily show the most up-to-date classification.

To attain a copy of the publicly released version of any materials maintained in the JFK Collection at the NARA facility in College Park, MD, you may contact the JFK Access Staff, at 301/713-6620.

The following materials were removed from this file and are maintained in the JFK Collection at NARA:

File & Serial Number	JFK Subject Identifier (for NARA purposes)
92-4204-3 pgs. A, B, 1-5	Joseph Civello

For Informational Purposes Only

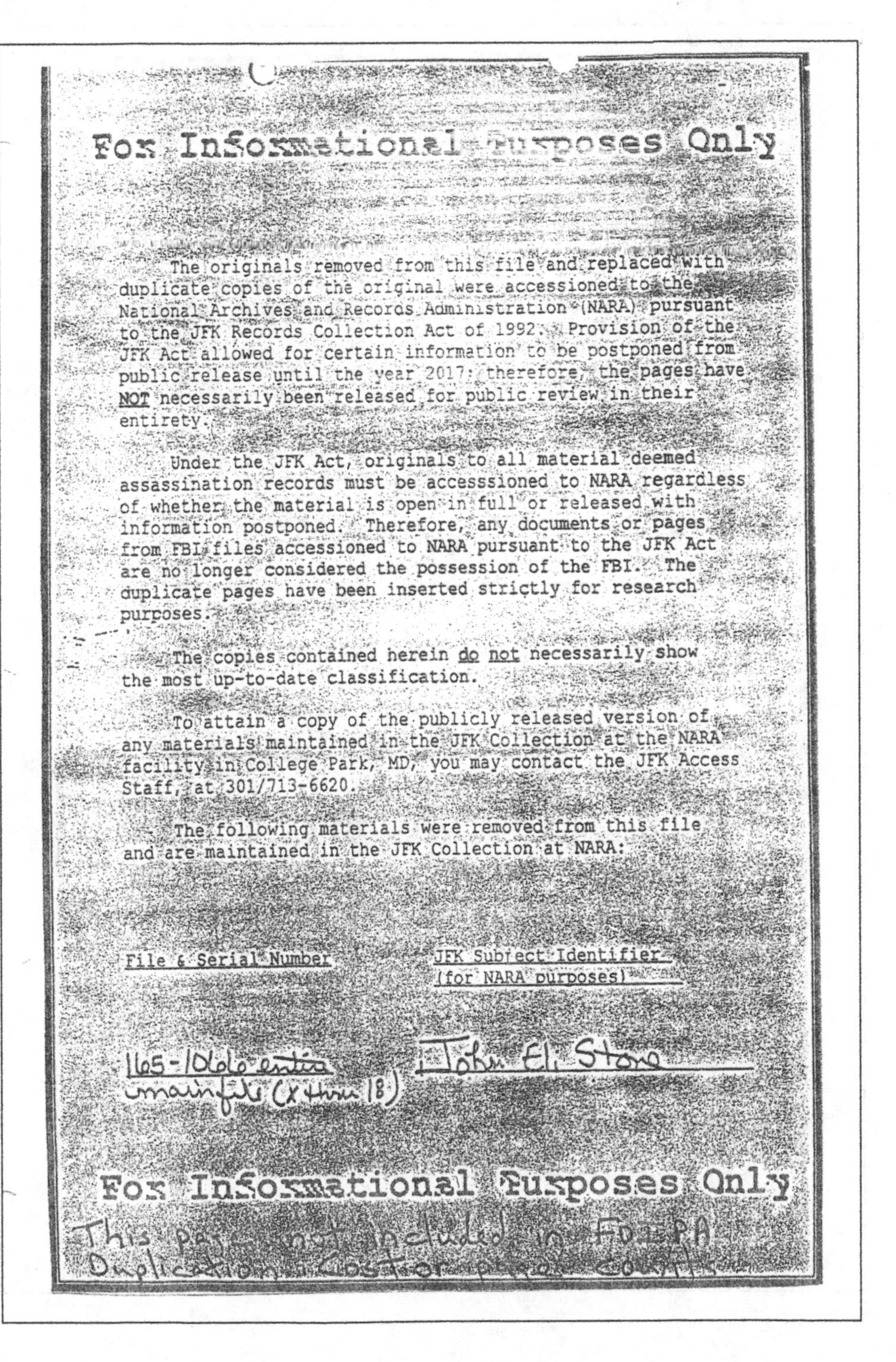

For Informational Purposes Only

The originals removed from this file and replaced with duplicate copies of the original were accessioned to the National Archives and Records Administration (NARA) pursuant to the JFK Records Collection Act of 1992. Provision of the JFK Act allowed for certain information to be postponed from public release until the year 2017: therefore, the pages have NOT necessarily been released for public review in their entirety.

Under the JFK Act, originals to all material deemed assassination records must be accesssioned to NARA regardless of whether the material is open in full or released with information postponed. Therefore, any documents or pages from FBI files accessioned to NARA pursuant to the JFK Act are no longer considered the possession of the FBI. The duplicate pages have been inserted strictly for research purposes.

The copies contained herein do not necessarily show the most up-to-date classification.

To attain a copy of the publicly released version of any materials maintained in the JFK Collection at the NARA facility in College Park, MD, you may contact the JFK Access Staff, at 301/713-6620.

The following materials were removed from this file and are maintained in the JFK Collection at NARA:

File & Serial Number	JFK Subject Identifier (for NARA purposes)
165-1066 entire main file (X thru 18)	John Eli Stone

For Informational Purposes Only

This page not included in FOI-PA Duplication cost or page counts

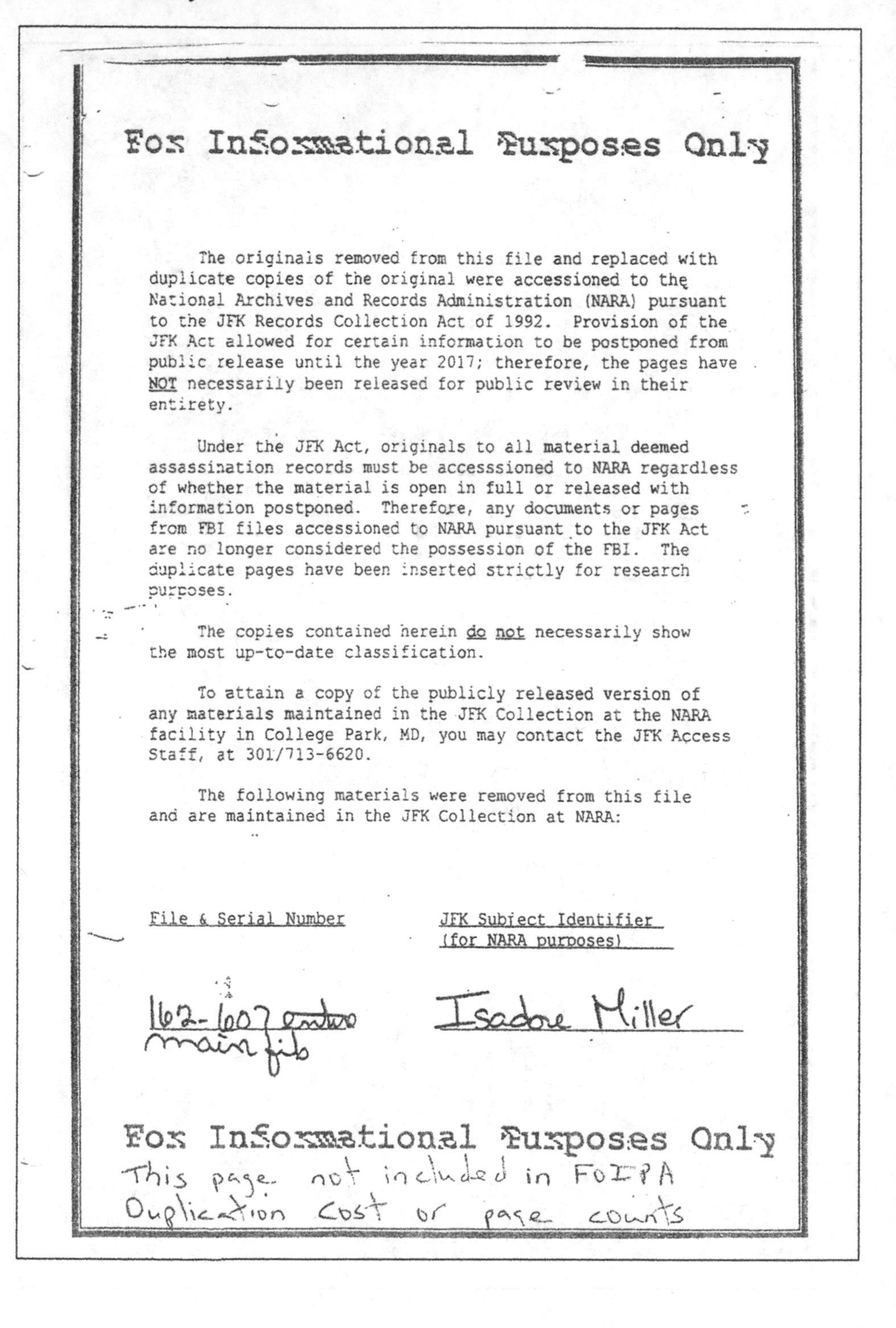

For Informational Purposes Only

The originals removed from this file and replaced with duplicate copies of the original were accessioned to the National Archives and Records Administration (NARA) pursuant to the JFK Records Collection Act of 1992. Provision of the JFK Act allowed for certain information to be postponed from public release until the year 2017; therefore, the pages have NOT necessarily been released for public review in their entirety.

Under the JFK Act, originals to all material deemed assassination records must be accesssioned to NARA regardless of whether the material is open in full or released with information postponed. Therefore, any documents or pages from FBI files accessioned to NARA pursuant to the JFK Act are no longer considered the possession of the FBI. The duplicate pages have been inserted strictly for research purposes.

The copies contained herein do not necessarily show the most up-to-date classification.

To attain a copy of the publicly released version of any materials maintained in the JFK Collection at the NARA facility in College Park, MD, you may contact the JFK Access Staff, at 301/713-6620.

The following materials were removed from this file and are maintained in the JFK Collection at NARA:

File & Serial Number	JFK Subject Identifier (for NARA purposes)
162-607 entire main file	Isadore Miller

For Informational Purposes Only

This page not included in FOIPA Duplication cost or page counts

For Informational Purposes Only

The originals removed from this file and replaced with duplicate copies of the original were accessioned to the National Archives and Records Administration (NARA) pursuant to the JFK Records Collection Act of 1992. Provision of the JFK Act allowed for certain information to be postponed from public release until the year 2017; therefore, the pages have NOT necessarily been released for public review in their entirety.

Under the JFK Act, originals to all material deemed assassination records must be accesssioned to NARA regardless of whether the material is open in full or released with information postponed. Therefore, any documents or pages from FBI files accessioned to NARA pursuant to the JFK Act are no longer considered the possession of the FBI. The duplicate pages have been inserted strictly for research purposes.

The copies contained herein do not necessarily show the most up-to-date classification.

To attain a copy of the publicly released version of any materials maintained in the JFK Collection at the NARA facility in College Park, MD, you may contact the JFK Access Staff, at 301/713-6620.

The following materials were removed from this file and are maintained in the JFK Collection at NARA:

File & Serial Number	JFK Subject Identifier (for NARA purposes)
165-1066-75	Russell Douglas Mathews

For Informational Purposes Only

This page not included in FOIPA Duplication Cost or page counts

UNITED STATES GOVERNMENT

Memorandum

TO : SAC, DALLAS [redacted] b2 b7D DATE: 2/20/68

FROM : SA [redacted] b7C

SUBJECT: [redacted] b7C b7D

☐ CI ☐ SI ☐ R (Prob)
☒ PCI ☐ PSI ☐ R
☐

Dates of Contact
1/29/68 (contacted by Agents [redacted] and [redacted]) b7C b7C

Titles and File #s on which contacted

[redacted] TGP	52-4932
TOP HOODLUMS & CRIMINAL INTELLIGENCE	92-625A
INTERSTATE GAMBLING ACTIVITIES	92-625B

Purpose and results of contact

☐ NEGATIVE ☒ POSITIVE ☐ STATISTICAL

DL 52-4932: PCI advised he had received no additional information concerning [redacted]

DL 92-36: PCI advised that he knew JOE CIVELLO and was very aware that CIVELLO was considered the top man among the Italian element in Dallas. He knew that CIVELLO was extremely close to JOE IANNI and stated that JOE IANNI's father, FRANK IANNI, was very close to JOE CIVELLO. PCI advised that about all of CIVELLO's group belong to the Zuroma Club [redacted] PCI advised that CIVELLO is also close to PHILIP S. BOSCO and CHARLES J. SANDONE, former detective of Dallas PD. PCI said he did not know the family relationship of SANSONE to CIVELLO. [redacted] is also a part of this group through his gambling activities with PHILIP BOSCO. JOHNNY ROSS PATRONO is

b7C b7D (handwritten in margin)

☒ Informant certified that he has furnished all information obtained by him since last contact.	Rating: Excellent	Coverage: Same

1-52-4932 (SA [redacted])
1-92-36 [redacted]
1-92-192 [redacted]
1-92-617 (Closed file)
1-92-331
1-92-292
1-165-61
1-92-332

1-92-551
1-92-586
1-92-339
1-162-289
1-162-417
1-92-625A
1-92-625B

92-192-147

Searched Indexed
Serialized Filed
FEB 20 1968
FBI DALLAS

b7C

HJE/bjc
(15)

EXHIBIT B

U.S. v. John Eli Stone, et al

Certificates of Search

Sanders letter to DOJ

Filed 21 day of October
1963 at 4:35 o'clock P M
JOHN A. LOWTHER, Clerk
By [signature] Deputy

IN THE UNITED STATES DISTRICT COURT

FOR THE NORTHERN DISTRICT OF TEXAS

UNITED STATES OF AMERICA	I	
VS.	I	NO. 3-63-186 CRIMINAL
	I	(18 USC Sections 1084 and 371)
JOHN EL STONE, JAMES WOODROW STONE and ISADORE MILLER	I	(26 USC Section 7203)

The Grand Jury Charges:

That during the period beginning on or about October 1, 1962, and ending June 30, 1963, in the Dallas Division of the Northern District of Texas, JOHN EL STONE did engage in the business of accepting wagers on sporting events as defined in Section 4421 of the Internal Revenue Code; that prior to engaging in said business he was required under the provisions of Section 4901 of the Internal Revenue Code to pay to the District Director of Internal Revenue for the Internal Revenue District of Dallas, at Dallas, Texas, the special occupational tax imposed under the provisions of Section 4411 of the Internal Revenue Code; that prior to engaging in said business he did knowingly and willfully fail to pay said special occupational tax to said District Director of Internal Revenue, or to any other proper officer of the United States.

In violation of Section 7203, Internal Revenue Code; 26 U.S.C., Section 7203.

This page: October 21, 1963, indictment of John Eli Stone, et, al. Dallas federal court document. **Following page**: Certificate of Search dated May 31, 1996, certified at the height of Barefoot Sanders's power on the Dallas bench. Does not list RFK's 1963 prosecution, "3:63cr186." **Third page**: After Sanders's death while still on the bench, a Certificate of Search now includes the October 21, 1963, Stone indictment. Clearly, Sanders saw to it that RFK's attempt to take down the Civello mob via Stone was kept out of the public record during his time on the federal bench in Dallas.

United States District Court
Northern District of Texas
Dallas Division

Nancy Doherty
Clerk of Court

1100 Commerce Street
Dallas, Texas 75242

Certificate of Search

I, NANCY DOHERTY, Clerk of the United States District Court for the Northern District of Texas, do hereby certify that after a diligent search of the records of this court, find **three criminal proceedings** in which the following named person(s) are a party to, from 01/01/1960 up to and including 01/01/1981, namely,

John Eli Stone : 3:74cr500
3:75cr251
3:77cr17

Witness my official signature and the seal of said court, at Dallas, Texas in said district on this day, May 31, 1996.

Nancy Doherty
Clerk of Court

By: Steve Tittle
Steve Tittle
Deputy Clerk

Fee: $15.00

United States District Court
Northern District of Texas
Office of the Clerk
1100 Commerce Street, Room 14523
Dallas, Texas 75242-1003

Certificate of Search

I, Karen Mitchell, Clerk of the United States District Court for the Northern District of Texas, do hereby certify that after a diligent search of the records of this court, found **(4) Criminal case proceedings** involving the following named persons, from October 21, 1963 up to and including September 15, 2010, namely,

John Eli Stone

Witness my official signature and the seal of said court, at Dallas, Texas in said district

on this day, September 15, 2010.

Karen Mitchell
Clerk of Court

By Marie Ramos
Marie Ramos
Deputy Clerk

CR-3-63-186

CRIMINAL DOCKET
UNITED STATES DISTRICT COURT

D. C. Form No. 100 Rev.

TITLE OF CASE	ATTORNEYS
THE UNITED STATES	For U.S.:
vs.	Barefoot Sanders
JOHN EL STONE, JAMES WOODROW STONE and ISADORE MILLER	Donald H. Stone
	For Defendants: Charles W. Tessmer, Emmett Colvin, Jr., Suite 400, 706 Main St., Dallas, Texas

Failure to pay occupational tax; to register with Internal Revenue; to make excise tax return; use of wire communication in ICC in placing bets & wagers and conspiracy to conduct business without paying occupational tax.

STATISTICAL RECORD	COSTS	DATE 1964	NAME OR RECEIPT NO.	REC.	DISB.
		9-26	E.C.Colvin	5 00	
J.S. 2 mailed 10-31-63	Clerk	9-28	Jas W. Stone	1000 00	
		9-29	SF201 C.D.T.		[illegible]
J.S. 3 mailed	Marshal	10-8	[illegible]		1000 00
				3000 00	3000 00
Violation	Docket fee	1965			
		4-19	I.Miller	5000 00	
Title 26 Sec. 7203; 18 Sec. 1084 & 371		4-30	[illegible]		5000 00

DATE 1963	PROCEEDINGS
Oct. 21	Filed INDICTMENT. (Received from Wichita Falls Division)
Oct. 22	Issued WARRANT FOR ARREST of John El Stone & given to U.S. Marshal.
Nov. 12	Filed cby defendant, Isadore Miller, MOTION TO QUASH SEARCH WARRANT, FOR RETURN, and FOR SUPPRESSION OF EVIDENCE, AFFIDAVIT of Mrs. Lucrecia Kennedy, Isadore Miller and Dave L. Miller.
Nov. 12	Filed by defendant, John El Stone, MOTION TO QUASH SEARCH WARRANT, FOR RETURN, and FOR SUPPRESSION OF EVIDENCE. Also AFFIDAVIT OF John El Stone.
Nov. 12	Filed by defendant, Isadore Miller, MOTION TO QUASH SEARCH WARRANT, FOR RETURN, and for SUPPRESSION OF EVIDENCE and AFFIDAVIT of Isadore Miller in support of motion to suppress.
Nov. 12	Filed by defendant, James Woodrow Stone, MOTION TO QUASH SEARCH WARRANT, FOR RETURN, and for SUPPRESSION OF EVIDENCE and AFFIDAVIT of James Woodrow Stone

DATE 1964	PROCEEDINGS
May 27	Filed plaintiff's REPLY to defendants' motion to quash search warrant, for return of and for suppression of evidence. (Original to STH)
May 27	Filed plaintiff;s BRIEF in reply to defendants' brief on motion to suppress. (Original to STH)
May 28	Filed by defendant, John El Stone, supplemental motion to quash warrant, for return and for suppression of evidence.
May 28	Filed by defendant, James Woodrow Stone, supplemental motion to quash warrant, for return, and for suppression of evidence.
May 28	Filed by defendant, Isadore Miller, supplemental motion to quash warrant for return, and for suppression of evidence.
June 4	Filed RETURN ON SUBPOENAS TO TESTIFY executed on May 26, 1964 as to Robert M.Parrott by phoning Robert P.Gamberling, agent, by mailing a copy to their office; as to Robert P.Gamberling, by phone and by mailing a copy as to Hugh Amos by leaving a copy with Lt.Eric Kamisky; executed on May 27, 1964 as to Mrs. Lucretia Kennedy by personal service.
June 15	Filed ORDER denying defendants motion to quash search warrants. Motion to suppress evidence obtained through an electronic device is granted in that it is inadmissible at the trial of this cause. STH
June 18	Filed MOTION FOR CONTINUANCE to next term of court.
June 24	Filed RETURN ON SUBPOENA on behalf of U.S. executed on June 12, 1964 by serving Henry Clinton Winfrey in person.
Aug. 10	Filed OPINION re motion to suppress (copies mailed counsel by Judge Hug[hes] Office)
Sept. 8	Filed defendant's MOTION TO DISMISS counts 1 through 7, counts 15 and 16 and MEMORANDUM OF AUTHORITIES in support thereof. (Original and carbon of motion & brief to STH)
Sept. 8	Filed supplemental motion to dismiss adding additional ground & Brief. (Original and carbon to STH)
Sept. 14	Filed plaintiff's REPLY to defendant's motion to dismiss.
Sept. 14	Filed ORDER ~~granting~~ denying defendant's MOTION to dismiss counts 1 through 12 and counts 15 and 16. S
Sept. 14	Filed ORDER denying defendant's motion to dismiss additional ground counts 1 through 12 and counts 15 and 16. S
Sept. 14	Filed defendant's MOTION FOR CONTINUANCE.
Sept. 14	Filed ORDER denying defendants motion for continuance. S
Sept. 14	Filed Order continuing cause as to Isidore Miller only....STH
Sept. 16	Filed plaintiff's PETITION for a writ of habeas corpus ad testificandum, (Joe Henry Hodges, Jr.)

PLEASE ADDRESS ALL MAIL TO
UNITED STATES ATTORNEY
P. O. BOX 158

Peterson
Stone

United States Department of Justice

UNITED STATES ATTORNEY RECEIVED
NORTHERN DISTRICT OF TEXAS
DALLAS 1, TEXAS 75221 SEP 1 0 1963
September 6, 1963
CRIMINAL DIVISION

Air Mail

Mr. Herbert J. Miller, Jr.
Assistant Attorney General
Criminal Division
Department of Justice
Washington, D. C. 20530

Attention: Mr. William G. Hundley, Chief
Organized Crime and Racketeering

Re: John Eli Stone, P-1449-63
Albert Meadows, P-1595-63 see copy

Dear Sir:

Recently Mr. Arnold Stone of Organized Crime and Racketeering Section visited me in our Dallas office and suggested that it might be advisable to utilize a Grand Jury in connection with the captioned matters. After discussion, it was my understanding that Mr. Stone was to furnish us a brief pertaining to the merits of the captioned cases, after which a decision would be made concerning the desirability and necessity for a Grand Jury investigation.

I was out of the office last week but I understand that Mr. Stone in a conversation with Mr. Hughes, Chief of our Criminal Division, indicated that he was planning to be in Wichita Falls to work with the Federal Grand Jury which we will have convened there September 23rd.

Before a final decision is made about using the Wichita Falls Grand Jury for this purpose, I would like to have from Mr. Stone (1) the promised memorandum opinion concerning the merits of these cases and (2) a memorandum as to what it is hoped will be accomplished by Grand Jury action at Wichita Falls, the witnesses to be subpoenaed and details with respect to the preparation and issuance of those subpoenas, and any and all other information on this project which may seem pertinent.

I will appreciate hearing from you at your early convenience.

Sincerely,

Barefoot Sanders
United States Attorney

RECEIVED
SEP 11 1963
ORGANIZED CRIME AND
RACKETEERING SECTION

164-93-5
DEPARTMENT OF JUSTICE
SEP 9 1963
RECORDS BRANCH
CRIMINAL DIVISION
Organized Crime and Racketeering Section

(1)

EXHIBIT C

Author's Letter to Sanders and Wade

P.O. Box 91196
Austin, TX 78709-1196

Honorable Judge Barefoot Sanders
Chief Judge, U.S. District Court
Northern District of Texas
1100 Commerce, Rm. 14A-20
Dallas, Texas 75242

September 3, 1996

Dear Judge Sanders,

I am the author of *Act Of Treason: The Role Of J. Edgar Hoover In The Assassination Of President Kennedy* (Carroll & Graf, 1991). Since the release of that book I have continued my research into the JFK/Oswald murders.

The purpose of this letter is to ask certain questions of you which have arisen during my research into your time as U.S. Attorney for the Northern District of Texas (1961-65).

From the mid 1920's into at least the mid 1970's there existed in Dallas a small, private Sicilian "social club" known as the Anonymous (or ZuRoma) Club, which met weekly. Meetings were held at a west side house near Love Field and occasionally in private residences and Italian restaurants. Membership and guest lists were published weekly in a local Italian newsletter by the name of La Tribuna Italiana (changed to Texas Tribune during WWII). My research into this club has revealed that in addition to dinner, guests also systematically indulged in gambling in the form of poker (See attached 1-A). Under Texas penal statutes this activity rendered the club a "gambling house" (attached 1-B). Membership in this club included Mafiosi such as convicted heroin trafficker and killer Joseph F. Civello, Texas Mafia boss Joseph Piranio, Assistant Dallas D.A. Angelo Piranio, and Dallas PD member Charles Sansone (attached 1-C). Guests included murderers Joe Campisi, Joe Ianni, and Sam Savalli, as well as other Mafiosi (e.g. Rosario and Sam Maceo, Sam Campisi, Philip S. Bosco, Ross Musso) (attached 1-D). Various law enforcement figures appeared as well (e.g. Tom Clark, Glenn Byrd, D.A. Henry Wade, Sheriff Bill Decker, Mayor Earle Cabell, to name a few) (attached 1-E). As I'm sure you are aware, member Joe Civello was arrested in November 1957 in New York at the Apalachin Mob conference and prosecuted (attached 1-F). In essence, the club fits the profile described by the U.S. Bureau of Narcotics in 1950's era analyses of Mafia infiltration (with the intent of corrupting local law enforcement) of legitimate Italian-American promotional organizations (attached 1-G). My questions are as follows:

1. Why did you, as an attorney and Texas State Legislator appear as a guest of the Anonymous Club the last week of April 1958 (attached 2-A)?

2. What was the nature of your relationship with member Peter Tamburo and Philip S.

"pump" Bosco, the latter appearing as a guest of the club the same night as yourself?

3. In your private associations with Bosco, Tamburo, and other Anonymous Club members, did you make disparaging or inflammatory remarks about President Kennedy or Organized Crime Task Force investigations during the 1961-63 time period? Was there ever any discussion about the removal of either Kennedy from public office?

4. Why in 1963 did you, as a U.S. Attorney, state that there was no organized crime in Dallas when FBI internal reports stated there was a Mafia crime family in Dallas with at least "25 members" (the Civello Mob) (attached 3-A,B)?

5. What was your reaction to the initiation of an Organized Crime Task Force investigation of the Dallas Mafia's bookmaking operation (Commerce Street, Enquire Shine and Press Shop, Carousel Club, Sol's Turf Bar) by Robert Kennedy in April 1963? (attached 4-A)

6. I have interviewed the lead attorney in that investigation, Arnold M. Stone. What was your reaction to his presence in Dallas?

7. What was your reaction to the indictment of Civello bookmakers John Eli Stone, James Stone, Isadore Max Miller in the fall of 1963 (U.S. v. Stone, et al) (See attached 4-A)?

8. What was your reaction to Task Force questioning of their Mob contact, Philip S. Bosco, in conjunction with the investigation (attached 5-A)?

9. Did your presence with Bosco at the Anonymous Club influence your handling of him?

10. Were you aware that Bosco was a criminal associate of Civello and his lieutenants, Joe Ianni and Ross Musso (attached 6-A)?

11. Were Ianni and Musso, both Italian aliens and key members of the Dallas Mafia, going to be deported as part of the Task Force assault in 1963?

12. Did you inform U.S. Attorney Stone and Attorney General Kennedy about your association with Anonymous Club members and Philip Bosco?

13. Did you discuss the Stone investigation and prosecution with Vice President Lyndon Johnson in the weeks prior to the assassination of President Kennedy?

14. What was your reaction to published reports in 1962 and 1963 suggesting that JFK did not intend to retain LBJ as a running mate in the 1964 presidential race?

15. On the afternoon of November 22, 1963, when you learned that District Attorney Henry Wade's office was preparing to file a conspiracy-based indictment against

Oswald for the murder of President Kennedy, did you contact Cliff Carter at the White House (attached 7-A)? Did you speak directly with LBJ?

16. Did Lyndon Johnson or Carter instruct you to call Wade and persuade him to delete all reference to conspiracy in the indictment, or did you do this on your own?

17. Why did you, as a federal official, interfere in the prosecution of a purely local crime when you had no legal jurisdiction? Your office had seen the Zapruder film that day, as well as WFAA (Jay Watson) coverage, both of which clearly revealed the presence of a shooter on the grassy knoll -- in *front* of the presidential limousine (attached 8-A). You also knew of the arrest of Oswald and the recovery of his rifle -- in a building *behind* the presidential limousine. Taken together, the evidence made a crossfire, and thus conspiracy (of whatever origin) obvious.

18. Why did you arrange to have Sarah Hughes, the presiding judge in the U.S. v. Stone prosecution, perform the swearing in ceremony on Air Force One (attached 9-A)?

19. Did you take control of the Stone and Albert Meadows prosecutions after the assassination? Why were these cases not prosecuted during the six month period following the assassination (attached 10-A, B)?

20. To what degree did you control the handling of FBI interviews of Dallas area Mafiosi and informants in the months following the assassination (attached 11-A)?

21. Were you involved in the physical examination and preparation of such affidavits for purposes of categorization as Warren Commission Documents and/or Exhibits?

22. Did you participate in the censorship of **Commission Document 84,** which became **Exhibit 1536** (attached 12-A)? If so, was it because the informant revealed that Jack Ruby was a criminal associate of both Civello and Philip S. Bosco?

23. With your knowledge of the Stone defendants and their direct connection to Ruby before the assassination (i.e. Ruby ran "book" with the Enquire and Turf Bar and was under IRS investigation as were the others), why did you, as U.S. Attorney to Dallas, not come forward with what you knew during the Warren Commission or Ruby trial deliberations (attached 13-A)? Was this because you had persuaded D.A. Wade not to file a conspiracy-based indictment against Oswald?

24. Did you testify in Executive Session before the Warren Commission?

25. When the U.S. House of Reps. reinvestigated the Kennedy assassination in the latter 1970's (HSCA), were you questioned at that time?

26. The timing of the U.S. Senate confirmation hearing approving your nomination to the Federal bench (Northern Dist. of Texas-Dallas) coincided exactly with the filing of

the HSCA's final Report (March 29, 1979), which overturned the Warren Report and found probable conspiracy in the murder of JFK (attached 14-A,B). Was your nomination a political reaction to the investigation and finding of conspiracy?

27. When the FBI supplied the Judiciary Committee (controlled by Ted Kennedy and Bob Dole) with your background report, which they used to make their decision, was the Committee made aware of your association with the Anonymous Club (attached 15-A)? With Bosco? With Tamburo? Handling of the Stone case? If not, did you make them aware of the association?

28. Were you asked about your intervention in the Oswald indictment?

29. Was the U.S. Fifth Circuit Court made aware of the facts supporting questions 1 through 28? Was the State Bar of Texas?

30. Were President Carter and/or Sen. Lloyd Bentsen made aware at the time of your nomination?

The above data is but a small part of the results of a four year investigation into this case, which I began in 1992. This data (with supporting documents) is included in a book I have just completed. In the interest of historical objectivity, your response to the above questions will be made a part of my book. There are certain time limitations beyond my control concerning your response to this questionnaire. If I have received no response by September 10, 1996, I will presume you decline to comment.

Sincerely,

Mark North, B.A., J.D.

P.O. Box 91196
Austin, TX 78709-1196

Henry M. Wade, Sr.
Attorney-at-law
16475 Dallas Pkwy, Suite 550
Dallas, Texas 75248

September 3, 1996

Dear Mr. Wade,

I am the author of *Act Of Treason: The Role Of J. Edgar Hoover In The Assassination Of President Kennedy* (Carroll & Graf, 1991). Since the release of that book I have continued my research into the JFK/Oswald murders.

The purpose of this letter is to ask certain questions of you which have arisen during my research into your time as Dallas County District Attorney (1951-86). As you may recall, earlier this year I contacted you by phone and you granted me a brief interview.

From the mid 1920's into at least the mid 1970's there existed in Dallas a small, private Sicilian "social club" known as the Anonymous (or ZuRoma) Club which met weekly. Meetings were held at a west side house near Love Field and occasionally in private residences and Italian restaurants. Membership and guest lists were published weekly in a local Italian newsletter by the name of La Tribuna Italiana (changed to Texas Tribune during WWII). My research has revealed that in addition to dinner, guests also systematically engaged in gambling in the form of poker (See attached 1-A). Under Texas penal statutes this activity rendered the club a "gambling house" (attached 1-B). Membership in this club included criminals such as convicted heroin trafficker and killer Joseph F. Civello, Texas Mafia boss Joseph Piranio, Assistant Dallas D.A. Angelo Piranio, and Dallas PD member Charles Sansone (attached 1-C). Guests included murderers Joe Campisi, Joe Ianni, and Sam Savalli, as well as other Mafiosi (e.g. Rosario and Sam Maceo, Sam Campisi, Philip S. Bosco, Ross Musso) (attached 1-D). In essence, the club fits the profile described by the U.S. Bureau of Narcotics in 1950's era classified analyses of Mafia infiltration (with the intent of corrupting local law enforcement) of legitimate Italian-American promotional organizations. (attached 1-E). My questions are as follows:

1. Why did you, as an attorney and District Attorney, also appear as a guest of this club? Texas Tribune columns (attached 2-A) reveal that you attended the meeting on at least four occasions. You no doubt recall that member Joe Civello was arrested at the New York Apalachin Mob conference in November 1957 and subsequently prosecuted (attached 2-B).

2. Given the week-to-week, ongoing poker game conducted by the club, why was it never raided as a "gambling house"?

3. Was this because of your presence and the appearance of other law enforcement officials (e.g., Tom Clark, Glenn Byrd, Sheriff Bill Decker, Judge Joe Brown, Mayor Earle Cabell, to name a few) (attached 3-A)?

4. Why, April 1962, did you publicly state that under your tenure, Dallas had been kept "free of organized crime," when FBI crime condition reports from that time period state that the Mafia had "25 members" in Dallas (i.e., the Joe Civello Mob)? (attached 4-A B).

5. The Tribune ceased publication in December 1962. Did you continue to appear as a guest of the club after 7/7/62? After the President's assassination?

6. During your guest appearances, did you (as a self-proclaimed supporter of Lyndon Johnson; attached 5-A) make any disparaging or inflammatory remarks about John or Robert Kennedy in any context? Was there any discussion that either Kennedy should be removed from office?

7. Did you discuss LBJ or his wife, Claudia (a woman of partial Italian extraction, mother's maiden name Minerva Patillo)?

8. To your knowledge, did LBJ, who ran political ads in the Tribune and was a friend of club favorites Peter Tamburo and Joe Gennaro, ever appear as a guest of the club (attached 6-A thru C)?

9. I have obtained copies of numerous letters between you and LBJ from the early 1950's onward, indicating a close political relationship (attached 7-A thru O). One of your letters indicates you conducted surveillance on his Senatorial opponents in election years. Did this involve electronic surveillance? Did this surveillance utilize any of your assistants? What time of the day did you conduct this surveillance?

10. Were you promised anything by LBJ for help in his bid to obtain the 1960 Democratic nomination for president? If so, was it a federal judgeship position in the Northern District of Texas?

11. In your letters to LBJ during the course of his *vice presidency*, why did you always refer to him as "Mr. President"?

12. Were you angered by media reports, which began appearing in late 1962 and ran into 1963, to the effect that President Kennedy would not retain LBJ as his running mate in 1964?

13. In April 1963, U.S. Attorney General Robert Kennedy's Task Force on Organized Crime began an investigation of the Dallas Mafia's Commerce Street gambling operation. This included such front operations as the Enquire Shine and Press Shop, Sol's Turf Bar, and the Carousel Club, which were conducting bookmaking. The U.S. Attorney in charge was Arnold M. Stone, whom I have interviewed. The investigation

involved electronic surveillance and resulted in the fall 1963 prosecution of John Eli Stone, James Stone, and Isadore Max Miller (attached 8-A). Their contact man, Mafioso Philip "pump" Bosco (a frequent guest of the Anonymous Club), was also questioned. Bosco worked closely with Joe Ianni and Joe Civello (attached 8-B). What was your reaction to this prosecution? Were you questioned by the Task Force about the club or the downtown bookmaking operation? About Jack Ruby's criminal association with Isadore and David Miller?

14. Did you know that, like yourself, Barefoot Sanders also appeared as a guest of the Anonymous Club (attached 9-A)? Did you know that one of those appearing along with him was Philip Bosco? You are presumably aware that Warren Commission Exhibit 1536 (Bobby Gene Moore FBI affidavit) was censored by the Commission to exclude reference to Ruby's association with Joe Civello and Philip Bosco (attached 9-B, C).

15. Did you investigate the March 1963 "suicide" of Joe Ianni's brother-in-law John Carcelli (shot through the left chest and brain) (attached 10-A)? Carcelli's WWII military service was used by U.S. A.G. Tom Clark and Maury Hughes to enable Truman's pardon of heroin trafficker Frank Ianni, which, in turn, prevented his deportation by the INS. Did LBJ prevent the second attempt to deport Ianni under the McCarran Act?

16. As D.A. in 1951, why did you not further investigate and reindict Joe Ianni for the beating death of a restaurant patron, when eyewitness accounts state that Ianni attacked and killed the man merely for arguing with one of his employees (attached 11-A)?

17. Were Joe Ianni and Civello brother-in-law Ross Musso, both aliens, under threat of deportation in 1963 by the INS?

18. The afternoon of November 22, 1963, you told the Dallas media that the evidence indicated that more than one person was involved in the JFK assassination (attached 12-A). Indeed, your's and Barefoot Sanders' offices viewed the Zapruder film. WFAA, Jay Watson, scooped the murder and interrupted local afternoon programming with a parade of witnesses reiterating what the Zapruder film clearly proved -- a shot from the *right front* of JFK's limousine. You also had Oswald and his rifle, located in a building many yards *behind* the limousine. Eyewitnesses also indicated shots from that building. Clearly, you had ample evidence of a cross fire, and thus conspiracy in JFK's killing. Hence, your public statement. Accordingly, your office prepared a conspiracy-based indictment against Oswald that afternoon. But as your Warren Commission testimony states, U.S. Attorney Barefoot Sanders, Texas Attorney General Waggoner Carr, and LBJ aid Cliff Carter personally contacted you and persuaded you to change the wording of the indictment to delete any charge of conspiracy (attached 12-B). Why, as District Attorney, with exclusive jurisdiction and clear evidence of at least two assassins (of whatever motivation), did you do this? As D.A., you knew that none of the above mentioned federal officials had *any* legal authority to intervene in a *local* murder prosecution.

19. Did LBJ contact you and instruct you not to pursue a conspiracy-based investigation? Did you cooperate because of your relationship with the Anonymous Club? Did you cooperate because of political ambition?

20. The day after your June 8, 1964 Warren Commission testimony you met with LBJ at the White House (attached 13-A). Did you discuss your suspicions of conspiracy (which you revealed to the Commission in testimony)? Did you discuss the fact that U.S. District Court Judge Sarah Hughes (the woman LBJ had swear him in on Air Force One) was also the presiding judge in the then ongoing Task Force prosecution (U.S. v. Stone, et al)?

21. My research indicates that when the U.S. House of Representatives reinvestigated the Kennedy assassination in the latter 1970's they were aware of at least some of the above data. Were you called to testify in Executive Session? If so, were you granted immunity for your testimony?

22. As a former D.A. and an attorney, you are aware of 18 U.S.C.A. 2383 (Misprision of Treason). With your knowledge of Ruby's ties to the Dallas Mafia, U.S. v. Stone, and the alteration of the Moore affidavit regarding Bosco, why have you not revealed to the proper authorities the Civello Mob's clear motive to assassinate President Kennedy and silence Oswald?

23. In the critical hours after the murder, when the other "killers" were most likely to have been apprehended, you directed the investigation away from anyone besides Oswald by deleting any reference to conspiracy from his indictment. The evidence you had by that evening clearly pointed in the direction of at least two assassins. Given the above data, what distinguishes your actions the afternoon and evening of November 22nd, 1963, from that of an "Accessory" in the murder of President Kennedy (attached 14-A)?

The above data is but a small part of the results of a four year investigation into this case, which I began in 1992, and is included in a book I have just completed. In the interest of historical objectivity, your response to the above questions will be made a part of my book. There are certain time limitations beyond my control with regard to your response to this questionnaire. Accordingly, I will presume that you decline to comment if I have received no response by September 10, 1996.

Sincerely,

Mark North
B.A., J.D.

EXHIBIT D

Lyndon Johnson Correspondence

Henry Wade

J Edgar Hoover

Barefoot Sanders

Joe Gennaro

Albert Thomas

John McKee

HENRY WADE
ATTORNEY - AT - LAW
DALLAS, TEXAS

PHONE R-3128

1434 M & W TOWER BLDG.

March 2, 1950

MAR 5 A.M.

Mr. & Mrs. Lyndon Johnson
United States Senate
Washington, D. C.

Dear Lyndon and Ladybird:

I really enjoyed seeing both of you while I was in Washington and appreciate very much the invitation to your cocktail party, which was very successful. If there is anything I can do for you down here, please call upon me.

Good luck to you in the tremendous responsibilities you have there in Washington.

Your friend,

Henry
HENRY WADE

HW/jo

P.S. - Sara enjoyed the party
Henry

March 8, 1950.

Dear Henry:

Lady Bird and I think you were mighty nice to write us such a thoughtful note upon your return to Dallas. We enjoyed having you and your brother out to the house and hope we will have the pleasure again some day.

Give my best wishes to all the Wade family.

Sincerely,

Lyndon B. Johnson.

Honorable Henry Wade,
Attorney at Law,
1434 M & W Tower Building,
Dallas, Texas.

HENRY WADE
DISTRICT ATTORNEY
RECORDS BUILDING
DALLAS, TEXAS

July 10, 1951

Senator Lyndon B. Johnson
United States Senate
Washington, D. C.

REC'D JUL 15 1951

Dear Lyndon:

I want you to know that I appreciate very much your kindness in sending me the autographed picture. It is now being framed and will be placed in a prominent spot in the office, and I shall be very proud of it as I am of you and the outstanding job you are performing.

Everything is going along fine here in this office, and I believe you are in excellent shape politically speaking in this part of the state.

If I can ever help you with anything, please command me.

Your friend,

Henry

HENRY WADE
District Attorney
Dallas, Texas

HW:jf

March 1, 1954

Dear Hank:

Jake Pickle has written me of his recent visit with you. He told me of your generous offer of assistance this summer in case, as seems likely, that you do not have an opponent.

I want you to know how much I appreciate this, Hank. I have always felt, of course, that I could count on the Wade brothers all the way down the line. At the same time, it makes me feel mighty good to hear from old and true friends who want to help for the pure sake of helping. Thanks for this and for all the other things you have done for me.

Best regards. I will appreciate your keeping me informed of any significant developments there, and of course I am always glad to have your suggestions and advice.

Sincerely,

Lyndon B. Johnson

Honorable Henry Wade
District Attorney
Records Building
Dallas, Texas
lbj/bm/sw
cc-jake

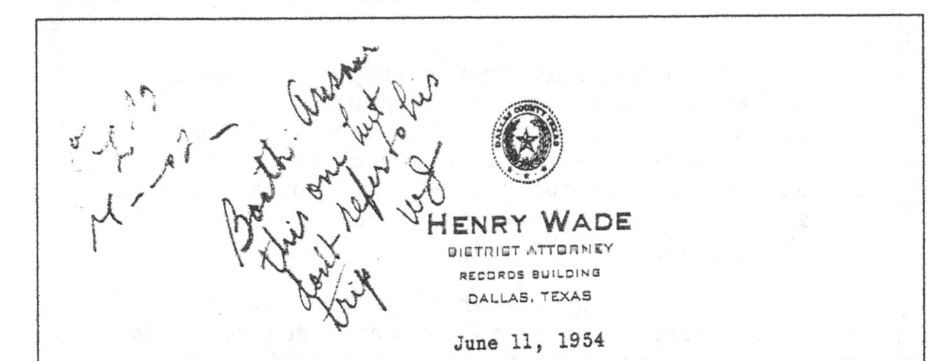

HENRY WADE
DISTRICT ATTORNEY
RECORDS BUILDING
DALLAS, TEXAS

June 11, 1954

Senator Lyndon B. Johnson
United States Senate
Washington, D. C.

Dear Senator:

I made the trip, as we discussed, to Beeville and stayed there four days waiting for the candidate to return after setting up a tentative appointment with him. It turns out that he had an appointment to visit the Dallas Morning News on Thursday afternoon at 3:00, this being the day that Mr. Ruggles is off duty, and he came down especially for the interview, but Mr. Daugherty did not arrive for the interview, but did come up Friday afternoon, a day later and discuss his candidacy with the News. I did not see any publicity growing out of this conference and do not think he was very successful in presenting his candidacy, although I have no information on this score.

I find that rather than return to Beeville, he and a group went out to Junction and spent the weekend with Coke Stevenson and since, have seen some publicity growing out of this conference. From all I could learn in Beeville, they have not been able to raise any money of a substantial nature, and that they have no definite plans as to the future of their campaign.

Jim, who was interested in it, as I told you, was very disgusted and said that he intended to have nothing further to do with it, and knew of very little being done there. He did tell me he would discuss the state senatorial race with Daugherty and let me know what, if any, progress he had along those lines.

I learned also from a very confidential but authentic source that the Republican Party had no intention of spending any big amount of money in an effort to defeat you in November, since it is their opinion it would take a million and a half dollars to put on any creditable campaign and in all probability it would be a failure at that.

I do not think your campaign could be in any better shape than it is now and I see no reason for any organized campaign in your behalf at this time.

I do think you should try to return here and make a few public appearances on two or three occasions between now and election, and see no reason for you to recognize there is an opponent running against you in any of those appearances.

I am sending a copy of this to Jake Pickle and hope both of you will treat all of the above information confidential, since I think we are in a good position to find out in advance any proposed big expenditures in behalf of Daugherty or any expected new developments in his campaign.

Your friend,

Henry Wade

HW:JF HENRY WADE

cc J.J.Pickle

June 7, 1955

Dear Hank:

I am glad to know that you are thinking of making the race for Congress from the Dallas District next year. I hope you will finally decide to run. We need men like you up here.

I have had your name placed on my own mailing list for the Congressional Record. If you need information about the votes cast so far by the present Congressman, I am sure the House Campaign Committee will be glad to provide it for you.

I appreciate your kind remarks about me. You are very flattering, my friend, but I am not a candidate for President. The job I have suits me fine.

Please keep me informed of your plans, and let me know if there is any way in which I can be of service.

Best personal regards.

Sincerely,

Lyndon B. Johnson

Honorable Henry Wade
District Attorney
Records Building
Dallas, Texas
LBJ:BM:gr

Let me know What you Want or need from me LBJ

September 11, 1955

Dear Henry:

With old and true friends like us, it would be superfluous to say it, but I just want to drop a reminder -- I'm for you lock, stock and barrel. I'm behind you in just about anything you undertake to do and I hope you know it.

We plan to be in Dallas October 13th for Johnson-Rayburn Day. Hope to see you then.

Sincerely,

Lyndon B. Johnson

Honorable Henry Wade
District Attorney
Records Building
Dallas, Texas

mmw

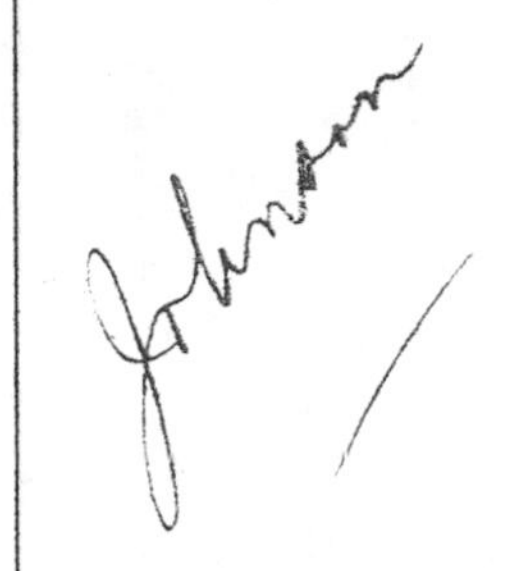

HENRY WADE
DISTRICT ATTORNEY
RECORDS BUILDING
DALLAS 2, TEXAS

July 21, 1959

Senator Lyndon Johnson
United States Senate
United States Capitol
Washington, D. C.

Dear Senator:

I have read with much interest the mouthings of Paul Butler and want you to know that I feel like you are a hundred percent right and that it has strengthened considerably your chances of being our next president.

I have thought some about running for Attorney General of the State next year, but now feel that I will remain here and do what I can in your behalf towards your nomination and whatever assistance I could be in your election.

If there is anything that you would like for me to do, please call on me.

Your devoted friend,

HENRY WADE

HW:JF

July 25, 1959

Dear Henry:

It was very thoughtful of you to write me as you did on July 21.

I have enjoyed your friendship for many years, and I am grateful for any help that you can give me to enable me to do a better job for my state and nation.

The Wade brothers have always been my strong supporters, and I will always be grateful.

Sincerely,

Lyndon B. Johnson

Honorable Henry Wade
District Attorney
Records Building
Dallas 2, Texas

SHJ:efj

HENRY WADE
DISTRICT ATTORNEY
RECORDS BUILDING
DALLAS 2, TEXAS

June 7, 1960

Mr. Walter Jenkins
c/o Honorable Lyndon B. Johnson
United States Senate
United States Capitol
Washington, D. C.

Dear Walter:

Belatedly I want to thank you for helping me and the First Citizens Bank with their application for the FDIC. They approved the move and said conditions would have to be made prior to moving, which apparently we can meet without too much difficulty.

I was out in California all last week trying to stir up some strength for the Senator and am in the process of making a report in detail to Irv Hoff. The Senator helped his own cause tremendously by his visit and made an excellent impression on those that saw or met him. I talked to some 40 delegates and all of them thought that the image that had been built of the Senator in California was changed and although the majority of the delegates seemed to be waiting on Pat Brown, I feel like a majority of them could in the final analysis end up in Johnson's camp, although I do not believe at present he has over 35 delegate votes.

I want to go back about a week before the convention and would like very much to be a delegate of some nature so that I would have access to the floor. I know that you all are swamped with requests, but if you have a chance to help me on this, I would appreciate it.

Your friend,

Henry Wade

HENRY WADE

HW:JF

P.S. Have not had any luck with the local group - most of whom have never been for the Senator - but say they are now - Hen

June 22, 1960

Dear Henry:

Walter showed me your good letter of June 7. I am deeply grateful to you for all your help and support. It is most rewarding for a man in public life to be able to count on friends like you.

Best wishes and kind regards.

Sincerely,

Lyndon B. Johnson

Honorable Henry Wade
Records Building
Dallas 2, Texas

LBJ:MCJ:edd

July 23, 1960

Hon. John B. Connally
1209 Ft. Worth National Bank Bldg.
Fort Worth, Texas

Dear John:

I enjoyed visiting with you in California and was sorry that we came out second best but was very impressed with the Kennedy organization there and believe that we have a strong ticket that will be elected in November.

I don't know who is going to be running the show in Texas but want you to know that I am available to do anything possible here for the ticket or for that matter in other states if it is felt that I could be of some value there.

I have two brilliant assistants here, Jim Bowie who is my Administrative Assistant and is a very capable, energetic young man who is very anxious to do anything possible for the Kennedy-Johnson ticket in Texas or in other places if it is felt that he could be of some service. He has expressed willingness to take a leave of absence from the office and devote full time to the campaign in question if someone would pay his salary and expenses. I think he could make a very valuable contribution to the campaign if the right place could be found for him.

Another of my assistants, Sam McCorkle, who was a law partner and Jerry Mann's campaign manager when he ran for Attorney General and I feel that he is very capable and

Hon. John B. Connally - 2 - July 23, 1960

he has expressed a desire to be active in the campaign. His son-in-law, Jack Vaughan, is in the oil business here and Sam has already contacted him with reference to a rather sizable contribution to the campaign and Jack has indicated willingness in this respect. Both of these men have considerable political savory and would know how to handle themselves under any circumstances.

I was down in East Texas one day this week and spent another day out in West Texas and believe that with some work that there would be no question that the ticket will carry Texas although I doubt whether it will carry Dallas County. As you know Dallas County is a problem since the democratic machinery is not under the control of good democrats to put it mildly.'

Nellie was sure looking young and chipper at the convention and it can be due only to the fact that her husband treats her so fine. Give my regards to her and the whole family.

Your friend,

Henry Wade

HENRY WADE

em

cc: Senator Lyndon Johnson
Austin, Texas

Sen John Kennedy
WasHingenateD C

HENRY WADE
DISTRICT ATTORNEY
RECORDS BUILDING
DALLAS 2, TEXAS

April 18, 1961

The Honorable Lyndon B. Johnson
Vice President of the United States
United States Capitol
Washington, D. C.

Dear Mr. Vice President:

Congratulations upon your Texas reception and treatment for Chancellor Adenauer. From all reports it was a huge success.

As you are probably aware, I can think of nothing more interesting or desirable for me than my appointment to one of these new Federal Judgships that are to be created in the Northern District of Texas.

I realize this usually comes under the patronage of the U. S. senators, but I had rather have you for me than all of the senators in Washington. I know you are busy on things much more important, and for that reason I have not taken your time in discussing it with you.

I have no idea what, if any, chance I have, but am enclosing some background information concerning myself of which you may not be familiar, and hope you find time to read it. I could and would come to Washington and visit with you in person, if you feel that advisable and would have the time.

If you have any recommendation you think I should follow, it would be greatly appreciated.

Your friend,

Henry Wade

HENRY WADE

HW:JF

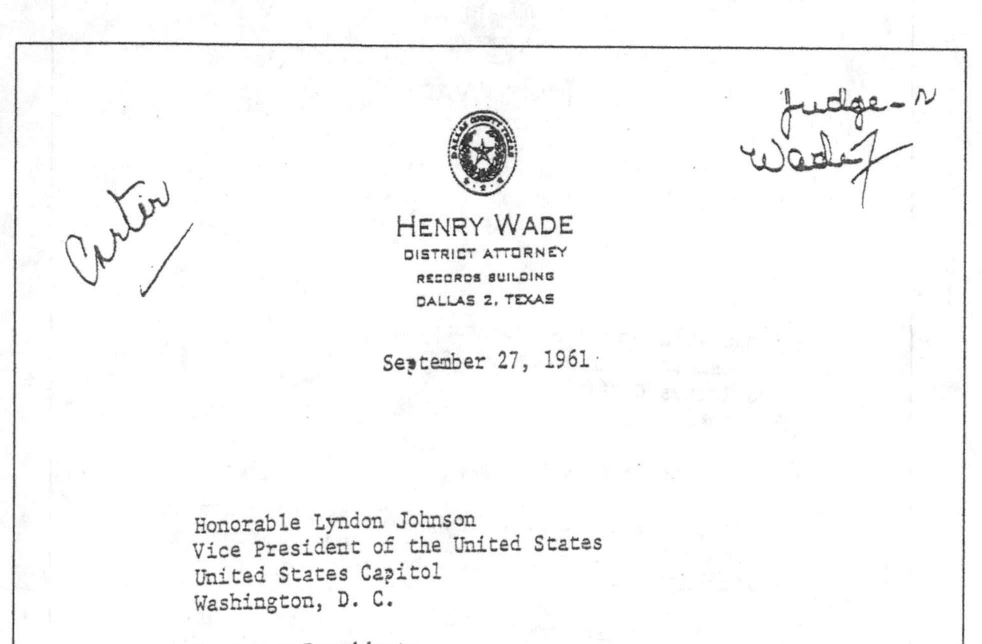

Judge-N
Wade-7

Carter

HENRY WADE
DISTRICT ATTORNEY
RECORDS BUILDING
DALLAS 2, TEXAS

September 27, 1961

Honorable Lyndon Johnson
Vice President of the United States
United States Capitol
Washington, D. C.

Dear Mr. President:

I want you to know that I deeply appreciate your consideration and help concerning the judgeship here. I know that without your support, I would have received no consideration, and I fully realize your problem and do believe that four appointments were made that will be a credit to the Judiciary of Texas.

I am very thankful of your friendship through the years and appreciate the leading role you are playing in the present Administration, and hope we are fortunate some day to have you as our President.

Your friend,

Henry Wade

HENRY WADE

HW:JF

Carter

HENRY WADE
DISTRICT ATTORNEY
RECORDS BUILDING
DALLAS 2, TEXAS

September 19, 1962

The Honorable Lyndon B. Johnson
Vice President of the United States
United States Capitol
Washington, D. C.

Dear Mr. President:

It was sure nice to see you at Bonham, and I enjoyed your talk, particular the things about Mr. Sam.

I am doing what I can for John and feel like he will win, but he does have a race on his hands.

We are all looking forward to working again for you, because we need you as President of this country.

Give my best regards to Lady Bird.

Your friend,

HENRY WADE

HW:JFL

HENRY WADE
DISTRICT ATTORNEY
RECORDS BUILDING
DALLAS, TEXAS 75202

November 5, 1964

Honorable Lyndon B. Johnson
President of the United States
L B J Ranch
Stonewall, Texas

Dear Mr. President:

I am so happy and jubilant over the election and so thankful that you are our president and will be our president, I hope, for many years to come. Your excellent record as president and your program for the future make all of us who have supported you for years very proud. Your leadership caused the sweeping Democratic victory, and most important we got rid of Bruce Alger and the air is much fresher in Dallas since Tuesday.

I know that you will succeed in your program and believe you will go down in history as our greatest president. I only hope that you can accomplish this without overworking yourself and was happy to see that you are going to spend a week or so at probably the only place you can relax, that of the LBJ Ranch.

Sincerely yours,

HENRY WADE

HW:sc

OFFICE OF THE DIRECTOR

Federal Bureau of Investigation
United States Department of Justice
Washington 25, D.C.

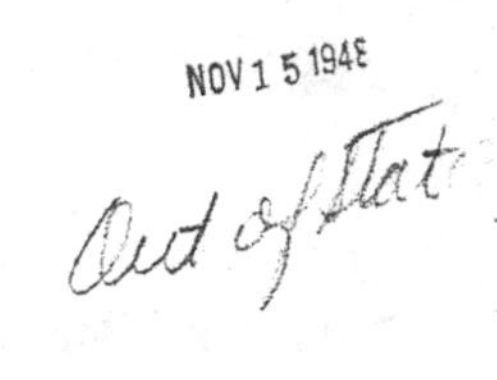

November 9, 1948

Honorable Lyndon B. Johnson
Member of Congress
Johnson City, Texas

My dear Congressman:

I want to take this opportunity to drop you a personal note and congratulate you on your election to the Senate. I also would like to express to you my appreciation for the fine assistance you have given us in the past, and to let you know that we will be only too glad to help you at any time in the future.

With expressions of my highest esteem and best regards,

Sincerely yours,

J. Edgar Hoover

fa done

November 18, 1948

Dear Mr. Hoover:

Thank you very much for your kind and thoughtful message. I sincerely appreciate it.

As a long-standing admirer of your own personal leadership andáability as well as the remarkable efficiency and integrity of your great organization, I want you to know that I will always consider it a privilege to assist you at anytime.

Mrs. Johnson and I hope to return to our home in Washington soon and move in as your neighbors on 30th Place once more.

With my warmest personal regards,

Sincerely,

Lyndon B. Johnson

hb -- out of state
Hon. J. Edgar Hoover
Washington, D. C.

COPY LBJ

OPTIONAL FORM NO. 10
MAY 1962 EDITION
GSA FPMR (41 CFR) 101-11.6
UNITED STATES GOVERNMENT

Memorandum

TO : SAC, DALLAS (92-331) DATE: 2/16/68

FROM : CLERK [redacted] b7C

SUBJECT: PHILIP STEPHENS BOSCO, aka,
Philip S. Bosco, Phil Bosco,
P. S. Bosco, Philip Steve Bosco,
Phillip Stevens Boscoe
ANTI-RACKETEERING

CORRELATION MEMORANDUM

All References on index cards have been reviewed and the following summaries set set out:

Subject file 165-92: PHILIP STEPHENS BOSCO. Interstate Transmission of Wagering Information.

Serial 4, Dallas Weekly Summary airtel to Director, dated 6/10/63. Informant [redacted] furnished information that BOSCO operated as a bookmaker over the telephones at his Gulf Service Station, 2701 Ross Avenue, Dallas. Customers come to the station to pay off or collect under the pretext of purchasing gasoline.

b2
b7C
b7D

Serial 6, Memo from SA [redacted] dated 6/28/63. [redacted] Special Agent, Intelligence Section, Internal Revenue Service, advised on 6/27/63, that it had been ascertained through a recording device attached in a pay telephone booth used frequently by JOHN ELI STONE, a known bookmaker, that STONE was receiving the betting line from Las Vegas, Nevada, and immediately disseminating this information to BOSCO.

Serial 8, Dallas letter to Director, dated 7/24/63. [redacted] Vice Squad, Dallas Police Department, advised that on 7/17/63, BOSCO was arrested at his service station, and charged with vagrancy. They searched him with a search warrant and made a search of the service station looking for bookmaking paraphernalia. The Dallas police officers obtained a baseball schedule sheet from BOSCO, which contained the betting odds for each individual game and the scheduled pitchers for that date. Also obtained was a 2x3 piece of paper containing several telephone numbers

92-331-246
SEARCHED ____ INDEXED ____
SERIALIZED ak FILED ____
FEB 19 1968
[redacted] LAS

b7C [redacted]

5010-108-01

Buy U.S. Savings Bonds Regularly on the Payroll Savings

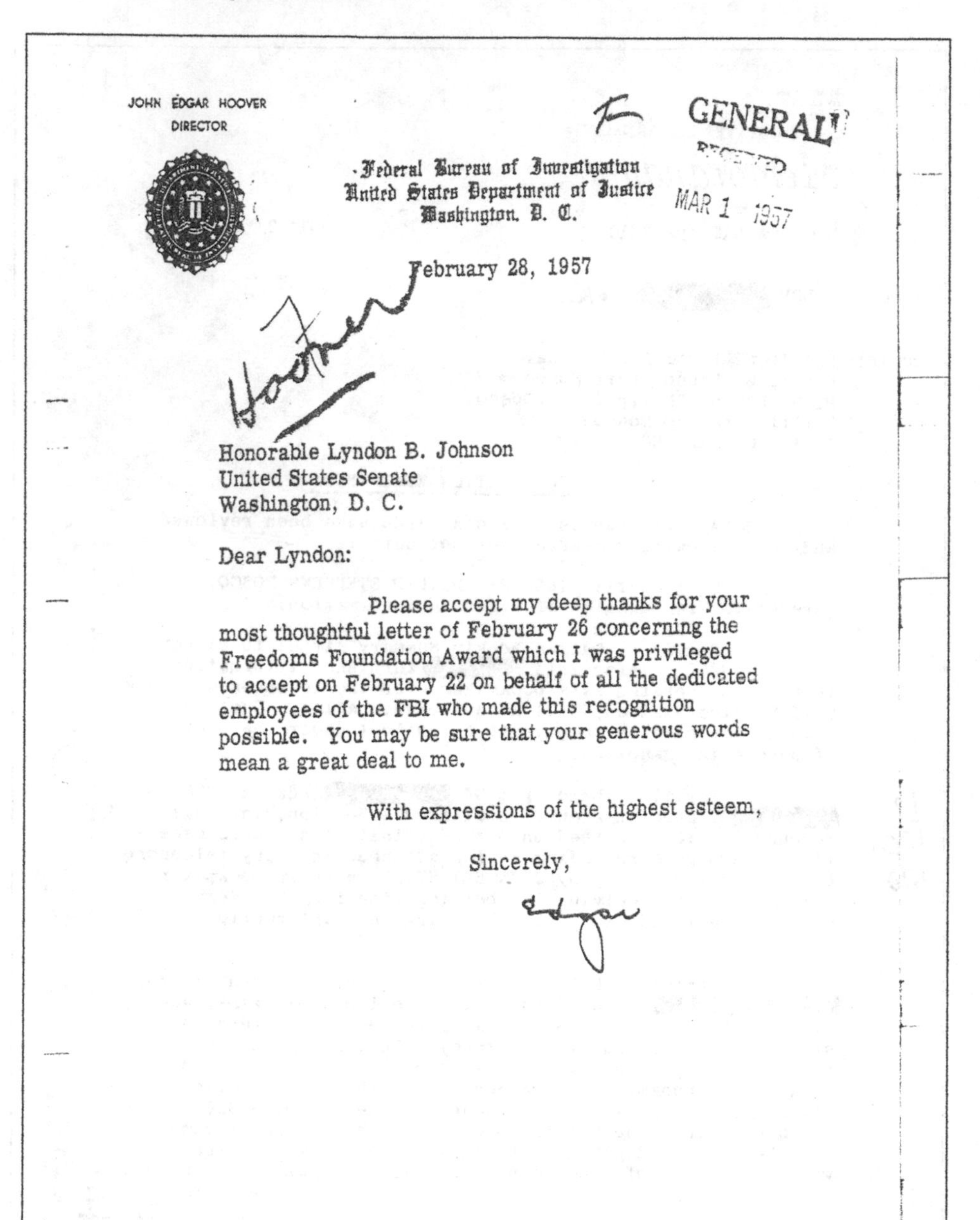

JOHN EDGAR HOOVER
DIRECTOR

GENERAL
RECEIVED
MAR 1 1957

Federal Bureau of Investigation
United States Department of Justice
Washington, D. C.

February 28, 1957

Hoover

Honorable Lyndon B. Johnson
United States Senate
Washington, D. C.

Dear Lyndon:

Please accept my deep thanks for your most thoughtful letter of February 26 concerning the Freedoms Foundation Award which I was privileged to accept on February 22 on behalf of all the dedicated employees of the FBI who made this recognition possible. You may be sure that your generous words mean a great deal to me.

With expressions of the highest esteem,

Sincerely,

Edgar

COPY LBJ LI

JOHN EDGAR HOOVER
DIRECTOR

Federal Bureau of Investigation
United States Department of Justice
Washington, D. C.

November 7, 1957

Honorable Lyndon B. Johnson
United States Senate
Washington, D. C.

Dear Lyndon:

I have received the copy of your letter of October 31, 1957, to Mr. Nichols. It was characteristically thoughtful of you to comment so generously regarding his career, and I know that he was deeply grateful to hear from you in this regard.

Your kind remarks concerning my administration of the FBI mean very much to me, and I want to thank you.

Sincerely,

Edgar

May 12, 1958

My Dear Mr. Hoover:

Just a brief note to express my warm congratulations to you upon the anniversary you celebrated over the weekend. I think it is a great tribute to you personally that you have served in such a responsible position for 34 years under Presidents and Attorneys General of both parties.

I think it is an equal tribute to our people that the overwhelming majority of our citizens have such great confidence in you.

It is my personal hope that you will continue in your position for many years to come, because I know of no man who has done more to defend our institutions from our enemies.

Warm regards,

Sincerely,

Lyndon B. Johnson

Mr. J. Edgar Hoover, Director
Federal Bureau of Investigation
Washington, D. C.

LBJ: GER:jas

POLICY

OFFICE OF THE DIRECTOR

Yes

UNITED STATES DEPARTMENT OF JUSTICE

FEDERAL BUREAU OF INVESTIGATION

WASHINGTON 25, D. C.

May 15, 1958

Honorable Lyndon B. Johnson
United States Senate
Washington, D. C.

Dear Lyndon:

Please accept my heartfelt thanks for your most thoughtful remembrance of my 34th Anniversary as Director of the FBI. You may be sure I deeply appreciate your kindness in writing.

Our work over the years has been made immeasurably easier by the support of good friends such as you, and I want you to know that I am truly grateful.

Sincerely,

Edgar

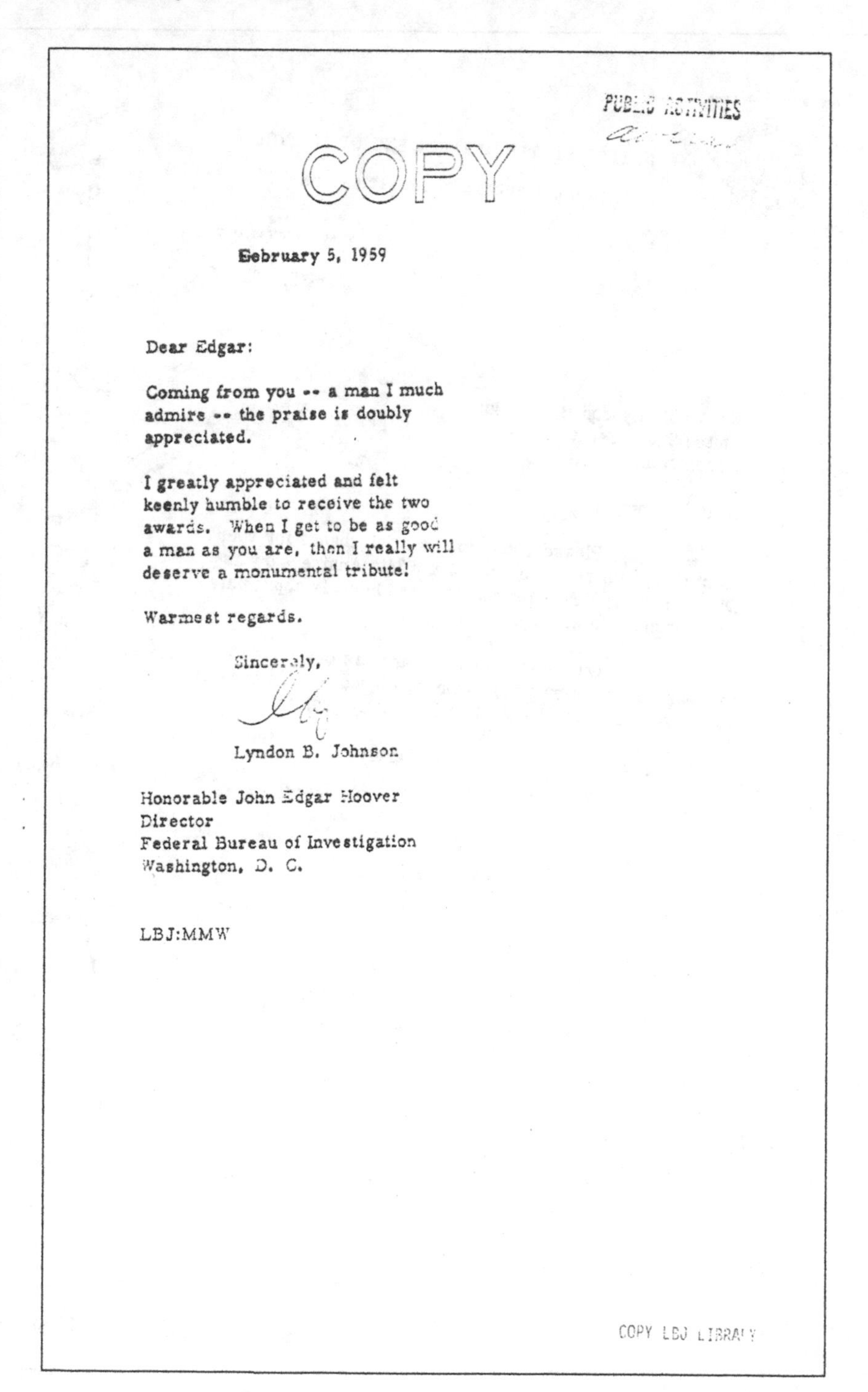

PUBLIC ACTIVITIES

COPY

February 5, 1959

Dear Edgar:

Coming from you -- a man I much admire -- the praise is doubly appreciated.

I greatly appreciated and felt keenly humble to receive the two awards. When I get to be as good a man as you are, then I really will deserve a monumental tribute!

Warmest regards.

Sincerely,

Lyndon B. Johnson

Honorable John Edgar Hoover
Director
Federal Bureau of Investigation
Washington, D. C.

LBJ:MMW

COPY

September 23, 1959

Dear Edgar:

My Austin friends are overjoyed that you find it possible to accept the invitation to address the United Fund's noon meeting on November ninth. They have assured me nothing will be spared to make this occasion a memorab le one and we all count ourselves fortunate to have you with us.

Lady Bird and I would consider it an additional blessing if you could come spend the weekend before Monday, the ninth with us at the ranch. We are just 65 miles west of Austin and could arrange to meet you at the Austin airport and drive with you out to Johnson City where we live.

The Austin United Fund has asked me to introduce you when you speak to them. That will be a very delightful and pleasant assignment.

With warm regards.

Sincerely,

Lyndon B. Johnson

Honorable J. Edgar Hoover
Director
Federal Bureau of Investigation
Washington, D. C.

P. S. On second thought, it might be better if you were to take either the Braniff jet leaving Washington at 9:20 am for Dallas or the American jet leaving about 11:15 am and my plane could pick you up in Dallas. This way you would have no lay-over in Dallas. Let me know your travel plans.

JOHN EDGAR HOOVER
DIRECTOR

Federal Bureau of Investigation
United States Department of Justice
Washington, D. C.

November 10, 1959

Honorable Lyndon B. Johnson
United States Senator
Johnson City, Texas

Dear Lyndon:

My trip to Austin and to your home yesterday was an unforgettable experience. It was certainly a great pleasure to be with Lady Bird, you, and your friends and associates.

I was tremendously impressed by the warmth and friendliness of your fellow citizens and I am truly sorry that I could not remain for a longer stay. I shall never forget your many kindnesses to me during my visit.

With kindest regards to Lady Bird and to you,

Sincerely,

Edgar

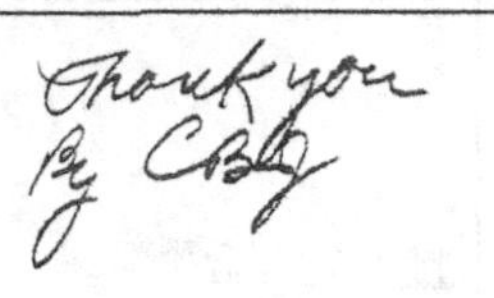

COPY

November 10, 1959

Dear Edgar:

I can't tell you how much we all enjoyed your visit with us yesterday. The people here are talking--and will be for a long time to come--of your speech, your visit to Huston-Tillotson and to the Texas Employees Association session.

I just wish that it had been possible for you to stay longer. Now that you have seen the ranch, both Lady Bird and I are counting on and looking forward to an early return. You saw the deer. They are there. Now it is up to you to come pick out your buck.

Beagle sends his apologies for the masterful job he did in transferring his hair to your suit.

We send our very warmest best wishes and many thanks.

Sincerely,

L

Lyndon B. Johnson

The Honorable J. Edgar Hoover
Director, Federal Bureau
of Investigation
Washington, D. C.

LBJ:CBL:gw
OFL

SANDERS & SANDERS
ATTORNEYS AND COUNSELORS
16TH FLOOR KIRBY BUILDING
DALLAS, TEXAS

HAROLD B. SANDERS, SR.
BAREFOOT SANDERS

LEFKOWITZ, GREEN, GINSBERG & EADES
ASSOCIATE COUNSEL

RIVERSIDE 7-4851

November 15, 1960

Senator Lyndon B. Johnson
L-B-J Ranch
Johnson City, Texas

Dear Senator:

Jan and I extend to you and Mrs. Johnson our warmest congratulations on your election victory and on the great work which you did in the campaign.

We were particularly delighted with the Texas results, although disappointed in our county - as were several hundred others here who had worked diligently for you and Senator Kennedy. Sometime I should like to discuss the Dallas situation with you.

Both you and Mrs. Johnson were magnificent on your Dallas visit, "Black Friday", November 4.

You have our profound respect and admiration for the terrific campaign which you made. We are glad to have had a part in the fight. If we can help in any way in the future, please let us know. With every good wish,

Sincerely,

Barefoot Sanders

BS/mvc

EXECUTIVE
PL/ST 43
PR8-1/G*
CO 127

October 7, 1964

Dear Mr. Gennaro:

In behalf of the President I am acknowledging your letter with your marginal note thereon to the President about your recent visit to the White House.

I know it gave Mr. Johnson pleasure to be with you on this occasion and, moreover, I know it is a source of great satisfaction to him to have the friendship and support extended by you and the members of your Committee.

I shall see that your letter is brought to his attention at the earliest opportunity.

Sincerely,

A. C. Perry

Arthur C. Perry,
Assistant

Mr. Joseph P. Gennaro, General Chairman
American-Italian Committee for Johnson
Box 1423
Dallas, Texas

ACP:pm

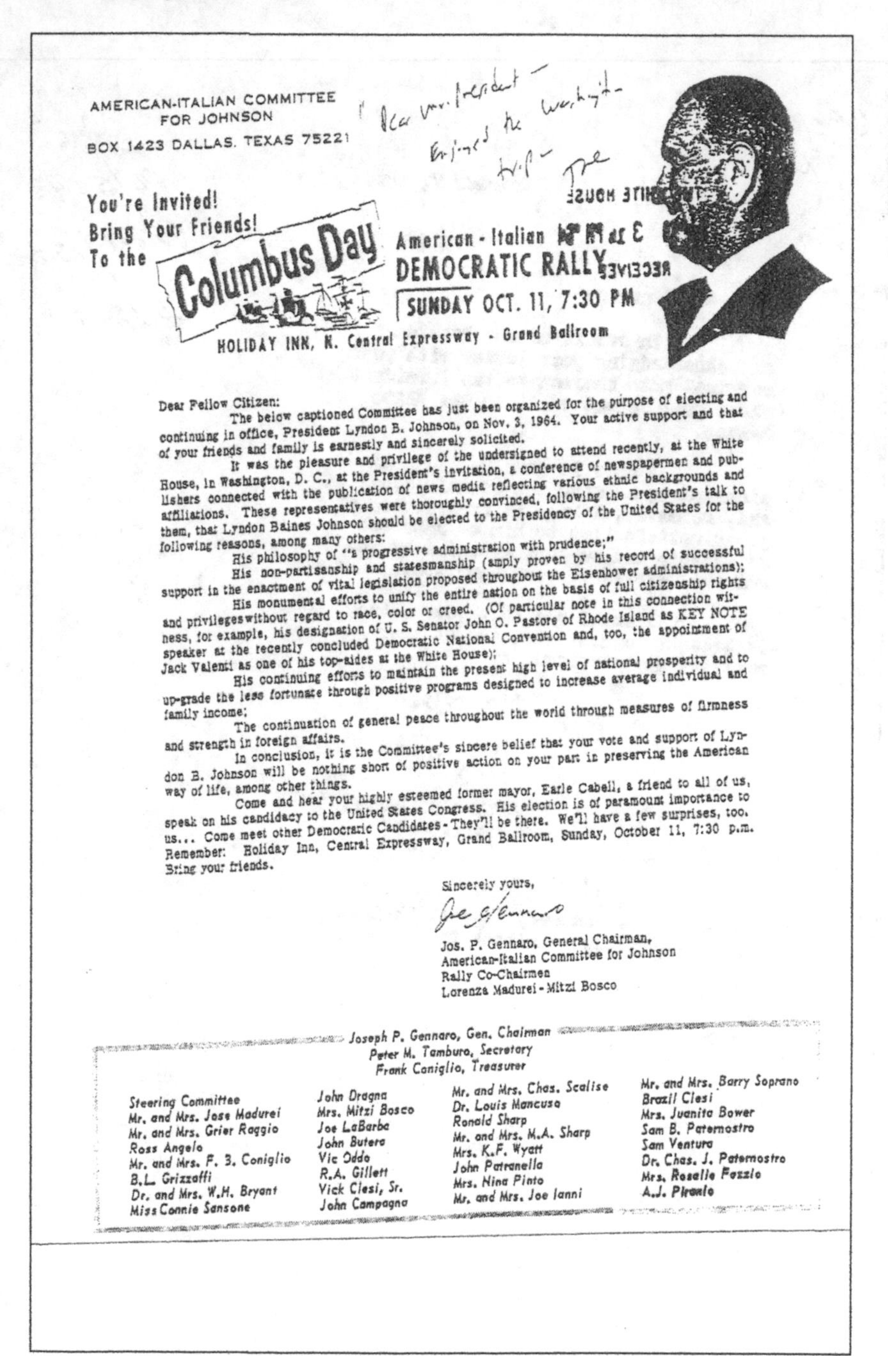

AMERICAN-ITALIAN COMMITTEE
FOR JOHNSON
BOX 1423 DALLAS, TEXAS 75221

You're Invited!
Bring Your Friends!
To the Columbus Day American-Italian DEMOCRATIC RALLY
SUNDAY OCT. 11, 7:30 PM
HOLIDAY INN, N. Central Expressway - Grand Ballroom

Dear Fellow Citizen:

The below captioned Committee has just been organized for the purpose of electing and continuing in office, President Lyndon B. Johnson, on Nov. 3, 1964. Your active support and that of your friends and family is earnestly and sincerely solicited.

It was the pleasure and privilege of the undersigned to attend recently, at the White House, in Washington, D. C., at the President's invitation, a conference of newspapermen and publishers connected with the publication of news media reflecting various ethnic backgrounds and affiliations. These representatives were thoroughly convinced, following the President's talk to them, that Lyndon Baines Johnson should be elected to the Presidency of the United States for the following reasons, among many others:

His philosophy of "a progressive administration with prudence;"

His non-partisanship and statesmanship (amply proven by his record of successful support in the enactment of vital legislation proposed throughout the Eisenhower administrations);

His monumental efforts to unify the entire nation on the basis of full citizenship rights and privileges without regard to race, color or creed. (Of particular note in this connection witness, for example, his designation of U. S. Senator John O. Pastore of Rhode Island as KEY NOTE speaker at the recently concluded Democratic National Convention and, too, the appointment of Jack Valenti as one of his top-aides at the White House);

His continuing efforts to maintain the present high level of national prosperity and to up-grade the less fortunate through positive programs designed to increase average individual and family income;

The continuation of general peace throughout the world through measures of firmness and strength in foreign affairs.

In conclusion, it is the Committee's sincere belief that your vote and support of Lyndon B. Johnson will be nothing short of positive action on your part in preserving the American way of life, among other things.

Come and hear your highly esteemed former mayor, Earle Cabell, a friend to all of us, speak on his candidacy to the United States Congress. His election is of paramount importance to us... Come meet other Democratic Candidates - They'll be there. We'll have a few surprises, too. Remember: Holiday Inn, Central Expressway, Grand Ballroom, Sunday, October 11, 7:30 p.m. Bring your friends.

Sincerely yours,

Jos. P. Gennaro, General Chairman,
American-Italian Committee for Johnson
Rally Co-Chairmen
Lorenza Madurei - Mitzi Bosco

Joseph P. Gennaro, Gen. Chairman
Peter M. Tamburo, Secretary
Frank Coniglio, Treasurer

Steering Committee
Mr. and Mrs. Jose Madurei
Mr. and Mrs. Grier Raggio
Ross Angelo
Mr. and Mrs. F. 3. Coniglio
B.L. Grizzaffi
Dr. and Mrs. W.H. Bryant
Miss Connie Sansone

John Dragna
Mrs. Mitzi Bosco
Joe LaBarba
John Butera
Vic Oddo
R.A. Gillett
Vick Clesi, Sr.
John Campagna

Mr. and Mrs. Chas. Scalise
Dr. Louis Mancuso
Ronald Sharp
Mr. and Mrs. M.A. Sharp
Mrs. K.F. Wyatt
John Patranella
Mrs. Nina Pinto
Mr. and Mrs. Joe Ianni

Mr. and Mrs. Barry Soprano
Brazil Clesi
Mrs. Juanita Bower
Sam B. Paternostro
Sam Ventura
Dr. Chas. J. Paternostro
Mrs. Roselle Fazzio
A.J. Piranio

EXHIBIT E

Anonymous (Zuroma) Club Meetings

November 13, 1943

Anonymous Club

Anonymous Club members were guests Thursday of last week of C. S. Papa at their usual meeting place. A home-cooked dinner was served, the specialty being ravioli, which was pronounced par excellent by everyone and enjoyed thoroughly.

Guests of the evening were Sgt. Paul Satariano, Mr. S. G. Martin, Mr. P. M. Tamburo and Lt. Angelo Piranio.

February 9, 1946

Dinner Dance*

Mr. Joe Ianni was host Wednesday evening... at a dinner and dancing party at the...Hotel Adolphus.... Those who attended were Mr. and Mrs. Joe Civello, Mr. and Mrs. Ross Musso, Mr. and Mrs. Charles Civello,... Mr. Philip Bosco,...and Mrs. Ianni.

March 13, 1948

Anonymous Club

Mr. Jack Barr was host to the Anonymous Club members and guests last week. He served one of those always superb dinners cooked especially for the club by Mrs. Vincent Parrino. Needless to say it was thoroughly enjoyed and many gave expression to their appreciation.

Guests were Messers Joe Ianni, Ralph Patrone, Joe Patrone, Dean Parrino, Judge W. L. Sterrett, R. H. Cummings, C. A. Farrell, Pat Parkinson, J. W. Monk.

After a short business session, the group went into their usual game session.

September 14, 1957

Anonymous Club Names Tamburo Honorary Member

Dallas — Mr. Joe Colletti and Mr. Phil Bosco hosted a most interesting meeting of the Anonymous Club Thursday evening of last week. Guests were Tony Ventura, Peter M. Tamburo, Nick Morale and Walter Strebey.

High point in the activities was the naming of Mr. Tamburo as a life-time honorary member of the club. This is regarded as a high compliment, since the club limits its membership, both active and honorary.

December 14, 1957

Entertain Stars

Mr. and Mrs. Phil Bosco and Mr. and Mrs. Nick Morale entertined two of the best known Notre Dame players Saturday night following the game. They had a wonderful dinner especially prepared by Joe Ianni at his "Ristorante Vesuvio". The guests were the famous Notre Dame star fullback Nick Pietrosante voted by Oklahoma the best individual player they opposed all year, and tackler Charles Puntilo. The boys plan to return to Dallas next year for the State Fair and already have a nievitation for another one of Joe Ianni's marvelous dinners with the same hosts.

---

fav comment

Jln

November 21, 1957

Dear Friend:

Thank you for sending me a copy of your letter of November 12th to Mayor Bob Thornton.

In the face of your generous comments about me, I lack words adequately to express my appreciation. You are more than kind. I am grateful to you and to all my other friends of the Italian-American Civic Federation.

I am looking forward to the meeting in Dallas. I hope to see you while I am there.

Warm good wishes. Please feel free to call on me at any time that I can be of service to you.

Sincerely,

Lyndon B. Johnson

Mr. Peter M. Tamburo, President
Italian-American Civic Federation
3332 Amherst Street
Dallas 25, Texas

LBJ:BM:ap

(VJ) SPECIAL

November 16, 1960

Dear Mr. Tamburo:

If I wrote you every day I couldn't thank you enough for all your interest and support.

But, from one un-hyphenated Democrat to another ---- thanks. Thanks for everything. And I do hope that I can, in the conduct of the office of the Vice President, merit your confidence.

With warm best wishes,

Sincerely

Lyndon B. Johnson

Mr. Peter M. Tamburo
3332 Amherst Street
Dallas 25, Texas

LBJ:MJDR

UNITED STATES DISTRICT COURT
FOR THE
NORTHERN DISTRICT OF TEXAS
DALLAS, TEXAS

Filed 11 day of July 1963 at ___ o'clock ___ M
JOHN A. LOWTHER, Clerk
By ___ Deputy

UNITED STATES OF AMERICA)
NORTHERN DISTRICT OF TEXAS)

AFFIDAVIT

Before Bill Adkins, United States Commissioner for the Northern District of Texas at Dallas, Texas.

I, Charles A. Bus, Jr., am a Special Investigator, Alcohol and Tobacco Tax Division, Internal Revenue Service.

On April 1, 1963, I was assigned to assist in the investigation of John Eli Stone, James Woodrow Stone, and Isadore Max Miller for alleged wagering tax violation.

The assignment involved surveillance of these individuals to determine their activities. ...

On June 19, 1963, while John Eli Stone was using the telephone booth in front of the Safeway store, EM 8-9257, I overheard him talking with someone whom he called Izzie. They were talking about baseball games to be played that day and discussed the various pitchers. At the end of that conversation I heard Stone say that he would call and get a line. Immediately thereafter I heard him dial and tell someone that he wanted to talk to Las Vegas, Nevada, telephone number REgent 5-3111. After depositing several coins in the telephone, I heard him ask for George Hunt. He then apparently received the baseball line for that day. ... Immediately after that, he telephoned someone and gave them the line, mentioning the names of pitchers and figures. At the end of that conversation I heard him say that he would call "Bosco." He then dialed someone and gave the line.

Peter M. Tamburo, president of Dallas's Italian-American Civic Federation (IACF), was closely tied to the Mafia infested Anonymous Club. Fluent in Italian and a Johnson confidant since 1948, he was made an honorary "life-time" member of the Club by Dallas Mafia boss Joe Civello and gambling lieutenant Philip Bosco, among others, in early September 1957. Tamburo told the group "in union there is strength." The IACF included members and guests of the Club. In mid November, just days after Civello's Apalachin Mob arrest, Tamburo wrote to Johnson. When I obtained review and opening of LBJ's correspondence with Tamburo, I discovered that the latter's letter is missing from the file (coded "fav. comment - gen.") All that remains is LBJ's November 21st response. His salutation is misleading. In pre-Kefauver days, Johnson addressed his letters "Dear Pete." Less than a year after Apalachin, LBJ wrote Tamburo: "I do not know what the future will hold but I will always feel grateful to people like you who have been so good to me over the years." Tamburo was also a prime backer of Johnson crony Barefoot Sanders, who appeared before the Club in early 1958 with Philip Bosco. And it was Bosco who was under investigation by RFK's Organized Crime Task Force in October 1963.

*Facsimile

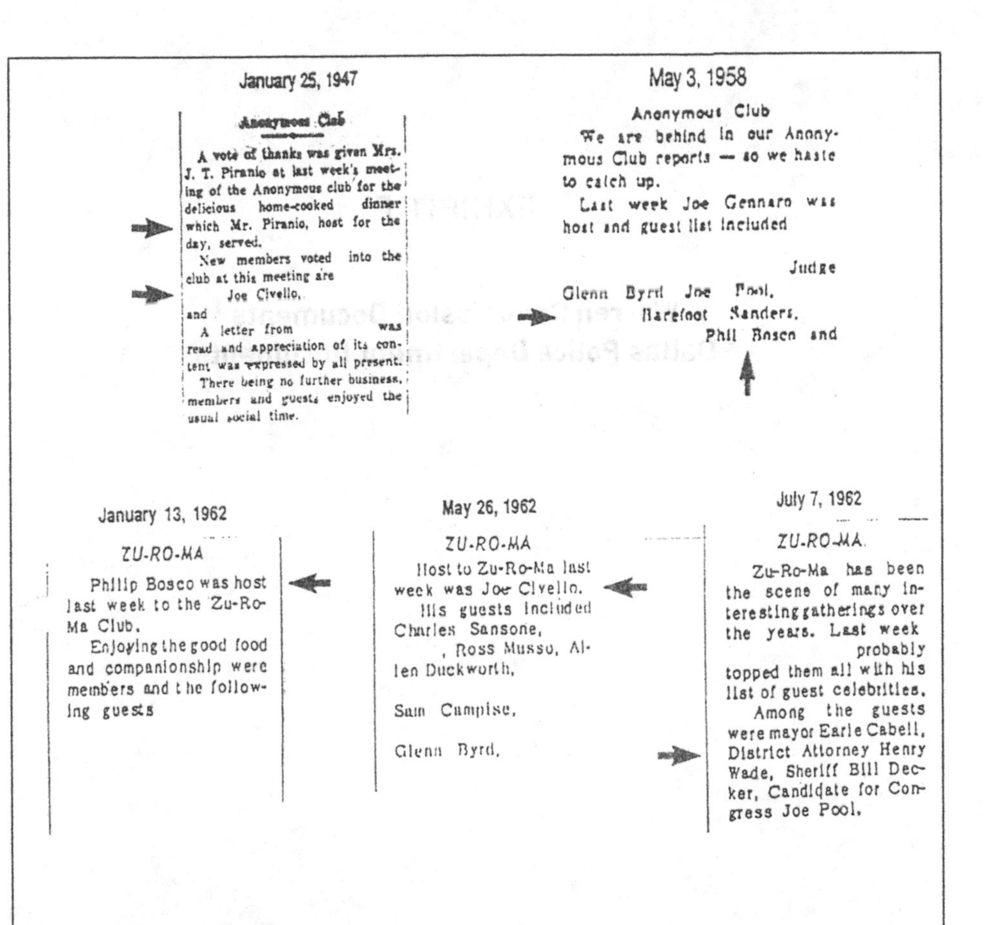

January 25, 1947

Anonymous Club

A vote of thanks was given Mrs. J. T. Piranio at last week's meeting of the Anonymous club for the delicious home-cooked dinner which Mr. Piranio, host for the day, served.

New members voted into the club at this meeting are Joe Civello, and

A letter from was read and appreciation of its content was expressed by all present.

There being no further business, members and guests enjoyed the usual social time.

May 3, 1958

Anonymous Club

We are behind in our Anonymous Club reports — so we haste to catch up.

Last week Joe Gennaro was host and guest list included

Judge Glenn Byrd Joe Pool, Barefoot Sanders, Phil Bosco and

January 13, 1962

ZU-RO-MA

Philip Bosco was host last week to the Zu-Ro-Ma Club.

Enjoying the good food and companionship were members and the following guests

May 26, 1962

ZU-RO-MA

Host to Zu-Ro-Ma last week was Joe Civello.

His guests included Charles Sansone, , Ross Musso, Allen Duckworth,

Sam Campise,

Glenn Byrd,

July 7, 1962

ZU-RO-MA.

Zu-Ro-Ma has been the scene of many interesting gatherings over the years. Last week probably topped them all with his list of guest celebrities.

Among the guests were mayor Earle Cabell, District Attorney Henry Wade, Sheriff Bill Decker, Candidate for Congress Joe Pool.

Dallas-based Italian-American social club, the Anonymous Club met every Thursday evening at a private house on northwest side of city. Membership included Dallas Mob boss Joe Civello. Predecessor Joe Piranio was evidently a member from the 1920's until his death in 1956. Club name was changed to Zu Roma Club in 1958, after Civello's arrest at national Mob summit meeting (Apalachin) in New York. Why Civello and Piranio were allowed to become members remains unknown. Weekly guest list was published in locally circulated *Texas Tribune*, an Italian-American news letter. Names of guests which bear no relevance to the subject of this book have been deleted for privacy considerations.

EXHIBIT F

Warren Commission Documents
Dallas Police Department Documents

Commission Exhibit No. 1754

UNITED STATES DEPARTMENT OF JUSTICE

FEDERAL BUREAU OF INVESTIGATION

In Reply, Please Refer to
File No.

WASHINGTON 25, D. C.

June 10, 1964

JACK L. RUBY
LEE HARVEY OSWALD - VICTIM

ISADORE MAX MILLER, Also
Known As Isadore "Izzy" Miller

INFORMATION CONCERNING

An investigation of Isadore Max Miller was instituted to ascertain if his gambling activities were in violation of Federal antigambling statutes.

It was determined that for the past several years Miller has operated as a bookmaker in the Dallas, Texas, area. In his gambling activities he is closely associated with known Dallas, Texas, bookmakers John Eli Stone, Henry Clinton Winfrey and James Woodrow Stone, brother of Eli Stone. These individuals use various apartments in Dallas as bookmaking headquarters and frequently change their base of operations. In most instances the apartments are rented and telephone service acquired under assumed names.

No violation of Federal statutes was developed and no prosecution resulted in connection with this investigation of Miller.

Jack Ruby's name does not appear in this file and he was not connected in any way in this investigation.

COMMISSION EXHIBIT NO. 1754

The Stone prosecution "disappears." In collusion with LBJ, FBI director Hoover simply denied the existence of the case via Ruby's confidant, Isadore Miller, co-defendant to Stone. The public never learned that RFK's Organized Crime Task Force had Miller's gambling front (The Enquire Shine and Press Shop, located two doors down from Ruby's Carousel Club) under investigation from late 1961 onward. Ruby acted as a low level bookmaker in the Stone-Miller operation. The Stone trial docket on the opposing page proves the prosecution was stopped after the JFK assassination until LBJ, Hoover, and the Warren Commission could sell the "lone nut" story to the American people.

CR-3-63-186.

CRIMINAL DOCKET
UNITED STATES DISTRICT COURT

D. C. Form No. 100 Rev.

TITLE OF CASE	ATTORNEYS
THE UNITED STATES	For U. S.:
vs.	Barefoot Sanders
JOHN EL STONE, JAMES WOODROW STONE and ISADORE MILLER	Donald M. Stone
	For Defendant: s Charles W. Tessmer Emmett Colvin, Jr. Suite 400, 706 Main St. Dallas, Texas
Failure to pay occupational tax; to register with Internal Revenue; to make excise tax return; use of wire communication in ICC in placing bets & wagers and conspiracy to conduct business without paying occupational tax.	

STATISTICAL RECORD	COSTS			DATE	NAME OR RECEIPT NO.	REC.	DISB.
				1964 9-24	E.C.Colvin	5 00	
J.S. 2 mailed 10-31-63	Clerk			9-28	Jas W.Stone	1000 00	
				9-29	57201 C.D. [illegible]		[illegible]
J.S. 3 mailed	Marshal			10-1	[illegible]		3000 00
						3000 00	3000 00
Violation	Docket fee			1965			
				4-19	I.Miller	5000 00	
Title 26 Sec. 7203 18 Sec. 1084 & 371				4-30	[illegible]		5000 00
Sec.							

DATE 1963	PROCEEDINGS
Oct. 21	Filed INDICTMENT. (Received from Wichita Falls Division)
Oct. 22	Issued WARRANT FOR ARREST of John El Stone & given to U.S. Marshal.
Nov. 12	Filed cby defendant, Isadore Miller, MOTION TO QUASH SEARCH WARRANT, FOR RETURN, and FOR SUPPRESSION OF EVIDENCE, AFFIDAVITS of Mrs. Lucretia Kennedy, Isadore Miller and Dave L. Miller.
Nov. 12	Filed by defendant, John El Stone, MOTION TO QUASH SEARCH WARRANT, FOR RETURN, and FOR SUPPRESSION OF EVIDENCE. Also AFFIDAVIT OF John El Stone.
Nov. 12	Filed by defendant, Isadore Miller, MOTION TO QUASH SEARCH WARRANT, FOR RETURN, and for SUPPRESSION OF EVIDENCE and AFFIDAVIT of Isadore Miller in support of motion to suppress.
Nov. 12	Filed by defendant, James Woodrow Stone, MOTION TO QUASH SEARCH WARRANT, FOR RETURN, and for SUPPRESSION OF EVIDENCE and AFFIDAVIT of James Woodrow Stone.

DATE 1964	PROCEEDINGS
May 27	Filed plaintiff's REPLY to defendants' motion to quash search warrant, for return of and for suppression of evidence. (Original to STH)
May 27	Filed plaintiff;s BRIEF in reply to defendants' brief on motion to suppress. (Original to STH)
May 28	Filed by defendant, John El Stone, supplemental motion to quash warrant, for return and for suppression of evidence.
May 28	Filed by defendant, James Woodrow Stone, supplemental motion to quash warrant, for return, and for suppression of evidence.
May 28	Filed by defendant, Isadore Miller, supplemental motion to quash warrant for return, and for suppression of evidence.
June 4	Filed RETURN ON SUBPOENAS TO TESTIFY executed on May 26, 1964 as to Robert M.Parrett by phoning Robert P.Gemberling, agent, tby mailing a copy to their office; as to Robert P.Gemberlin, by phone and by mailing a cop as to Hugh Amos by leaving a copy with Lt.Eric Kamisky; executed on May 27, 1964 as to Mrs. Lucretia Kennedy by personal service.
June 15	Filed ORDER denying defendants motion to quash search warrants. Motion to suppress evidence obtained through an electronic device is granted in that it is inadmissible at the trial of this cause. STH
June 18	Filed MOTION FOR CONTINUANCE to next term of court.
June 24	Filed RETURN ON SUBPOENA on behalf of U.S. executed on June 12, 1964 by serving Henry Clinton Winfrey in person.
Aug. 10	Filed OPINION re motion to suppress (copies mailed counsel by Judge Hu Office)
Sept. 8	Filed defendant's MOTION TO DISMISS counts 1 through 7, counts 15 and 16 and MEMORANDUM OF AUTHORITIES in support thereof. (Original and carbon of motion & brief to STH)
Sept. 8	Filed supplemental motion to dismiss adding additional ground & Brief. (Original and carbon to STH)
Sept. 14	Filed plaintiff's REPLY to defendant's motion to dismiss.
Sept. 14	Filed ORDER ~~granting~~, denying defendant's MOTION to dismiss counts 1 through 12 and counts 15 and 16. S
Sept. 14	Filed ORDER denying defendant's motion to dismiss additional ground counts 1 through 12 and counts 15 and 16. S
Sept. 14	Filed defendant's MOTION FOR CONTINUANCE.
Sept. 14	Filed ORDER denying defendants motion for continuance. S
Sept. 14	Filed Order continuing cause as to Isidore Miller only....STH
Sept. 16	Filed plaintiff's PETITION for a writ of habeas corpus ad testificandum, (Joe Henry Hodges, Jr.).

FD-302 (Rev. 1-25-60)

FEDERAL BUREAU OF INVESTIGATION

CD 84

Date November 27, 1963

1

BOBBY GENE MOORE, 865 43rd Street, Oakland, California, was interviewed at his home. He stated that he desired to furnish information regarding JACK RUBY, who he had known in Dallas, Texas. He stated that he had observed an interview on television with an associate of RUBY in which the associate said that RUBY had no gangster connections. MOORE furnished the following information:

He was raised in Dallas, Texas, having been born in that city on December 12, 1927. About 1951 or 1952, he was living at a rooming house at 1214 Ball Street, Dallas. This house was at the rear of Hill's Liquor Store at the corner of Ross Avenue and Ball Street. This liquor store was a front for a bookie-type operation where bets were taken on all types of athletic events and horse races. It was operated by a man named HILL, first name unknown, and his son. This gambling place was patronized by most of the gambling element in Dallas and RUBY was a frequent visitor. MOORE did not know whether or not RUBY was actually connected with the operation of the gambling place or was merely a participant.

During that time MOORE was employed by Cirello and LaMonte Italian Importing Company, 3400 Ross Avenue. MOORE suspected that his employers, JOSEPH CIRELLO and FRANK LA MONTE, were engaged in racket activities because on occasion they would not allow him to open certain cartons containing cheese imported from Italy, although that was his alleged job. It was his opinion, based on this, that they might be importing narcotics. He had no additional information to substantiate this. RUBY was also a frequent visitor and associate of CIRELLO and LA MONTE.

Two officers, CHARLIE SANSONE (PH), white, male, American, about 40, a detective in the Dallas Police Department, and MARVIN BLUNT, a Texas State Policeman, were regular patrons at Hill's Liquor Store and MOORE felt that they were obviously either aware of the gambling action if they were not actually involved.

Judge O'BRIEN, a Municipal Judge in Dallas, was a friend of CIRELLO and LA MONTE and MOORE frequently put hams and other food stuffs in O'BRIEN's car at their request.

on 11/26/63 at Oakland, California File # SF 44-494, DL 44-1639

by Special Agent DONALD F. HALLAHAN & ~~THOMAS G. [illegible]~~ 91 Date dictated 11/27/63

This document contains neither recommendations nor conclusions of the FBI. It is the property of the FBI and is loaned to your agency; it and its contents are not to be distributed outside your agency.

Commission Document No. 84

What LBJ and the Warren Commission knew. The above FBI document, generated just five days after the assassination, clearly tied Ruby to the Pearl Street Mafia and the *Stone* prosecution via Joe Civello and Philip Bosco. It became internal Commission Document. 84.

SF 44-[illegible]
DL 44-[illegible]

2

RUBY was also friendly with PHIL BOSCO, owner of the Gulf Service Station which was across the street from [illegible]'s Liquor Store, and MOORE felt that BOSCO was also engaged in criminal activities in Dallas, although he had no specific information to substantiate this.

In about [illegible], RUBY hired MOORE as a part-time piano player and he played periodically after hours at the Vegas Club from 1952 until 1956, when MOORE left Dallas and moved to California. While at the Vegas Club, he saw RUBY on numerous occasions with a revolver. RUBY was friendly for awhile with CANDY BARR, a well-known Dallas stripper. He is also well known to JIM JOHNSON, leader of a quartet who played at the Vegas Club regularly from 1955 until January, 1963, when MOORE last visited Dallas.

MOORE felt that from RUBY's association with (FNU) HILL, CIRELLO, LA MONTE, and PHIL BOSCO that he was connected with the underworld in Dallas.

MOORE had no information regarding any connection between RUBY and Dallas Police Officers. MOORE did not know OSWALD and knew of no connection between RUBY and OSWALD. He knew of no radical extremist views by RUBY or any racial extremist views. He had no information concerning RUBY being in California. He knew RUBY between approximately 1952 until 1956, when MOORE left Dallas and went to California. He saw RUBY again previously on a visit to Dallas in January, 1963. He had no additional factual information.

What they told the public. In order hide the Dallas Mob's culpability in the assassination (as well as Ruby's motive to kill Oswald), the Commission suppressed all but the first two paragraphs of Document 84, publishing it as CE1536. Treason by any measure.

2

LA 44-895

ABADIE advised that he had no knowledge as to RUBY's association with OSWALD. ABADIE was never in RUBY's Carousel Club or in any of his other clubs, pointing out that his social status and income did not incline him to be in places such as this. He stated that the only thing he knew about any background was hearsay to the effect that RUBY had come to Dallas from Detroit, Michigan, in 1934 or 1935; that he was related to the RUBINSTEINs, who were mixed up in the "poker crowd" and a part of the old "Purple Gang" in Detroit. ABADIE stated that he had heard this type information while a bellhop at the Wolverine in Detroit, Michigan, at about this time. ABADIE advised that he did not know who RUBY's parents were, did not know their names, or whether or not JOSEPH and FANNIE RUBINSTEIN were in fact part of the family described just previously by him.

He also stated that he knew of no associates of RUBY amongst the gamblers in Dallas or amongst the other racketeers. He stated that working in his warehouse, however, it was obvious that to operate gambling in the manner that he did, that he must have racketeering connections with other individuals in the City of Dallas, as well as Fort Worth, Texas. He also said that this opinion applied also to police connection with the two cities and that this had to be obvious in order to operate. While he was making book for RUBY's establishment, he did observe police officers in and out of the gambling establishment on occasion. He knew none of these officers and could not identify any.

During his employment with the two enterprises owned by JACK RUBY he observed nothing to indicate that RUBY had any subversive connections, any interest in the Fair Play for Cuba Committee, or any radical or extremist views, either communistic or views of the far right.

Because of his lack of closeness to RUBY, himself, he knew none of RUBY's close relatives, associates, or girl friends. He stated that RUBY's reputation in the working establishment was that he had no close friends, stayed completely to himself, and was interested solely and entirely in his businesses and in gambling.

4

LA 44-895

He advised that he had other guns as follows:

One was a .38 caliber snub-nose Smith & Wesson revolver, traded to an aircraft surplus dealer in San Antonio, Texas, in 1959. This individual has a wife who runs a motel and can be identified by the Piper Airplane dealers in Houston, CUMMINGS and GROVES, as there was a law suit between the two. In 1957 he had a .38 automatic, which was stolen while he lived at 106 Newhouse Street, Houston, Texas. Earlier than that his previous wife, BARBARA JEAN ABADIE, stole a .32 caliber Police Colt Special and gave it to some girl friend somewhere in the State of California.

ABADIE concluded by saying that he wanted to make it plain that he had never had any close association with RUBY, although RUBY had known his father, WILLIAM G. ABADIE, many years prior to the time of employment. Even this was never mentioned to him by RUBY. He advised that while he was employed by RUBY he received no impressions of extremism any place he worked on RUBY's part or on the part of anyone else, except that everyone in the shop and everyone he worked with were anti-integrationists in their views. He said they did not like Negroes; that he, himself, did not; that they would not allow Negroes to place bets and did not want to associate with them. ABADIE heard no views expressed indicating that anyone he worked with wanted to take any extremist action in support of their views.

The following descriptive data was obtained by personal observation and interview:

Name	WILLIAM B. ABADIE
Sex	Male
Race	White
Date of Birth	September 3, 1908
Place of Birth	Houston, Texas
Hair	Black with grey temples
Eyes	Brown
Height	5' 10½"
Weight	138 pounds

281

COMMISSION EXHIBIT No. 1750—Continued

3

LA 44-895

His particular impressions of RUBY were that he was a quiet, intense racketeer, gambler and hustler. He advised that he never saw him angry or appearing upset during the period of time that he was an employee. He appeared calm, not one to express his emotions; had the reputation amongst the workers of neither drinking nor being addicted to narcotics. His one outstanding characteristic, which was mentioned, was his own personal intense interest in gambling of any kind.

ABADIE advised that he had no gun in his possession; that to the best of his memory, which he said is extremely clouded because of his constant drinking, the last time that he had his 1941 Colt blue, single-action revolver was in February, 1960, when he hocked it in a Birmingham, Alabama, pawn shop, along with his watch. He could not recall the name of the pawn shop but stated that there are only three or four in the city; that they are all in one block and it was one of these. He stated that he had no gun at the time that he was employed by RUBY; that he had not sold him any gun, loaned him any gun, or, along with the previous information mentioned, had not even had any contacts with him of any kind.

As to his wife, Mrs. RUBY ABADIE, whose whereabouts is not known to him, ever having met RUBY in his, ABADIE's company, he maintained that this was absolutely not true. He said his wife was never around either of RUBY's establishments where he was employed and he at no time ever met RUBY out any place socially when his wife was present, or any other time. He further advised that Mrs. SHIRLEY GATLIN was a friend of both him and his wife, but that she had not been in Dallas during the time that he was employed by RUBY, which was the only time that he ever knew who RUBY was or had ever observed him any place. He advised, therefore, that it would have been impossible for the three of them to have ever run into RUBY in Dallas.

5

LA 44-895

Immediate Relatives	Wife: RUBY ABADIE, address unknown.
Education	High school, plus night school, Detroit University.
Profession	Instrument mechanic
Employment	October 14, 1963, to present: Scott Instrument Company, 3734 West Slauson, Los Angeles, California
Arrest Records	1930: Illegal possession of liquor; fined $100. at Wichita, Kansas.
	1932: Disturbing the peace; fined $10. at Wichita, Kansas.
	1960: Fraud; $25.00, Houston, Texas.
Peculiarities	Both hands crippled by arthritis.

In addition, at the time of the interview ABADIE described himself as an alcoholic and "bum," advising that he had been a constant alcoholic for the past ten years.

He advised that prior to going to work for Scott Instrument Company he was employed by the Salvation Army, San Bernardino, California, for five weeks, and in the hospital for three weeks, both San Bernardino.

282

COMMISSION EXHIBIT No. 1750—Continued

The Abadie Suppression. Like Document 84, the FBI's interview of Ruby employee William Abadie was sanitized by the Commission. Page one of the interview (following page) was deleted from CE1750 in order to hide Ruby's status as a Mob bookmaker at precisely the time when RFK's bookmaking investigation of Stone began, April 1963.

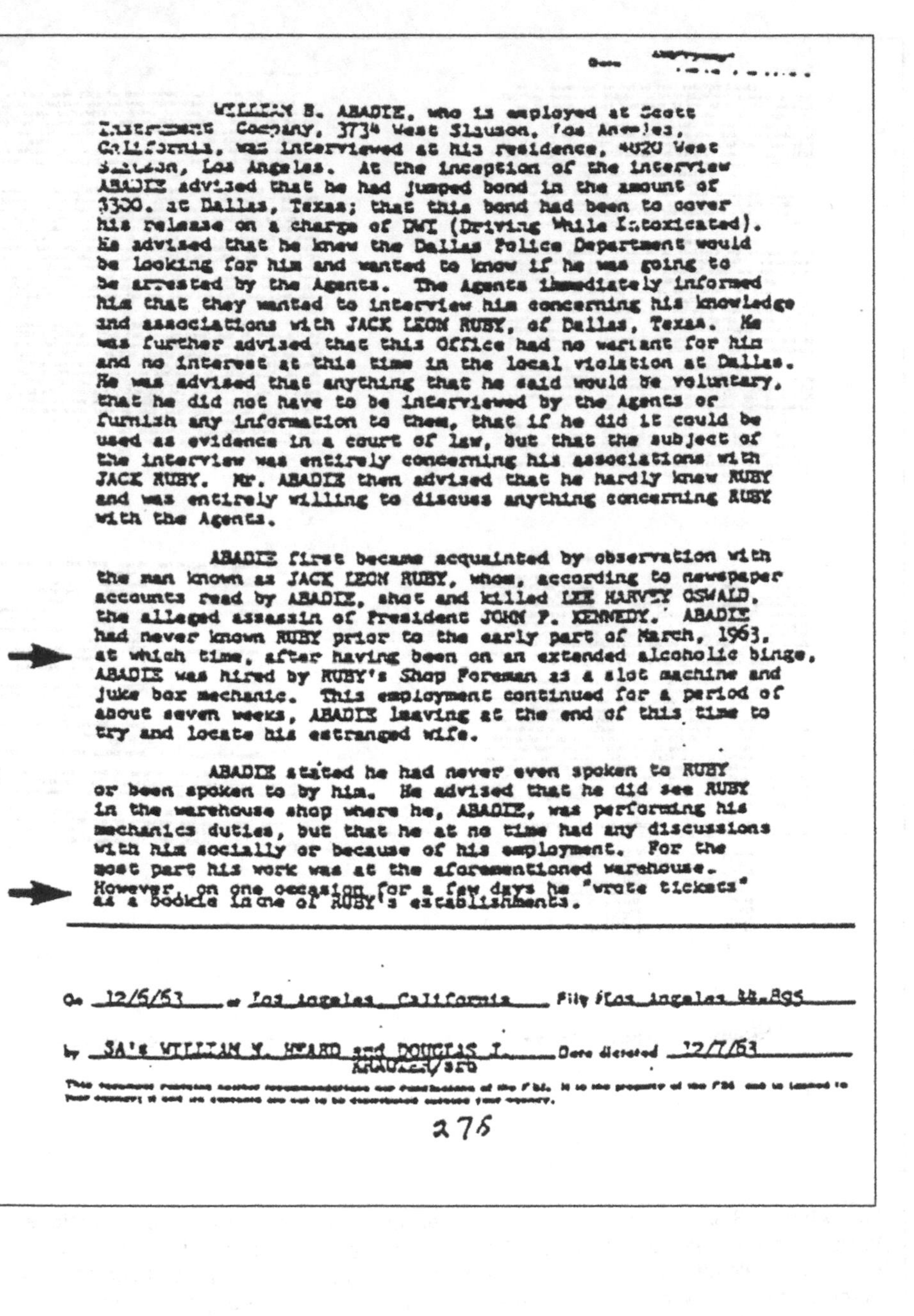

WILLIAM B. ABADIE, who is employed at Scott Instrument Company, 3734 West Slauson, Los Angeles, California, was interviewed at his residence, 4020 West Slauson, Los Angeles. At the inception of the interview ABADIE advised that he had jumped bond in the amount of $300. at Dallas, Texas; that this bond had been to cover his release on a charge of DWI (Driving While Intoxicated). He advised that he knew the Dallas Police Department would be looking for him and wanted to know if he was going to be arrested by the Agents. The Agents immediately informed him that they wanted to interview him concerning his knowledge and associations with JACK LEON RUBY, of Dallas, Texas. He was further advised that this Office had no warrant for him and no interest at this time in the local violation at Dallas. He was advised that anything that he said would be voluntary, that he did not have to be interviewed by the Agents or furnish any information to them, that if he did it could be used as evidence in a court of law, but that the subject of the interview was entirely concerning his associations with JACK RUBY. Mr. ABADIE then advised that he hardly knew RUBY and was entirely willing to discuss anything concerning RUBY with the Agents.

ABADIE first became acquainted by observation with the man known as JACK LEON RUBY, whom, according to newspaper accounts read by ABADIE, shot and killed LEE HARVEY OSWALD, the alleged assassin of President JOHN F. KENNEDY. ABADIE had never known RUBY prior to the early part of March, 1963, at which time, after having been on an extended alcoholic binge, ABADIE was hired by RUBY's Shop Foreman as a slot machine and juke box mechanic. This employment continued for a period of about seven weeks, ABADIE leaving at the end of this time to try and locate his estranged wife.

ABADIE stated he had never even spoken to RUBY or been spoken to by him. He advised that he did see RUBY in the warehouse shop where he, ABADIE, was performing his mechanics duties, but that he at no time had any discussions with him socially or because of his employment. For the most part his work was at the aforementioned warehouse. However, on one occasion for a few days he "wrote tickets" as a bookie in one of RUBY's establishments.

On 12/6/63 at Los Angeles, California File # Los Angeles 44-895

by SA's WILLIAM Y. HEARD and DOUGLAS I. ARRAUZ/srb Date dictated 12/7/63

This document contains neither recommendations nor conclusions of the FBI. It is the property of the FBI and is loaned to your agency; it and its contents are not to be distributed outside your agency.

276

FD-302 (Rev. 1-25-60) FEDERAL BUREAU OF I Commission Exhibit No. 1752

1

Date December 3, 1963

ROBERT DONALD LAWRENCE, was interviewed at his residence, 237 Lana Street, Apartment 1A, Las Vegas, telephone number 736-4785.

LAWRENCE was questioned concerning his knowledge of, and/or association with, JACK RUBY. LAWRENCE advised that he has not seen RUBY since he departed Dallas, Texas, approximately six or seven years ago. He advised that he was acquainted with RUBY in Dallas, when the latter owned and operated the "Vegas Club" in that city. He recalled RUBY as at one time the operator of the "Professional Club" in Dallas.

LAWRENCE related that he knew RUBY well, describing him as a "hot head" with a "short fuse."

He stated that he has no information that RUBY has been in the Las Vegas area recently and added that he has never seen RUBY in Las Vegas, Nevada.

LAWRENCE recalled that RUBY at one time operated a beer and wine establishment in Dallas, Texas. He further recalled that RUBY was always friendly with the police in Dallas. He mentioned that RUBY was a very excitable person and used to become heated in the midst of poker games when things did not go his way. He also advised that RUBY spoke like a high pressure salesman when in conversation with others. LAWRENCE related that he knew the following persons were friends and associates of RUBY in the Dallas, Texas area:

JOHNNY ROSS, liquor store owner;
"Chicken Louie," well known hood, deceased;
R. D. MATTHEWS, strong arm man;
CHARLEY TISH, employed Prime Rib Restaurant, Las Vegas;
ABE WEINSTEIN and BARNEY WEINSTEIN, brothers who operated the Colony Club and Theatre Lounge respectively.

LAWRENCE advised that he had never heard of LEE HARVEY OSWALD until his name appeared in the newspapers.

On 11/28/63 at Las Vegas, Nevada File # Las Vegas 44-48

by SAS FRANCIS J. SCHMIDT and JOSEPH A. MURRAY: JAM/nph Date dictated 11/28/63

This document contains neither recommendations nor conclusions of the FBI. It is the property of the FBI and is loaned to your agency; it and its contents are not to be distributed outside your agency.

198

"Friends and associates of Ruby." This December 3, 1963 FBI document, published by the Warren Commission, illustrates the lengths to which both would go to hide Ruby's Mob connections. "Johnny Ross" was actually John Ross Patrono, Dallas gambler and frequent guest of the Anonimo Club. His father, Ralph Patrono, was a Club member. "Chicken Louie" was in reality Louis Ferrantello, Mafia gambler. The real names of both were well known to the Dallas FBI and local law enforcement. Ferrantello took the "Fifth Amendment" over one hundred times when called before the Texas state legislature's "Little Kefauver" crime committee in 1951, was cited for contempt, and spent a year in jail.

DALLAS POLICE

PERMANENT PASS
Please Admit Party of 4 or Less
Extend Special Consideration to Same
Courtesy of CAROUSEL CLUB
Pass Good Only by Person Registered with management
Name JOHN M. GRIZZAFFI
Re: Glenn Byrd № 206
Bus. Address
Signed
CORNER OF FIELD & COMMERCE RI 7-2362
Valid any nite except Sat., Holidays & Special Occasions
This Pass Revokable, Discretion of Management

PERMANENT PASS
Please Admit Party of 4 or Less
Extend Special Consideration to Same
Courtesy of CAROUSEL CLUB
Pass Good Only by Person Registered with management
Name № 241
Bus. Address
Signed
CORNER OF FIELD & COMMERCE RI 7-2362
Valid any nite except Sat., Holidays & Special Occasions
This Pass Revokable, Discretion of Management

TO ALL PUBLIC OFFICIALS
To MR. JACK RUBY
4727 Homer Street, # 105
Signature
Kindly extend to the individual whose signature appears above, any and all assistance which may be properly given in keeping with your official duties and obligation
1957 1961
GLENN W. BYRD
JUSTICE OF THE PEACE, PRECINCT 1
DALLAS COUNTY, TEXAS
No. 1960

The "connected" Jack Ruby. Found among Ruby's possessions by Dallas PD and suppressed by the Warren Commission, the "Permanent Pass" cards prove association with the Pearl Street Mafia. The third card was used by Ruby to avoid arrest. All were evidently part of Commission Document 102. The National Archives has revealed that almost all of CD 102 was "missing...when received from the Commission." I found the the Grizzaffi and Byrd cards among police documents at the Texas State Archives.

INVESTIGATION OF ASSASSINATION
OF PRESIDENT JOHN F. KENNEDY
NOVEMBER 22, 1963

SUPPLEMENTAL REPORT

CD 107

could make a positive determination of what the object is. It was concluded, however, that the image seen does not depict the form of a person or persons and is possibly a stack of boxes later determined to have been in the room.

When Oswald was interviewed on November 23, 1963, regarding the photograph which portrays him holding a rifle and wearing a holstered pistol, he would not discuss the photograph without the advice of an attorney. He admitted that the head of the individual in the photograph could be his but suggested the possibility that the police had superimposed this part of the photograph over the body of someone else. However, Marina Oswald, when questioned regarding this photograph, stated that she had taken it. (Exhibit 9)

The FBI Laboratory has examined this photograph and has concluded that, while the rifle in the photograph is similar in appearance to the assassination weapon and while there are no apparent differences between them, there is insufficient detail to identify the rifle in the photograph as the assassination weapon.

C. Paper Bag

The FBI Laboratory examined the brown wrapping paper in the shape of a long bag which was found near the window from which the shots were fired. It was determined that the wrapping paper and the three-inch manila tape used to construct the bag were the same as that used by the Texas School Book Depository.

\- 4 -

FD-302 (Rev. 3-3-59) FEDERAL BUREAU OF INVESTIGATION

Date 11/30/63

NOV 30 1963

1

Lt. CARL DAY, Dallas Police Department, stated he found the brown paper bag shaped like a gun case near the scene of the shooting on the sixth floor of the Texas School Book Depository Building. He stated the manager, Mr. TRULY, saw this bag at the time it was taken into possession by Lt. DAY. TRULY, according to DAY, had not seen this bag before. No one else viewed it. TRULY furnished similar brown paper from the roll that was used in packing books by the Texas School Book Depository. This paper was examined by the FBI Laboratory and found not to be identical with the paper gun case found at the scene of the shooting. The Dallas police have not exhibited this to anyone else. It was immediately locked up by DAY, kept in his possession until it was turned over to FBI Agent DRAIN for transmittal to the Laboratory. It was examined by the Laboratory, returned to the Dallas Police Department November 24, 1963, locked up in the Crime Laboratory. This bag was returned to Agent DRAIN on November 26, 1963, and taken back to the FBI Laboratory.

Lt. DAY stated no one has identified this bag to the Dallas Police Department.

The framing of Lee Harvey Oswald. FBI Director J. Edgar Hoover's January 1964 "Supplemental Report" to the Warren Commission flatly concluded that the paper "gun case" used to connect Oswald to the assassination crime scene came from the School Book Depository, where he worked. But the Bureau's own internal report on the "FBI Laboratory's" findings, dated November 30, 1963, concluded the *opposite.*[3] Despite this obvious fraud, the Warren Commission (serving at President Johnson's pleasure) did not publicly challenge the Report, and continued to work closely with Hoover. Its own final report, in most respects simply echoed Hoover's original "conclusions" about the assassination. A few months after Hoover's Supp. Report, LBJ issued an executive order waiving Hoover's compulsory retirement, bypassing federal law.

Source Notes to Glossary

1. *Dallas Morning News*, July 16, 1928, I, p.7; July 28, 1928, I, p.1; November 16, 1957, I, p.1;*U.S. Bureau of Narcotics, Traffic In Opium and Other Dangerous Drugs, 1936 Report*, p.37; *U.S. Senate Committee on Government Operations, Organized Crime and Illicit Traffic In Narcotics, 1963-4*, Part 4, p.1098.
2. *Dallas Morning News*, January 9, 1937, II, p.1; April 3, 1937, II, p.1; *Dallas Journal*, January 9, 1937, I, p.1; April 2, 1937, I, p.1; *Dallas Times Herald*, January 9, 1937, I, p.10; U.S. v Smith, et al ; *U.S. Penitentiary-Leavenworth, Ks, imprisonment record card, Joseph Civello.*
   G. Robert Blakey and Richard N. Billings, *The Plot to Kill the President* (New York: Times Books, 1981), p.322; *Texas Tribune*, January 25, 1947, p.2.
3. *Texas Tribune*, April, 19, 1947, p.5; October 15, 1949, p.8; May15, 1954, See "Civello's" ad; June 2, 1956, p.2; October 12, 1957, p.8; *U.S. Senate Committee on Government Operations, Organized Crime and Illicit Traffic In Narcotics, 1963-4*, Part 4, p.1098.
4. *U.S. Bureau of Narcotics, Special Report, The Mafia*, June 14, 1950; *Papers of Waggoner Carr, Inventory of Donations, August 20, 1962*, p.2, "Special Reports;" *Dallas Morning News*, April 2, 1953, I, p.18; January 14, 1960, I, p.6.
5. *Dallas Morning News*, October 28, 1956, I, p.15; November 16, 1957, I, p.4; December 2, 1959, I, p.16:*Dallas Times Herald*, October 28, 1956, A, p.8; Blakey, *Plot to Kill the President*, p.314.
6. *Dallas Morning News*, October 25, 1950, III, p.1; February 21, 1953, III, p.1; March 13, 1959, I, p.14; March 14, 1959, III, p.9; March 25, 1959, I, p.1; May 22, 1959, I, p.1; *Dallas Times Herald*, May 22, 1959, C, p.21.
7. *Dallas Morning News*, December 19, 1959, I, p.1; January 14, 1960, I, p.6; *Houston Post*, March 23, 1960, I, p.1; *New York Times*, November 29, 1960, I, p.32.
8. *Dallas Morning News*, January 14, 1960, I, p.6; October 7, 1963, IV, p.1.
9. *Warren Commission Exhibits*, vol.22, p.303; vol.23, p.27; Blakey, *Plot to Kill the President*, p.314.
10. *Dallas Times Herald*, January 19, 1970, B, p.17., C, p.8.
11. *Texas Tribune*, May 22, 1954, p.2; June 18, 1960, p.1; December 22, 1962, p.1; *LBJ-Gennaro correspondence*, 1950's-60's.
    Texas tribune, May 15, 1954, p.3; July 17, 1954, p.2; See *Photo Inset, American-Italian Commitee for Johnson; LBJ-Presidential Daily Logs, August 3, 1964 and March 28, 1968*, See "Foreign language Press, Editors and Publishers;" *LBJ-Gennaro correspondence, 1964.*
12. *HSCA*, vol.9, p.517; *Texas Tribune*, July 23, 1955, p.2; May 18, 1957, p.1; *Warren Commission Hearings*, vol.2, pp.295-6, 323, 325-6. *Dallas Morning News*, August 19, 1993, A, p.32.

13. *Texas Tribune*, January 18, 1958, p.2; *Dallas Morning News*, October 29, 1953, I, p.9; *Houston Post*, April 20, 1975, I. p.1; *Dallas Morning News*, January 9, 1937, II, p.1; January 10, 1937, IV, p.1; April 3, 1937, II, p.1; U.S. v. Smith, et al.
Dallas Morning News, October 29, 1953, I, p.9; *Houston Post*, April 20, 1975, I. p.1; *TexasTribune*, September 20, 27, 1947, p.2; October 4, 1947, p.2; December 13, 20, 1947, p.2; May 29, 1954, p.2; January 18, 1958 p.2; *Death certificate of Frank Ianni, Texas Bureau of Health, Bureau of Vital Statistics, #1272.*

14. *Houston Post*, April 20, 1975, I p.1; See *Appendix- Anonimo Club Guests, Italian-Americans, Joe Ianni;* See *Photo Inset,, American-Italian Committee for Johnson.*
HSCA, vol.9, pp.989, 1009-10; *Texas Tribune*, November 2, 1946, p.2; September 13, 1947, p.2, See Campisi-Ianni photo; *Calvary Hill Cemetary (Catholic Arch Diocese), Dallas, Tx.*, Joe Ianni, date of burial June 1, 1973.

15. *Texas Tribune*, February 21, 1957, p.5; U.S. v. Smith, et al, See Praecipe For Subpoena, Ross Musso; *Dallas Morning News*, November 16, 1957, I, p.4; February 1, 1975, See "Deaths, Ross Musso;" *Worley's City Directory-Dallas*, 1937, 1959, 1970, 1975; *La Tribuna Italiana*, June 1, 1940, p.2.

16. See *Appendix-Anonimo Club Guests, Italian-Americans, J.R. Patrono, Ralph Patrono; Warren Commission Exhibits*, vol.23, pp.356-7, 362; *HSCA*, vol.9, pp.382-3, 419; *Texas Tribune*, January 23, 1943, p.2

17. *Dallas Morning News*, February 22, 1930, I, p.14; November 17, 1953, III, p.1; May 3, 1957, III, pp.5,13; May 4, 1957, III, p.14; *Worley's City Directory-Dallas*, 1930-2, !941-6, See "Angelo Piranio;" *Texas Tribune*, July 29, 1944, p.2; August 3, 1946, p.2; *Dallas Times Herald*, May 3, 1957, D, p.7.

SOURCE NOTES

AAS Austin American Statesman
CT Chicago Tribune
DJ Dallas Journal
DMN Dallas Morning News
DTH Dallas Times Herald
HP Houston Post
HSCA U.S. House Select Committee on Assassinations
LTI La Tribuna Italiana
MFCD Morrison & Fornys City Directory
NOTP New Orleans Times Picayune
NYT New York Times
PCD Polks City Directory
TA Texas Almanac
TBJ Texas Bar Journal
TT Texas Tribune
WC Warren Commission
WCD Worley City Directory
WP Washington Post

To avoid excessive footnoting, in some instances sources have been grouped under one citation at the end of a given paragraph.

Chapter 1

1. G. Robert Blakey, *The Plot to Kill the President* (Times Books, 1981), preface xiv.
2. Hearings before the Select Committee on Assassinations of the U.S. House of Representatives, 95th Congress, 2nd Session (Hearings and Report).
3. *U.S. v. John Eli Stone, et al.*, CR–3-63-186, U.S. District Court, Northern District of Texas–Dallas; MISUR recordings (Enquire Shine and Press shop, pay telephones, Dallas area, 1963); June 9 and 15, 1964, proceedings docket, ruling of Judge Sarah Hughes, granting defense motion to suppress evidence obtained through an electronic device. Dallas FBI file, Isadore Miller 162-96, section 3, July 1, 1963, AIRTEL, Dallas SAC to Hoover, re John Eli Stone, et al.
4. Dallas FBI file, Philip Bosco DL 182-14, section 1, Nov. 27, 1961 AIRTEL Dallas SAC to Hoover, CID summary.

Chapter 2

1. DMN, Aug. 28, 1948, II, p. 2.
2. U.S. Bureau of Narcotics, Special Report, The Mafia, June 14, 1950; LTI, Aug. 22, 1925, p. 3; LTI, March 13, 1926, p. 2; LTI, June 24, 1939, p. 6; TT, Nov. 13, 1943, p. 2; TT, Oct. 12, 1946, p. 1; TT, Jan. 25, 1947, p. 2; TT, Sept. 14, 1957, p. 1; LBJ Library, Senate corr. Johnson to Peter Tamburo, Nov. 24, 1948, Dec. 2, 1948, June 10, 1953, June 23, 1953, Nov. 12, 1953, Nov. 13, 1953, March 9, 1961, March 13, 1961.
3. TT, June 21, 1941, p. 2; DMN, June 22, 1941, II, p. 1; June 27, 1941, I, p. 7; Sept. 28, 1948, I, p. 6. Only source for TT is Center for American History, LBJ Library complex, Austin, TX. TT issues corresponding to LBJ campaign ads and swings through Dallas are missing.
4. DMN, Aug. 30,1948, I, p. 1; II, p. 2; Aug. 31, I, p. 1; Sept. 1, I, p. 1; II, p. 2; Sept. 2, I, p. 1; II, p. 2; Sept. 3, I, p. 1; Sept. 4, I, p. 1; Sept. 5, I, p. 1; Sept. 6, I, p. 1; II, p. 2; Sept. 7, I, p. 1; Sept. 8, II, p. 2; Sept. 13, I, p. 1; II, p. 2; Sept. 14, I, p. 1; Sept. 17, I. p. 1; Sept. 18, I, p. 1; Sept. 19, V, p. 2; Sept. 21, I, p. 1; II, p. 2; Sept. 22, I, p. 1; Sept. 23, I, p. 1; II, p. 2; Sept. 25, I, p. 1; Sept. 26, I, p. 1; Sept. 28, I, pp. 1 and 19, Sept. 29, I, p. 1; Sept. 30, I, p. 1; Oct. 1, I, p. 1; Oct. 3, I, p. 1; Oct. 5, I, p. 1; Oct. 6, I, p.1; Oct. 7, II, p. 2; Oct. 7, I, p. 3; Oct. 13, I, pp. 1 and 6; Oct. 14, II, p. 2; Oct. 15, I, pp. 1 and 13; II, p. 2; Oct. 16, II, p. 2; Oct. 17, IV, p. 2; Oct. 18, I, p. 1; Oct. 20, I, p. 20; II, p. 2; Oct. 22, I, p. 1; II, p. 2; Oct. 23, II, p. 2; Oct. 25, I, p. 15; Oct. 26, I, p. 4; Oct. 27, II, p. 2; Oct. 29, I, pp. 1 and 9; Oct. 30, I, p. 7; Oct. 31, I, p. 1; V, p. 11; Nov. 1, I, p. 1; II, p. 10; Nov. 2, II, p. 2; Nov. 3, I, p. 1; Nov. 4, 1948, I, p. 10; TT, Oct. 16, 1948; Oct. 23, 1948, G.O.P. Invades Texas Politics; Nov. 6, 1948, "Election Upset Gives Victory To Truman, Barkley and Johnson." DMN, Sept. 3, 1948, II, p. 2; Sept. 11, I, p. 1; Sept.24, 1948, I, p. 1. Richard G. Powers, *Secrecy and Power: The Life of J. Edgar Hoover* (NY: MacMillon, 1987), p. 394.
5. Mark North, *Act of Treason: The Role of J. Edgar Hoover in the Assassination of President Kennedy* (NY: Carroll & Graf, 1991), pp. 23–24; Powers, *Secrecy and Power*, pp.398–9; DMN, June 13, 1951, I, p. 11; generally, Johnson-Hoover letters.
6. DMN, Sept. 11 and 17, 1948, I, p. 1; DMN, Sept. 17, I, p. 12; Sept. 20, I, p. 1; Sept. 22,

I, p. 3; Sept. 24, 1948, I, p. 3; Oct. 28 and 30, 1948, I, p. 1

7. DMN, Sept. 8, 1948, I, p. 1; Sept. 10, 1948, II, p. 3; DMN, Sept. 12, I, pp. 1 and 13; Sept. 14, I, p.6; Sept. 17, 1948, I, p. 12; TA, 1958-59, p. 455; LBJ Library, Johnson to Clark, Nov. 5, 1957, corr. files; DMN, Feb. 17, 1944, II, p. 7; LTI, Oct. 7, 1939, p. 2; Robert Ferrell, ed., *Off the Record: The Private Papers of Harry S. Truman* (NY: Harper & Row, 1980),p. 37; DMN, June 14 and 29, 1945, I, p. 1; July 1, II, p. 1; July 14, 1945, I, p. 5; Oct. 11, I, p. 1; Oct. 12, 1945, II, p. 7; Dec. 9, I, p. 14; Dec. 25, 1945, I, p. 1; April 1,1946, II, p. 1; May 16, 1946, II, p. 13; Oct. 27, 1946, I, p. 10; June 6, 1947, I, pp. 1 and 20; TT, Oct. 6, 1945, p. 2; CT, Aug. 14, I, p. 9; Aug. 15, 1947, I, p. 21; DMN, Mar. 3, I, p. 17; Cong. Rec., Aug. 18, 1949, p. 11704; *Chicago Tribune*, Aug. 16, 1947, I, p. 10; G. Robert Blakey and Richard N. Billings, *The Plot to Kill the President* (NY: Times Books, 1981), p. 249; Congressional Record, August 18, 1949, pp. 11703-704 and 11720; DMN, July,29, 1949, I, p. 1.
8. Cong. Rec., Feb. 27, 1951, p. 1574–5; Truman Proc. 3000.
9. DMN, Nov. 11, 1952, I, p. 1; Jan. 3, 1953, I, p. 1; Oct 29, 1953, I, p. 9; Nov. 17, 1953, III, p. 1; Nov. 25, 1953, II, p. 3; April 29, 1954, III, p. 14; Sept. 30, 1954, I, p. 14; April 22, 1955, I, p. 1; Jan. 10, 1958, I, p. 4; Author's files, Dallas INS letter to author, Sept. 3, 1996.
10. TT, Aug. 31, 1957, p. 1; TT, Sept. 7, 1957, p. 1; Aug. 27, 1960, p. 2, LBJ U.S. Sen., Master File Index, Box 164, "Sca.- Scha. 236." LBJ Library, Austin, TX, LBJ U.S. Sen., Master File Index, Boxes 62 and 67, Gau.- Gen. 95, Savalli; DMN, July 15, 1970, D3, D4; TT, Nov. 19, 1955, p. 1; Congressional Record, April 15, 1954, p. 5238; DMN, March 10, 1963, I, p. 27; TT, Oct. 4, 1958; TBJ, May 1963, p. 434; Joe Bonds v. State, 161 Tex. Crim., p. 660, May 4, 1955.
11. Ibid. DMN, Jan.10, 1958, I, p. 4; July 15, 1970, D3, D4.
12. Author's files, letter from UT-Austin office of the Registrar, 1/14/11; UT Austin Bulletin, 1933–34, Student Directory; U.S. Census, Texas, 1880-1920, Soundex Index Cards for Pattillo surname and variations; Emidio De Felice, *Nomi E Cultura* (Sarin, Societa servizi Ausiliari E Ricera Informatica P.A., Pomezia, 1987), pp. 58, 76–7, 272, 280; Joseph G. Fucilla, *Our Italian Surnames* (Balt., Md: Genealogical Pub., Inc., 1987), p. 49; Andrew F. Rolle, *The Immi-*

grant Upraised (Norman, OK: Univ. of OK Press, 1968), p. 260; Ruth Montgomery, *Mrs. LBJ*, p.8; David Dobson, *Directory of Scots in the Carolinas*, 1680-1830 (Balt., Md: Genealogical Pub., Inc., 1986), p. 260; George F. Black, *The Surnames of Scotland* (NY: The NY Pub. Library, 1962), p. 649; Barri Blackwell and David Mattingly, *An Atlas of Roman Britain* (Camb., Mass.: Basil Blackwell, Inc., 1990), pp. 64, 74 and 76; Tenth Census of the United States, Alabama, 1880, Autauga County, ED No. 5, p. 105; LBJ Presidential Library, Austin, TX, *Mrs. Johnsons Family*, Taylor Genealogy; Joseph G. Fucilla, *Our Italian Surnames*, p. 210; Marie Smith, *The President's Lady* (NY: Random House, 1964), pp. 31-32; Ruth Montgomery, *Mrs. LBJ* (NY: Holt, Rinehart & Winston, 1964), pp. 8-9; *One on One* (w/Judy Maggio) ABC-Austin, May 22. 1996; LBJ, PBS miniseries, Sept. 30, 1991, Oct. 1, 1991; *20/20* ABC TV, Claudia Johnson interview, March 24, 1995.

13. TT, Aug. 18, 1956, p. 1; TT April 6, 1957, p. 1; TT, Sept. 7, 1957, p. 1.
14. LBJ Library, LBJ-Hoover, LBJ-Carr corr. 1959–1960.
15. Texas State Bar Assoc., Austin, Texas, Sarah Hughes file, Bio. Data-Sarah T. Hughes; *Who's Who in the South and Southwest* (Chicago: Marquis-Who's Who, Inc., 1963), Hughes, Sarah T.; DMN, May 10, 1946, II, p. 1; LTI, Mar. 2, 1935, p. 2; June 24, 1939, VII, p. 5; TT, June 29, 1946, p. 2; TT, Feb. 17, 1945, p. 3; TT, April, 27, 1946, p. 2; TT, Aug. 14, 1943, p. 2; DMN, Aug. 1, 1943, I, p. 1; Aug. 2, 1943, II, p. 1; DMN, Aug. 3, 1943, II, p. 1; DMN, Aug. 7, 1943 I, p. 7; Aug. 8, I, p. 3; II, p. 1; Aug.10, II, p. 1; Aug. 11, II, p. 10; Aug. 12, II, p. 12; Aug. 18, II, p. 1; Aug. 26 and 28, 1943, II, p. 1; DMN, Aug. 7, 1943, I, p. 1; DMN, Aug. 13, 1943, I, p. 5; Aug. 14, 1943, I, p. 2; DMN, Aug. 17, 1943, I, p. 6; Aug. 21 and 22, 1943, II, p. 1; DMN, Aug. 26, I, p. 3; II, p. 1; Aug. 27 and 29, 1943, II, p. 1;Texas Bar Journal, Nov. 1943, p. 515; DMN, Sept. 17, 1943, II, p. 1; Authors files, May 7, 1994 letter; LBJ Library, Austin, TX, LBJ U.S. Sen., Box 443, Dallas, W; Box 453, Dallas, VWXYZ; Box 463, Dallas, W; Master File Index, Boxes 191, Waa-Wak; Box 192, Waa-Wak; Case & Project, 1953, W-Wak; Box 1180, Sv-Sz; Gen.File, 1954, Box 518, Dougherty; Case & Project, 1956, Box 1221; LBJA Selected Names, Box 35, Wa-Wh; Sen. Polit. Files, Johnson for Pres., 1959–'60;

Sen. Subject Files, Box 731, Sen., U.S. Leadership.

16. LBJ Library, Austin, TX, LBJ U.S. Sen., Box 443, Dallas, W; Box 453, Dallas, VWXYZ; Box 463, Dallas, W; Master File Index, Boxes 191, Waa-Wak; Box 192, Waa-Wak; Case & Project, 1953, W-Wak; Box 1180, Sv-Sz; Gen.File, 1954, Box 518, Dougherty; Case & Project, 1956, Box 1221; LBJA Selected Names, Box 35, Wa-Wh; Sen. Polit. Files, Johnson For Pres., 1959–1960; Sen. Subject Files, Box 731, Sen., U.S. Leadership.
17. Ibid.
18. Ibid. See LBJ-Wade corr., June 7, 1955.
19. Ibid. See Sept. 11, 1955 corr.
20. Ibid. Wade to LBJ, July 21, 1959.
21. Ibid. LBJ to Wade, June 22, 1960.
22. DMN, May 2, 1951, I, p. 10; DMN, June 19, 1951, I, p. 3; DMN, Dec.21, 1951, I, p. 17; DMN, May 22, 1952, I, p. 6.
23. DMN, Sept. 9, 1951, I, p. 7; HP, April 20, 1975, I.
24. TT, July 7, 1962, p. 3; June 28, 1958, p. 3; May 24, 1958, p. 2; Dec. 21, 1957, p. 3.
25. DMN, April 4, 1943, II, p. 1; July 9, 1944, II, p. 1; April 7, 1951, III, p. 1; Aug. 20, 1955, III, p. 1; Gambling file, Texas History floor, Dallas Pub. Lib. for Jan. 1951 media analysis of 1950 murders, incl. Russell. art.; DMN, Sept. 13, 1936, I, p. 1; June 19, 1940, II, p. 1; Jan. 2, 1941, II, p. 1; Nov. 30, 1949, III, p. 1; Feb. 11, 1950, I, p. 9; March 14, 1950, I, p. 1; Nov. 23, 1950, I, p. 1; Mar. 24, 1951, III, p. 1; Aug. 9 and 10, 1951, III, p. 1; May 1, 1952, III, p. 1; April 5, 1955, I, p. 1; Dec. 25, 1959, I, p. 5; DTH, Nov. 30, 1949, I, p. 1; Feb. 7,1951, "Bomb Blast Rocks West Dallas Grocery"; DMN Aug. 29, 1946, II, p. 1; Sept. 26, 1946, II, p. 1; Sept. 27, 1946, II, p. 6.; DMN, Feb. 15, 1947, II, p. 1; DMN Feb. 16, 1956, I, p. 1; DMN, Oct. 23, 1958, IV, p. 1.

Chapter 3

1. DMN, Nov. 26, 1960, IV, p. 3; NOTP, June 6, 1961, I, p. 1; Dallas FBI file, Philip Bosco DL 182-14, section 1, Nov. 27, 1961 AIRTEL Dallas SAC to Hoover, CID summary; DMN, Nov. 15, 1961, I, p. 1.
2. DMN, Nov. 25, 1951, IV, p. 1; DMN, June 30, 1950, I, p. 23; Dec. 23, 1951, I, p. 8;DMN , June 27, 1951, III, p. 3; Dec. 24, 1953, I, p. 3; Jan. 6, 1954, III, p. 1; DMN Feb. 11, 1954, III, p. 1; DMN Mar. 30, 1955, I. p. 12; DMN, Sep. 20, 1955, I, p. 12; DMN Dec. 8, 1955, I, p. 17; DMN, July 12, 1953, IV, p. 2; DMN, May 4, 1956, III,

p. 17; DMN, Jan. 1, 1961, III, p. 1; DMN, Oct. 23, 1958, IV, p. 1; DMN, Oct. 21, 1955 I, p. 1; Jan. 4, 1959, I, p. 3; May 31, 1955, III, p. 3; DMN Mar. 25, 1959, I, p. 2; DMN, May 9, 1962, IV, p. 1; DMN, July 12, 1956, III, p. 18; DMN, Dec. 16, 1938, II, p. 1; DMN, Dec. 6, 1955, I, p. 5; DTH, Aug.24, 1952, "Crackdown Boosts Illicit Drug Prices"; DTH, July 12, 1959, "Is Dallas Southwest Hub for Activities of Mafia?"; DMN Feb. 12, 1956, I, p. 1; DMN, June 7, 1960, IV, p. 1; DMN April 26,1954, III, p. 2; Annual Reports, Federal Bureau of Narcotics, 1951-63; DMN Feb. 26, 1956, I, p. 1; DMN Jan. 8, 1955, I, p. 8; Annual Reports, Dallas Police Dept, 1951-63,escalation in burglary and theft.

3. DMN, May 9, 1955, I, p. 1; DMN, Sept. 20, 1955, I, p. 12; LBJ Library, Austin, TX, U.S. Sen. Files, Master File Index, Johnson-Daniel corr., April 7, 1954, Sept. 22, 1954, Sept. 7 and 20, 1955, Oct. 6, 1955, Oct. 9, 1956, May 13, 1957, June 21,1957, Aug. 2, 1958, Sept. 1, 1958, March 21, 1960; July 16, 1955; DTH, Sept. 29, 1955, "Dallas Hearings Due Oct. 19-20 in Drug Probe"; Daniel Hearings, Part 6, pp. 2148-49; DMN, Sept. 2, 1955 I, p. 1; Sept. 24, III, p. 1; Sept. 27, III, p. 4; Sept. 29, I, p. 11; Oct. 3, 1955, II, p. 10; DTH, Oct. 10, 1955,"Top Mexicans Invited to Texas Drug Probe"; Daniel Hearings, Preliminary Report - The Illicit Narcotics Traffic, No. 1440, Jan. 23, 1956, p. 1.
4. Daniel Hearings, Part 7, p. 2359; Ibid., Part 1, pp.55, 79–83, 108, 130–31, 170–72, Part 6, p. 2145–6, Part 7, pp. 2401, 2403, 2455–60, 2631–33, 2673; Mafia: U.S. Treasury Dept-Bureau of Narcotics, ed. Sam Giancana (Harper Collins Pub., NY, 2007), pp. 755,750,726, 728; Stephen Schneider, *Iced: The Story of Organized Crime in Canada* (John Wiley and Sons, Canada, LTD, 2009), p. 230; Skyrock (France), Paul Mondoloni: Sponsor of the Shadows, 2004, 2009, see ref. to Mondoloni arrest in Texas, "early 1953"; Lamar Waldron, *Legacy of Secrecy: The Long Shadow of the JFK Assassination* (Counterpoint, 2008), p. 71, note 43.
5. DMN, Nov. 9, 1955, I, p. 17.
6. DMN, Jan. 8, 1955, I, p. 8; Feb. 12, 1956, I, p. 1; June 7, 1960, IV, p. 1; DTH, Feb. 25, 1954, "Police Chief Cites Narcotic Traffic"; DMN, April 26, 1954, III, p. 2.
7. DMN, Jan. 8, 1955, I, p. 8; Feb. 12, 1956, I, p. 1; June 7, 1960, IV, p. 1.
8. NOTP, Aug. 26, 1951, I, p. 10; U.S. v. Dick Smith, et al.; New Orleans States Item, Jan.

30, 1951, I, p. 1; DMN, Oct. 6, 1937, I, p. 1; Oct. 9, 1938, I, p. 12; HSCA, vol. 4, p. 498; vol. 9, pp. 194, 422; Cong. Record, Aug. 6, 1970, p. 27,751; LTI, July 4, E 1931. NOTP, Mar. 25, 1959, I, pp. 1 and 52.

9. See note 23, chapter 2; see LTI, TT, weekly Anonymous/ Zuroma Club guest lists, 1930–1962.
10. DMN, Jan. 27, 1939, II, p. 6; Aug. 11, 1940, *This Week Magazine*, p. 4; June 24, 1948, II, p. 3; Sept.11, V, p. 1; Sept. 12, 1949, I, p. 6; Nov. 1, 1953, *This Week Magazine*, p. 7; Feb. 8, I, p. 1; July 19, 1954, I, p. 12; Dec. 31,1956, I, p. 1; April 27, 1959, I, p. 10; July 16, I, p. 6; Oct. 8, I, p. 17; Oct. 29, I, p. 17; Oct. 30 and 31, 1959, I, p. 10; IV, p. 1; Oct. 24, 1960, I, p. 6; DMN, May 9, II, p. 3; Nov. 14, I, p. 17; Dec. 19, 1947, I, p. 20; Feb. 28, 1953, III, p .2; May 30 1954, III, p. 2; Oct. 28, 1955, III, p. 2; Jan. 25, 1957, III, p. 2; June 3, 1959, IV, p. 2. Re pro Hoover news stories: DMN, July 28, 1936, II, p. 2; April 19, I, p. 1; Sept. 9, 1937, II, p. 2; Jan. 12, 1940, II, p. 2; Jan. 15 and 16, I, p. 1; Jan. 16, 1940, II, p .6; Nov. 29, 1960, I, p. 6; March 21, 1942, I, p. 16; March 7, 1947, II, p. 2; March 27, I, pp. 1 and 13; Mar. 29, II, p. 1; April 30, II, p. 1; June 15, I, p. 1; Oct. 15, I, p. 4; Nov. 18, 1947, II, p. 2; May 27, 1948, II, p. 20; Jan. 2, 1949, I, p. 3; June 25, I, p. 3; July 4, 11, II, p. 2; Aug. 21, VI, p. 6; Oct. 14, III, p. 4; Oct. 25, III, p. 5; Nov. 27, V, p. 2; Dec. 1, III, p. 2; Dec. 5, III, p. 6; Dec. 15, 1949, I, p. 13; May 26, 1950, I, p. 2; June 9, I, p. 1; June 21, 1950,I, p. 2; Jan. 15, 1951, I, p. 2; April 9, I, p. 2; April 28, I, p. 2; July 12, III, p. 3; Aug. 30, I, p. 2; Oct. 21, I, p. 1; Oct. 22, III, p. 2; Dec. 14, 1951, III, p. 2; Mar. 4, 1952, I, p. 9; Mar. 7, III, p. 15; Mar. 25, II, p. 8; July 11, III, p. 2; Aug. 30, I, p. 1; Sept. 25, 1952, III, p. 2; Jan. 19, 1953, I, p. 1; Feb. 10 , I, p. 1; Mar. 6, III, p. 2; Mar. 30, I, p. 1; May 28, III, p. 2; July 30, I, p. 5; Nov. 18, I, pp. 1 and 8; Nov. 23, I, p. 3; Nov. 24, III, p. 2; Nov. 26, III, p. 2; Dec. 1, III, p. 2; Dec. 1, I, p. 6; Dec. 4,III, p. 2; Dec. 13, IV, p. 2; Dec. 22, 1953, I, p. 7; Feb. 8, 1954, I, p. 1; Feb.18, I, p. 8; Mar. 16, III, p. 2; April 8, I, p. 4; May 6, I, p. 1; May 12, III, p. 2; May 29, III, p. 2; July 15, I, p. 5; July 21, I, p. 4; Aug. 22, IV, p. 1; Aug. 24, I, p. 1; Sept. 11, I, p. 1; Sept. 14, III, p. 2; Sept. 23, I, p. 3; Nov. 20, 1954, II, p. 4; April 4, 1955, II, p. 12; May 1, I, p. 10; Sept. 27, III, p. 2; Nov. 23, I, p. 4; Nov. 25, I, p. 3; Dec. 5, 1955, I, p. 5; Jan.15, 1956, I, p. 10; Jan. 26, III, p. 2; Mar. 5, III, p. 2; April 11, I, p. 2; April

20, III, p. 2; May 5, III, p. 2; May 11, I, p. 3; June 11, I, p. 1; June 12, III, p. 2; July 18, I, p. 1; Aug. 13, I, p. 23; Nov. 14, 1956, I, p. 1; Jan. 5, 1957, III, p. 2; Jan. 5, I, p. 1; March 13, I, p. 2; March 14, III, p. 2; May 9, I, p. 3; June 4, I, p. 8; June 5, III, p. 1; June 20, I, p. 1; June 30, I, p. 14; Aug. 14, I, p. 1; Aug. 15, IV, p. 4; Aug. 27, I, p. 1; Sept. 28, I, p. 1; Oct. 1, I, p. 4; Nov. 18, 1957, II, p. 5; Feb. 14, 1958, I, p. 1; Mar. 9, I, p. 1; Mar. 21, I, p. 6; April 29, IV, p. 4; May 25, III, p. 2; June 7, IV, p. 13; Aug. 30, IV, p. 5; Oct. 28, I, p. 1; Nov. 24, 1958, IV, p. 1; Mar. 3, 1959, IV, p. 4; April 12, IV, p. 2; May 11, I, p. 1; May 12, IV, p. 4; Oct. 18, I, p. 2; Oct. 22, I, p. 18; Oct. 30, I, p. 6; Dec. 21, I, p. 24; Dec. 21, I, p. 10; Dec. 24, 1959, I, p. 2; Jan. 17, 1960, I, p. 3; Mar. 14, I, p. 4; April 2, I, p. 1; July 5, IV, p. 2; July 9, I, p. 9; Sept. 1, I, p. 13; Sept. 26, I, p. 8; Oct. 5, II, p. 10; Oct. 6, IV, p. 2; Oct. 21, 1960, IV, p. 5; DMN, Jan. 12, 1936, I, p. 1; Jan. 3, 1948, I, p. 1; Nov. 11, II, p. 4; Nov. 12, II, p. 16; Nov. 26, I, p. 21; Dec. 7, I, p. 22; Dec. 8, II, p. 8; Dec. 9, I, p. 26; Dec. 10, 1948, I, p. 13; March 7, 1949, I, p. 1; April 20, III, p. 2; Dec. 9, 1950, III, p. 2; Feb. 8, 1953, III, p. 2; Feb. 21, 1954, I, p. 1; Feb. 22, III, p. 1; Feb. 23, 1954, I, p. 1; Oct. 7, 1955, III, p. 2; Jan. 1, 2, 3, 4, 5, 8, 9 of 1957, I, p. 1; July 23, IV, p. 3; Nov. 26, 1957, I, p. 4; Nov. 24, 1958, IV, p. 1; Mar. 2, 1959, I, p. 2; Jan. 6, 1961, I, p. 10; Mar. 2, IV, p. 1; May 29,1962, I, p. 16; DMN, May 10, 1951, III, p. 2; May 15, 1953, III, p. 2; Jan. 25, 1955, III, p. 2; Feb. 8, 1955, III, p. 2; Jan. 14, 1956, III, p. 2; Feb. 7, III, p. 2; Feb. 12, III, p. 2; May 12, III, p. 2; May 24,III, p. 2; Nov. 23, III, p. 2; Dec. 6, 1956, III, p. 2; Aug. 30, IV, p. 2; July 10 and 28, 1957, III, p. 2; Sept. 25, IV, p. 4; Oct. 12, 1957, IV, p. 6; Jan. 16, 1958, III, p. 7; Feb. 6, 1958, IV, p. 5; Oct. 30, 1959, IV, p. 4; Nov. 14, 1959, IV, p. 2; DMN, Mar. 1, 1939, I, p. 1; July 18, 1947, I, p. 6; Nov. 25, 1949, I, p. 9; Dec. 4, 1951, "Decker Thanked by FBI Chief for Breaking Railroad Case"; April 26, 1954, III, p. 1; Oct.19, 1954, III, p. 1; Jan. 18, 1957, III, p. 1; NYT Nov. 14, 1954, p. 88; William Sullivan, *My Thirty Years in Hoover's FBI* (W.W. Norton & Co., NY, 1979, p. 80–82, 110–111.

11. See chapter 2, note 23.
12. DMN, May 16, 1961, I, p. 8, IV, p.1; DMN, April 27, 1960, IV, p. 1; DMN, June 17, 1960, I, p. 9.
13. LBJ Library, Johnson-Wade corr., Wade letter to LBJ, Sept., 27, 1961; Texas State Bar Assoc., Austin, Texas, Sarah Hughes file, Bio. Data-

Sarah T. Hughes; *Who's Who in the South and Southwest* (Chicago: Marquis-Who's Who, Inc., 1963), Hughes, Sarah T.; DMN, Aug. 19, 1948, I, p. 2; DMN, May 10, 1946, II, p. 1; LTI, Mar. 2, 1935, p. 2; June 24, 1939, VII, p. 5; TT, June 29, 1946, p. 2; TT, Feb. 17, 1945, p. 3; TT, April, 27, 1946, p. 2; TT, Aug. 14, 1943, p. 2; DMN, Aug. 1, 1943, I, p. 1; Aug. 2, 1943, II, p. 1.

14. LBJ Library, Johnson-Gennaro corr. (Savalli case);DMN Oct 29,1953 I, p. 9; DMN Nov. 17, 1953 III, p. 1; DMN Nov. 25, 1953, II, p. 3; Jan. 10, 1958, I, p. 4.
15. DMN, Mar. 27, 1941, II, p. 1; DMN, Dec. 3, 1950, V, p. 1; DMN, Feb. 11, I, p. 2; Feb. 16, 1959, I, p. 8; DMN, Sept. 10, 1959, IV, p. 1; DMN, June 17, 1950, III, p. 1; DMN Oct.18, 1951, III, pp. 1 and 14.
16. DMN, Sept. 9, 1951, I, p. 7; HP, April 20, 1975, I, p. 1; FBI HQ file, Joseph Ianni, vols. 1–3, June 29, 1959 report, arrest record, p. 3.
17. G. Robert Blakey, *The Plot to Kill the President* (NY: Times Books, 1981), pp. 188,287; U.S. v. John Eli Stone, et al., 1963.
18. Dallas FBI file, Joseph Ianni, DL92-192, vol. 1, July 14, 1961, p. 3.
19. U.S. v. John Eli Stone, et al., CR-3-63-186, U.S. District Ct, N. Dist of Texas–Dallas.
20. Hearings before the Permanent Subcommittee on Investigations of the Committee on Government Operations, U.S. Senate, 87th Cong., 1st sess. (Gambling and Organized Crime), part 1, p. 513; DMN, Nov. 26, 1960, IV, p. 3; July 9, 1962, IV, p.3; General Investigative Committee Report to the House of Representatives of the 57th Legislature of Texas, vol. II, 1961, p. 170; Hearings before the Committee on the Judiciary, U.S. Senate, 87th Cong., 1st sess. (The Attorney Generals Program To Curb Organized Crime and Racketeering), 1961, pp. 2 and 4; Ed Reid, *The Grim Reapers* (Chicago: Henry Regnery Co., 1969), p. 17; U.S. Treasury Dept., Bureau of Narcotics Traffic in Opium and Other Dangerous Drugs (Wash., D.C.: GPO, 1960), pp. 23–24.
21. *Life*, Jan. 25, 1960, p. 24 and 90; *Life*, Feb. 1, 1960, p. 59.
22. LTI and TT social columns (1940–'60s) for general travel activity of Civello; U.S. House Select Committee on Assassinations (HSCA), vol. 9, p. 71.

Chapter 4

1. DMN, Feb. 2, 1961, I, p. 1.
2. DMN, Dec. 19, 1960, III, p. 12; Cong. Qrtrly. Almanac (CQA), 87th Cong., 1st sess., 1961, vol. 17, p. 381.

3. CQA, 87th Cong., 1st sess., 1961, vol. 17, p. 382.
4. Ibid.
5. Ibid., p. 383.
6. Ibid.
7. Ibid.
8. CQA, 87th Congress, 1st sess., 1961, vol. 17, p. 383.
9. Ibid, p. 384.
10. Ibid.
11. NOTP, Mar. 17, 1961, I, p. 3.
12. NOTP, April 6, 1961, pp. 1–2; April 11, 1961; April 16, 1961, p. 1.
13. NOTP, April 6, 1961, p. 2.
14. NOTP, April 11, 1961, p. 1.
15. Ibid.
16. NOTP, April 12, 1961, I, p. 4.
17. NOTP, April 14, 1961, I, p. 12.
18. NOTP, April 13, 1961, I, p. 6.
19. NOTP, April 17, 1961, I, p. 22; April 22, I, p. 1; April 25, I, p. 6; April 26, I, p. 1; April 27, I, p. 1; April 28, I, p. 1; May 4, 1961, I, p. 1.
20. NOTP, May 4, 1961, I, p. 1.
21. NOTP, May 5, 1961, I, p. 1; May 6, II, p. 7; May 7, I, p. 1; May 8, I, p. 2; May 11, I, p. 3; June 3 and 6, 1961, I, p. 1.
22. NOTP, May 13, 20, 1961, I, p. 1.
23. NOTP, June 2, 1961, I, p. 1.
24. NOTP, June 4, 1961, I, p. 1.
25. NOTP, June 6, 1961, I, p. 1.
26. NOTP, Dec. 29, 1960, I, p. 1; NOTP, April 6, 1961, I, p. 16; NOTP, April 7, 1961, I, p. 4; July 11, 1961, I, p. 1.
27. NOTP, July 11, 1961, I, p. 1.
28. NOTP, June 8, 1961, I, p. 1.
29. Ibid.
30. Ibid; June 17, 1961, I, p. 7; June 22, 1961, I, p. 1.
31. NOTP, June 28, 1961, I, p. 1; June 29, 1961, I, p. 5; HP, June 28, 1961, I, p. 1; DMN, June 28, 1961, I, p. 3
32. Ibid.
33. NOTP, June 28, 1961, I, p. 1.
34. NOTP, July 12, 1961, I, p. 1.
35. NOTP, Aug. 22 and 27, 1961, I, p. 1.
36. NOTP, Aug. 25 and 30, 1961, I, p. 1.
37. Ibid.
38. Ibid.; Aug. 31, 1961, I, p. 1.
39. NOTP, Aug. 31, 1961, I, p. 1.
40. NOTP, Sept. 1, 1961, I, p. 1; Hearings, Gambling and Organized Crime, part 1, p. 509.
41. Ibid.
42. NOTP, Sept. 2, I, p. 3; Sept. 8, 1961, I, p. 1; Hearings, Gambling and Org. Crime, pt. 3, pp. 664–678.
43. Hearings before Subcommittee No. 5 of the Com. on the Judiciary, House of Reps., 87th Cong., 1st sess. (Leg. Rel. to Org. Crime) 1961, ser. no. 16, p. 23; DMN, May 18, 1961, I, p. 1.
44. Ibid.; DMN, Oct. 26, 1959, I, p. 1.
45. General Investigating Committee Report to the House of Reps. of the 57th Leg. of Texas, Jefferson

County Investigation, 1961, vol. II, pp. 13 and 18.
46. Ibid.
47. Ibid.
48. Ibid., p. 116.
49. Ibid., p. 148.
50. John Bainbridge, *The Super Americans* (NY: Doubleday & Co. Inc., 1961), pp. 263–64
51. See note 45, p. 149.
52. DMN April 7, 1960, IV, p. 1; DMN, Feb. 3, 1961, I, p. 1; Feb. 4, 1961, IV, p. 1; Feb. 11, 1961, II, p.4; Feb. 28, 1961, I, p. 10; May 15, 1961, I, p. 6; DMN July 21, 1961, IV, p. 3; DMN, Dec. 10, 1961, I p. 12; DMN Jan. 30, 1962, II, p. 6;
53. DMN, Feb. 3, 1961, I, p. 1; Feb. 4, 1961, IV, p. 1; Feb. 11, 1961, II, p. 4; Feb. 28, 1961, I, p. 10; May 15, 1961, I, p. 6.
54. DMN, May 20, 1961, IV, p. 2; Sept. 12, 1961, IV, p. 4.
55. NOTP, Sept. 14, 1961, I, p. 1.
56. Ibid.
57. DMN, Oct. 13, 1961, I, p. 4.
58. NOTP, Sept. 14, 1961, I, p. 8.
59. Ibid.
60. NOTP, Oct. 24, 1961, I, p. 4.
61. NOTP, Oct. 25, 1961, I, p. 14.
62. Ibid.
63. Ibid.
64. NOTP, Oct. 31, 1961, I, p. 1; Nov. 30, 1961, I, p. 1.
65. NOTP, Dec. 21, 1961, I, p. 3.
66. DMN, Jan. 2, 1962, I, p. 2.
67. U.S. Treasury Dept., Bureau of Narcotics, Traffic in Opium and Other Dangerous Drugs (Wash., D.C.: GPO, 1962), pp. 33.
68. Ibid., pp. 28–31.
69. Ibid., pp. 4 and 61.
70. Public statement of U.S. Attorney General Robert F. Kennedy, Jan. 1962.

Chapter 5

1. Arthur M. Schlesinger, Jr., *Robert Kennedy and His Times* (Boston: Houghton Mifflin Co., 1978), p. 203.
2. LBJ Library, Austin, TX, Harry McPherson, *A Political Edu tion*, 1972, p. 13.
3. DMN, April 20, 1956, I, p. 1; May 24, 1956, III, p.2; May 24, 1956, I, p. 1; Oct. 29, 1959, I, p. 4; Nov. 1, 1959, I, p. 15; Aug. 5, 1960, IV, p. 2.
4. DMN May 24, 1956, III, p. 2.
5. DMN, April 18, 1960, IV, p. 4; Arthur M. Schlesinger, Jr., *Robert Kennedy and His Times* (Boston: Houghton Mifflin Co., 1978), pp. 206–211.
6. Arthur M. Schlesinger, Jr., *Robert Kennedy and His Times*, pp. 51 and 56; Robert Blakey, *The Plot to Kill the President*, p. 86.
7. Hearings before the Committee on Intrst. and Foreign Commerce, U.S.

House of Reps., 87th Cong., 2nd Sess., (Gambling Devices), Jan. 16, 18 and 19, 1962, p. 10.
8. Ibid., pp. 22–23 and25.
9. Ibid., p. 11.
10. Ibid., p. 25; Prohibiting the Transportation of Gambling Devices in Interstate Commerce, U.S. Sen., 87th Cong., 1st sess., Report No. 645, July 27, 1961, p. 3.
11. Ibid.; Cong. Record, Senate, Mar. 28, 1962, p. 5208.
12. Ibid.
13. Ibid., DMN, Feb. 2, 1962, I, p. 2.
14. See note 11, p. 5210.
15. Report of the Committee on Government Operations, Perm. Subcommittee on Investigations U.S. Sen., 87th Cong., 2nd sess. (Gambling and Org. Crime), Mar. 28, 1962, pp. 9–12.
16. *Atlantic Monthly*, April 1962, p. 76.
17. Ibid.
18. *Life*, Jan. 26, 1962, p. 78.
19. Ibid., p. 87.
20. Prohibiting the Transportation of Gambling Devices in Intrst. Commerce, U.S. House of Reps., 87th Cong., 2nd sess., Rpt. No. 1828, June 15, 1962; DMN, Jan. 17, 1962, I, p. 2.
21. *Time*, Jan. 12, 1962, p. 15.
22. NOTP, Jan. 9, 1962, I, p. 15; Jan. 19, 1962, I, p. 23.
23. NOTP, Jan. 25, 1962, I, p. 22.
24. NOTP, March 17, 1962, I, p. 12.
25. NYT, March 13, 1962, p. 9.
26. DMN, March 16, 1962 II, p. 1; Mar. 23, II, p. 2; Mar. 29, II, p. 1; Mar. 30, II, p. 1; May 16, 1962, II, p. 1.
27. DMN, Mar. 10, 1962, II, p. 3; DMN, May 20, 1962, II, p. 1.
28. Official Report of House General Investigating Committee to the House of Reps. of the 58th Legislature of Texas, Part II, Basketball Investigation, 1963, p. 21.
29. Ibid., pp. 45–46.
30. See note 28, p. 55.
31. Ibid., p. 44.
32. Ibid.
33. See note 28, p. 55.
34. DMN, April 10, 1962, I, p. 8; *Life*, Jan. 26, 1962, p. 90.
35. See note 10, p. 337.
36. Ibid. p. 348.
37. *Life*, Jan. 26, 1962, p. 90.
38. DTH, Nov. 25, 1963, A, p. 34; DMN, Nov. 27, 1963, I, p. 4.
39. DMN, April 8, 1962, I, p. 9; April 19, I, p. 11; May 5, III, p. 6; May 6, I, p. 22; July 16, IV, p.1; July 19, 1962, IV, p. 1.
40. DMN, June 26, 1962, IV, p. 3; June 28, 1962, I, p. 12.
41. Center for American History, Austin, TX, Papers of Will Wilson, AG files, Wilson to Freeman, May 4, 1962. LBJ Library, LBJ/Sanders corr., Mar. 15, 1961; LBJ to Sanders, Dec.11, 1961; DMN, Mar. 30, 1962, I, pp. 6–7; DMN, May 13, 1962, I, p. 13; May 4, 1962, I, p. 10; May 23, 1962,

I, p. 1; June 8, 1962, I, p. 1; June 18, I, p. 12; July 13, I, p. 4; July 20, I, p. 1; Aug. 19, 1962, I, p. 15.
42. Ibid.
43. DMN Sept. 6, 1961, I, p. 6. "Attorney Emphasizes States Rights Theme"; LBJ Library, U.S. Senate Daily Diary, Aug.6, 1960, Sept. 17, 1960.
44. DMN Nov. 30, 1961, I, p. 10; DMN Dec. 12, 1961, I, p. 8; DTH, Nov. 30, 1961, B,p. 24; DTH Dec.12, 1961, B, p. 18; DMN, April 4, 1962 I, p. 4.
45. DTH, Jan. 7, 1962, "Wilson Sees Battle for Dem Nomination"; Jan. 17, 1962, "Wilson Sees John Connally as Agent of Vice President"; DMN, April 4, 1962, "Daniel Building Up Fortune While Serving, Wilson Says"; HP, Feb. 17, 1962, "Wilson Lists Changes He Will Seek if Elected."
46. DMN, May 25, 1962, I, p. 6; Papers of Will Wilson, Wilson to Freeman, May 4, 1962.
47. DMN Sept. 24, 1962, I, p. 9. "Wilson Ending Career on Note of Activity"; DTH, Sept. 3, 1962, "Wilson Planning to Practice Law."
48. Edward B. Claflin, Ed., *JFK Wants To Know: Memos from the President's Office 1961-63* (NY: William Morrow & Co, 1991), p. 174.
49. Ibid., p.175.
50. DMN, May 10, 1962, IV, p. 2; July 23, IV, p. 2; July 29, IV, p. 2; Aug. 10, 1962, IV, p. 2.
51. DMN, Aug. 9, 1962, IV, p. 4.
52. LBJ Library, LBJ to Sanders, April 4, 1962.
53. Congressional Record-House, June 29, 1962, p. 12310–11.
54. DMN, July 9, 1962, IV, p. 3.
55. Ibid.
56. Traffic in Opium and Other Dangerous Drugs (Wash., D.C.: GPO, 1963), pp. 25, 29–31, 35.
57. 57. NOTP, June 14, 1962, I, p. 21; June 15, I, p. 3; June 16, I, p. 1; June 28, 1962, I, p. 27.
58. 58. NOTP, June 16, 1962, I, p. 1.
59. NOTP, July 28, 1962, I, p. 6.
60. NOTP, May 8, 1962, I, p. 4; Aug. 6, 1962, I, p. 1.
61. NOTP, Aug. 6, 1962, I, p. 1.
62. Ibid.
63. Ibid., NOTP, Aug. 7, 1962, I, p. 31.
64. Annual Report of the Attorney General of the United States, 1962, p. 192.
65. NYT, July 31, 1962, p. 19.
66. NYT, July 10, 1961, p. 12.
67. NYT, Sept. 20, 1961, p. 6.
68. NYT, Jan. 13, 1961, p. 14; Sept. 13, p. 34; Sept. 22, p. 32; Sept. 28, p. 1; Nov. 1, 1961, p. 1; April
69. 23, 1962, p. 1; JFK Library, WHCN File, Box 2778, Albert Thomas.
70. NYT, July 21, 1962, I, p.1.
71. LBJ Library, V.P. Daily Diary, Aug. 9-13, 1962; AAS, Aug. 14, 1962, I, p.23.

Chapter 6

1. Texas Police Journal, (Dallas, TX) Feb. 1962, p. 1.
2. Hearings before the Perm. Subcommittee on Investigations of the Committee on Gov. Operations, U.S. Sen., 88th Cong., 1st sess. (Org. Crime and Illicit Traffic in Narcotics), part 2, pp. 525–527.
3. DMN, Aug. 20, 1962, I, p. 2.
4. Attorney General Will Wilson, Address to United Citizens for Law Enforcement, Inc., Beaumont, Texas, August 22, 1961 (Leg. Ref. Library, Austin, TX), pp. 4 and 10.
5. DMN, Sept. 8, 1961, I, p. 6; Attorney General Will Wilson, letter to U.S. Sen., Perm. Subcommittee on Investigations, Sept. 20, 1961 (Leg. Ref. Library, Austin, TX).
6. See note 2, part 1, p. 23.
7. Ibid., part 2, p.401, part 4, p. 783.
8. Part 4, p. 782.
9. Ibid., p. 990.
10. Ibid., p. 1047.
11. Ibid., p. 1098.
12. Ibid., p. 928.
13. Ibid.
14. See note 7, part 4, p. 919.
15. Ibid.
16. Ibid.
17. Ibid., p. 920.
18. Ibid., p. 937.
19. Ibid., p. 958.
20. Ibid., p. 955.
21. Ibid., pp. 912, 955, 979.
22. Ibid., pp. 879, 899, 907; Traffic in Opium, Dec.31, 1954, p. 18; Dec. 31, 1958.
23. Traffic in Opium, Dec. 31, 1960, p. 44; Dec. 31, 1961, p. 37.
24. See note 7, p. 782; Traffic in Opium, Dec. 31. 1961, p. 38.
25. Traffic in Opium, Dec. 31, 1962, p. 47.
26. NYT, June 26, 1962, pp. 25 and 65; Traffic in Opium, Dec. 31, 1962, p. 47.
27. Traffic in Opium, Dec. 31, 1962, p. 47.
28. NYT, July 11, 1962, p. 22; Traffic in Opium, Dec. 31, 1962, p. 47.
29. See note 7, p. 652; John L. McClellan, *Crime Without Punishment* (New York: Duell, Sloan and Pierce, 1962), p.119.
30. Ibid., p.1047.
31. See note 7, p.885, 889; Traffic in Opium, Dec.31, 1961, pp.29–30; Dec.31, 1962, pp. 25, 29, 30,
34. Traffic in Opium, Dec. 31, 1963, p.34.
32. Ibid.
33. Ibid., p. 888.
34. Traffic in Opium, Dec. 31, 1962, p.3.
35. Ibid., pp.9 and 21.
36. Ibid.
37. Hearings before the Permanent Subcommittee on Investigations of the Committee on Government Operations, U.S. Sen., 87th Cong., 1st sess., part 3, Sept. 7, 1961, p. 769.

Chapter 7

1. LBJ Library, Austin, TX, Master File Index, LBJ to Thornton, Aug. 17, 1962; TT, April 5, 1958, p. 1; LBJ Library, Mrs. Johnson's Schedule for Friday, Sept. 7, 1962, Johnson Middle East tour, Aug.–Sept. 1962.
2. TT, April 5, 1958, p. 1.
3. HSCA, Vol.9, pp. 335–336, 1099; TT Sept. 8, 1962; Dallas FBI file, Sam Campisi, Memo, October 29, 1966.
4. LBJ Library, Middle East tour file, Unclassified Telegram Outgoing, Embassy, Rome, (CODEL JOHNSON) Sept. 4, 1962. Ibid.; NYT, Sept. 5, 1962, p. 11; *Avanti* (Rome, Italy), Sept. 5, 1962, p. 2; Sept. 6, p. 2; Sept. 7, pp. 2 and 6; Sept. 8, 1962, p. 2.
6. NYT, Sept. 7, 1962, p. 3.
7. HP, Sept. 7, 1962, I, p. 10.
8. LBJ Middle East Tour, Johnson speech, Naples shipyard, Sept. 6, 1962.
9. NYT, Index, 1945, p.968; LBJ Library, House of Representatives Files, Box 158; DMN, May 15, 1945, II, p.3; NYT, Sept. 6, 1962, p. 7; LBJ Library, House of Representatives Files, Box 158.
10. See note 9, Box 158.
11. HP, Sept. 6, 1962, V, p. 14.
12. Hearings before the Permanent Subcommittee on Investigations of the Committee on Gov. Operations, U.S. Sen., 87th Cong., 1st sess. (Gambling and Org. Crime), part 2, p. 522; DMN, Sept. 3, 1961, I, p.2; NOTP, Sept. 3, 1961, I, p.7.
13. *San Antonio Express*, Sept. 6, 1962, 17-B.
14. LBJ Middle East Tour, (CODEL JOHNSON) Sept. 7, 1962, #4779.
15. Ibid., #5884.
16. LBJ Library, LBJ VP Daily Diary, Sept. 10-15, 1962; HP, Sept. 13, 1962, I, pp.1, 15; VI, p.1.
17. HP, Sept. 14, 1962, I, p.7.
18. Ibid.
19. Ibid.
20. HP, Sept. 13, 1962, VI, p.1.
21. AAS, Sept. 13, 1962, I, p.1.
22. LBJ Library, Vice president's Daily Diary
23. HP, Sept. 13, 1962, I, p.9.
24. *Washington Post*, Feb. 19, 1962, A7; LBJ Library, LBJ VP Public Statements, Box 70, Sept. 16 (Bonham) and 18 (Miami), 1962 speeches; Daily Diary, Sept. 18, 1962.
25. HSCA, Vol. 5, p.311; see note 28, *Grim Reapers*, pp. 158–9.
26. Ibid.
27. Ibid.
28. Ed Reid, *The Grim Reapers* (Chicago: Henry Regnery Co., 1969), pp. 158–9.
29. Ibid.
30. HSCA, Vol. 9, p. 80.
31. LBJ Library, VP Public Stmts., Box 70, Sept. 11, 1962; JFK Presidential Library, Boston, Mass., WHCN File, Box 2 7778, JFK/Thomas corr.
32. LBJ Library, Johnson-Wade corr., 1961 onward.

33. AAS, Aug. 10, 1962, p. 14; Aug. 11, 1962, p. 11; Sept. 14, 1962, I, p.27.
34. Ibid.
35. LBJ Library, VP Daily Diary, July 23, 1962.
36. DMN, Mar. 28, 1963, I, p.18.
37. LBJ Library, VP Daily Diary, Mar. 7, 1963; April 10, 1963, Diary Backup.
38. DMN, April 24, 1963, I, p. 10.
39. DMN, April 24, 1963, I, p. 1.
40. Ibid.
41. Ibid.; G. Robert Blakey and Richard N. Billings, *The Plot to Kill the President* (NY: Times Books, 1981), p. 357.
42. LBJ Library, Master File Index, LBJ to Sanders, April 25, April 27, May 6, 1963.
43. JFK Presidential Library, Boston, Mass., WHCN File, Box 2778, JFK/Thomas corr., Thomas to JFK, April 20, 1963, w/ attachment; DMN, April 13, 1963, I, p. 5.
44. DMN, June 27, 1963, IV, p. 4; WP, April 14, 1963, A5.

Chapter 8

1. Dallas FBI file, Herbert Miller to Lynum, re Stone, IRS.
2. Ibid.
3. Dallas FBI, weekly summary reports, Dallas SAC to Hoover re Stone, et al.
4. FBI Identification Division: 245-126, arrest record of John Eli Stone.
5. Dallas FBI files, Philip Bosco, Joe Ianni.
6. DMN, June 30, I, p. 21; July 3, 1963, IV, p. 1; *U.S. v. John Eli Stone, et al.*, CR - 3 - 63 - 186, U.S. Dist. Court, N. Dist. of TX–Dallas, Natl. Archives SW Region (Fort Worth, TX), Affidavit of SA Charles A. Bus, Jr., June 27, 1963, pp.3-4; Affidavit of SA (FBI) Robert P. Gemberling, June 27, 1963, pp.1–2; Affidavit for Search Warrant, SA Kenneth E. Slane, June 27, 1963 (#375), p. 2.
7. Ibid.
8. Ibid; Texas State Archives, Austin, TX, John F. Kennedy Assassination files, Texas Court of Inquiry, Dallas Police file, R-33, Izzy Miller–Dave Miller entry, R-38, 161 thru 165 Dave Miller, V-4, Gannaway to Curry, Jan. 15, 1964.
9. Warren Commission Exhibit 1755.
10. Dallas FBI file, Isadore Miller, 1963-4.
11. Ibid.
12. DMN, April 1, 1963, IV, p.5; April 2, 1963, II, p.6; Death Cert. of John G. Carcelli, #23607, Texas Bur. of Health, Bur. of Vital Stats.; Dallas FBI file John Carcelli.
13. Ibid.
14. Dallas FBI files, Isadore Miller, Joe Ianni, Philip Bosco, John R. Patrono, see informant reports.

15. See note 12.
16. DMN, April 23, 1963, I, p.8; DMN, March 31, 1963, I, p.27.
17. DMN, July 3, 1963, IV, p. 1; See note 6, Affidavit of SA Robert Gemberling, p. 2; Affidavit for Search Warrant, SA Kenneth E. Slane, June 27, 1963 (#372), p. 3; Search Warrants, (#s372 and 375), June 27, 1963; Affidavit of SA Slane, May 14, 1964; Warrant of Arrest, June 29, 1963, Isadore Miller, James W. Stone, John Eli Stone; Polks City Directory, Dallas, TX, 1960-63, See "John E. Stone."
18. Ibid.
19. Ibid.
20. Ibid.
21. Dallas FBI file Philip S. Bosco, 182-14, sect. 2, sub file 162-292, Interstate Gambling Activity; 92-625, serial 38. July 17, 1963 arrest, interview of Bosco.
22. Ibid.
23. *Saturday Evening Post*, Aug. 10 and 17, 1963, Dallas FBI file, Isadore Miller, Sept. 3, 1963. Hoover to Shanklin re AIRTEL of Aug. 26, 1963, p.2.
24. DOJ, FOIA request, author's files, Sanders to Miller, Sept. 6, 1963; DMN, Sept. 28, 1963, I, p. 16.
25. Ibid.

Chapter 9

1. DMN, Sept. 20, 1963, IV, p. 3.
2. G. Robert Blakey and Richard N. Billings, *The Plot to Kill the President* (NY: Times Books, 1981), pp. 235–236.
3. LBJ Library, VP papers, Master File Index, LBJ to Sanders, Sept. 20, 1963.
4. NYT, Sept. 27, 1963, p. 3.
5. Ibid.
6. JFK Library, WHCN File, Box 2778, JFK to Thomas, Sept. 23, 1963.
7. James Reston, Jr., *The Lone Star: The Life of John Connally* (NY: Harper & Row, 1989), p. 259.
8. DMN, March 10, 1968, C2.
9. Hearings before the Perm. Subcommittee on Investigations of the Comm. on Gov. Operations, U.S. Sen., (Org. Crime and Illicit Traffic in Narcotics), 88th Cong., 1st sess., Sept. 25, 1963.
10. Ibid., Part 1, p. 11.
11. Ibid., pp. 18-19.
12. Ibid., p. 20.
13. Ibid.
14. Ibid., p. 30.
15. Ibid., pp. 78, 134, 158.
16. Ibid., pp. 198, 281–282.
17. DMN, Oct. 7, 1963, IV, p. 1.
18. See note 9, Part 2, p. 339.
19. Ibid., p. 342.
20. See ch. 8, note 17.
21. See note 9, Part 2, p. 422.
22. Ibid., p. 263.

23. Traffic in Opium, Dec. 31, 1963, p. 40.
24. Ibid., pp. 42–43.
25. Ibid., pp. 633–634.
26. Ibid., p. 615.

Chapter 10

1. Jim Marrs, *Crossfire* (Caroll & Graf, Pub., NY, 1989), pp. 177–8.
2. DMN, Aug. 26, 1963, IV, p. 4.
3. DMN, Oct. 20, 1963, III, p. 2; DMN, Oct. 7, 1963, IV, p. 1.
4. DMN, Oct. 8, 1963, I, p. 8.
5. DMN, Sept. 28, 1963, IV, p. 6.
6. *Wichita Falls Times*, Oct. 1, 1963, p. 20A; Oct. 2, 1963, p. 10B; DMN, Oct. 1, 1963, I, p. 10.
7. *Wichita Falls Times*, Oct. 2, 1963, p. 10B.
8. *Wichita Falls Times*, Oct. 2, 1963, p. 10B.
9. Ibid.
10. Ibid.
11. DMN, Oct. 2, 1963, I, p. 5; DMN, Oct. 1, 1963, I, p. 10.
12. Ibid., DMN, Oct. 3, 1963, I, p. 7; *U.S. v. Edward V. Driscoll and Albert Meadows*, CR - 3 - 63 – 174 U.S. Dist. Court, N. Dist. of Texas–Dallas, Natl. Archives SW Region (Ft. Worth, TX), Crim. Court Docket sheet.
13. DMN, Oct. 22, 1963, I, p. 10; *Wichita Falls Times*, Oct. 21, p. 1A; Oct. 14, 1963, p. 16D.
14. *Wichita Falls Times*, Oct. 22, 1963, p. 16D.
15. Dallas PD, Letter to Chief Curry, Jan. 15, 1964, Ruby appt. with Dr. Ulivitch.
16. HSCA, vol. 4, p. 498; vol. 9, pp. 194 and 422; Cong. Record, Aug. 6, 1970, p. 27 and 751; Scheim, *Contract on America* (Argyle Press, Silver Spring, MD, 1983),p. 94; LTI, July 4, E, 1931.
17. *Wichita Falls Times*, Oct. 21, 1963, p.1A; Oct. 25, 1963, p. 4A; Note 63, Crim. Court Docket sheet; Govt.'s Reply to Defendants Motion to Quash Search Warrant, for Return of and for Suppression of Evidence, May 27, 1964; U.S. v. John Eli Stone, et al., CR - 3 - 63 - 186, U.S. Dist. Court, N. Dist. of Texas – Dallas, Natl. Archives SW Region (Fort Worth, Texas), Crim. Ct. Docket sheet.
18. NOTP, Oct. 12 and 13, 1962, I, p. 15.; Nov. 1, I, p. 1; Dec. 18, I, p. 12; Dec. 20, I, p. 1; Dec. 21, 1962, I, p. 25; Feb.12, 1963, I, p. 6; May 11 and 28, I, p. 1; Aug. 31, III, p. 5; Oct. 11, I, p. 13; Oct. 29, I, p. 8; Nov. 5, I, p. 10; Nov. 6, I, p. 11; Nov. 8, I, p. 1; Nov. 13, I, p. 10; Nov.14, I, p. 5; Nov. 15, III, p. 13; Nov. 20, 1963, I, p. 6.
19. NOTP, Oct. 22, 1963, I, p. 15; NOTP, Oct. 25, 1963, I, p. 6.
20. NOTP, Nov. 14, 1963, I, p. 5.

21. NOTP, Nov. 16, 1963, I, p. 2; Nov. 17, 1963, I, p. 1; Nov. 19,1963, I, p. 1.
22. NOTP, Nov. 21, 1963, I, p. 9.
23. Ibid.
24. Ibid.
25. DMN, Aug. 22, 1962, IV, p. 4; July 26, 1963, IV, p. 2; Aug.18, 1963, III, p. 2; Aug. 19, IV, p. 2; Aug. 20, IV, p. 2; Aug. 21, IV, p. 2; Aug. 22 and 23, IV, p. 2; Aug. 29, IV, p. 4; Sept. 2, III, p. 2; Sept. 3, IV, p. 2; Sept. 7, IV, p. 2; Sept. 9, IV, p. 4; Sept. 15, III, p. 2; Sept. 16, IV, p. 4; Sept. 19, IV, p. 4; Sept. 20, III, p. 4; IV, p. 2; Sept. 21, IV, p. 2; Sept. 23, IV, p. 4; Sept. 24, IV, p. 2; Sept. 27, IV, p. 2; Sept. 28, 1963,IV, p. 6; Oct. 2, IV, p. 4; Oct. 3, IV, p. 2; Oct. 4, IV, p. 2; Oct. 5, IV, p. 2; Oct. 6, III, p. 2; Oct. 7, IV, p. 2; Oct. 18, IV, p. 4; Oct.8, IV, p. 4; Oct. 9, IV, p. 4; Oct. 10, IV, p. 4; Oct. 12, I, p. 4; IV, p. 4; Oct. 13, I, p. 9; Oct. 13, III, p. 2; Oct. 15, IV, p. 4; Oct. 15, I, p. 11; Oct. 19, IV, p. 2; Oct. 20, 1963, IV, p. 8; Oct. 21, IV, p. 4; Oct. 26, IV, p. 2; Oct. 28, IV, p. 4; Oct. 29, IV, p. 4; Oct.30, IV, p. 2; Nov. 14, IV, p. 2; Nov. 17, I, p. 1; Nov. 21, IV, p. 4; DMN, Nov. 22, I, p. 14; DMN, Nov. 22, 1963, IV, p. 2.
26. DMN, Nov. 1, 1963, IV, p. 1; DMN, Nov. 29, 1962, IV, p. 1; Jan. 11,1963, IV, p. 2; Jan. 12, 1963, IV, p. 1; Feb. 17, 1963, I, p. 20; June 22, 1963, II, p. 6; Aug. 11, 1963, I, p. 23; Oct. 24, 1963, I, p. 11; Oct. 25, 1963, IV, p. 1; Oct. 29, 1963, IV, p. 3; Oct. 30, 1963, I, p. 10; Nov. 5, 1963, IV, p. 6; Nov. 17, 1963, I, p. 1; DMN, Mar. 3, 1963, I, p. 14.
27. DMN, June 6, 1963, IV, p. 1.
28. DMN, Nov. 1, 1963, IV, p. 1.
29. Ibid.
30. Ibid.
31. Ibid.
32. DMN, Oct. 1, 15, 1962, IV, p. 4; Nov. 5, 1962, IV, p. 2.
33. DMN, May 10, 1962, IV, p. 2; DMN, July 23, 1962, IV, p. 2; DMN, Aug. 10, 1962, IV, p. 2; DMN, Nov. 11, 1962, IV, p. 2; Dec. 30, 1962, IV, p. 2; May 4, 1963, I, p. 4; May 11, 1963, IV, p. 2; July 28,1963, III, p. 2; Aug. 3,1963, IV, p. 2; DMN, Feb. 20, 1963, IV, p. 14; DMN, Jan. 1, 1963, IV, p. 2.
34. Ibid.; DMN, Feb. 20, 1963, IV, p. 14.
35. DMN, Jan. 16, 1963, IV, p. 2.
36. DMN, Oct. 11, 1963, I, p. 16; Oct. 12, 1963, IV, p. 5; Nov. 7, 1963, I, p. 14; Sept. 13, 1965, A, p. 7;. Sept. 14, 1965, A, p. 11; Sept. 15, 1965, A, p. 15; Sept. 15, 1965, A, p. 11; Sept, 21, 1965, A, p. 6; Sept. 22, 1965, A, p. 1.
37. DMN, Oct. 12, 1963, IV, p. 4.
38. DMN, Sept. 13, 1963, IV, p. 4.
39. DMN, Nov. 1, 1963, I, p. 1.

40. LBJ Library, Johnson-Wade corr., 1963.
41. NYT, Oct. 8, 1963, pp.1, 26.
42. Ibid.
43. LBJ Library, LBJ/Thomas corr. 1963, Re JFK dinner, Houston.
44. DMN, Nov. 16, 1963, I, p. 1.
45. DMN, Nov. 20, 1963, IV, p. 1.
46. John F. Kennedy Library, WHCN File, Box 2778, JFK test. speech, Houston, TX, re Albert Thomas, Nov. 21, 1963.
47. DMN, Nov. 21, 1963, IV, p. 1.
48. *Lubbock Avalanche Journal*, Nov. 22, 1963, I, p .1.
49. NOTP, Nov. 22, 1963, I, p.3; Scheim, *Contract on America* (Argyle Press), p. 261.

Chapter 11

1. AAS, Nov. 23, 1963, I, p. 8; *San Antonio Express News*, Nov. 23, 1963, A, p. 16; DMN (early city ed.), Nov. 23, 1963, IV, pp. 1 and 5; May 5, 1979, 18A; *Fort Worth Star Telegram*, Nov. 23, 1963, p. 1; TPA Messenger, June 1980, John C. Taylor, *The First Hundred Years*, pp. 9 and 47; HP, April 25, 1965, "Judge Hughes Can't Be Pushed Around"; FOIA CRM-961547F, Oct. 16, 1996 Mark North; Miller letter to Sanders, Dec. 19, 1963.
2. U.S. v. John Eli Stone, et al., court docket.
3. Ibid; see court documents, post Nov. 22, 1963.
4. Ibid; Miller letter to Sanders, Dec. 19, 1963.
5. See note 1.
6. LBJ Library, Nov. 22, 1963, Daily Presidential photography, LBJ swearing in sequence.
7. Ibid.
8. LBJ Library, Telephone Notes, The Pres. to Cong. Albert Thomas, Dec. 23, 1963, 1:30 pm.
9. DMN (early city ed.), Nov. 23, 1963, I, p. 2; IV, p. 1; CDTH, Nov. 22 (final ed.), p. 1; Nov. 23, 1963, A, pp. 5 and 17; *San Antonio Express News*, Nov. 23, 1963, A, p. 16; *Fort Worth Star Telegram*, Nov. 23, 1963, p. 2; AAS, Nov. 23, 1963.
10. WFAA TV (Dallas, Channel 8, ABC affiliate) news coverage of assassination, Nov. 22, 1963. Jay Watson footage.
11. Ibid.
12. Ibid.
13. Ibid.
14. Ibid.; DMN, Nov. 23, 1963, I, p .3
15. Ibid.
16. Ibid.
17. DTH, Nov. 22, 1963 (final ed.), p. 1.
18. DMN (early city ed.), Nov. 23, 1963, IV, p. 5; DTH, Nov. 23, 1963, I, p. 1.
19. DMN (early city ed.), Nov. 23, 1963, IV, p. 5.

20. *San Antonio Express-News*, Nov. 23, 1963, A, p. 16; AAS, Nov. 23, 1963, I, p. 8; *Fort Worth Star Telegram*, Nov. 23, 1963, p. 5; DTH, Nov. 23, 1963, A, p. 7; DMN (early city ed.), Nov. 23, 1963, EI, p. 2; *Lubbock Avalanche*, Nov. 24, 1963, A, p. 14.
21. DTH, Nov. 23, 1963, A, p. 1; DMN (early city ed.), Nov. 23, 1963, I, p. 2; *Fort Worth Star Telegram*, Nov. 23, 1963, III, p. 7.
22. WC, vol. 5, pp. 213 and 254.
23. Ibid., pp. 218-19, 229, 230, 232, 235-36, 240, 251.
24. Ibid.; Testimony of Henry Wade and Waggoner Carr before Warren Commission, WC Hearings, vol. 5.
25. Ibid., pp. 258–60.
26. *Lubbock Avalanche*, Nov. 24, 1963, A, p. 14; DTH, Nov. 23,1963, A, p. 1; *Fort Worth Star Telegram*, Nov. 23, 1963, I, p. 1.
27. Ibid.
28. Ibid.
29. WC, E2169, pp. 5 and 22; E2170, p. 2; E2172.

Chapter 12

1. Hoover directive to field offices, Nov. 22, 1963, 2:33 pm (EST).
2. North, *Act of Treason*, pp. 412-6.
3. North, *Act of Treason*, pp. 341-3.
4. WC, E2146, p. 13.
5. WC, E2144, pp.1–2; Jesse Curry, *JFK Assassination File* (Dallas: American Poster & Printing Co., Inc., 1969), bio. in intro.; DTH, Nov. 24, 1963, A, p. 3.
6. WC, E2144, p. 2..
7. WC, E2144, p. 6.
8. WC, E2146, pp. 4 and 6.
9. WC, E2147, pp. 1, 2, 4, 8.
10. WC, E2153.
11. WC, E2154.
12. LBJ Library, JFK Assassination File, Hoover to LBJ memo, Nov. 24, 1963; U.S. Code (1958 ed.), 18 USC241.
13. WC, vol. 5, pp. 189–90; vol. 14, pp. 434–35; vol. 15, pp. 91, 254–7, 267-8, 350–51, 356–57, 364–65, 458–59, 485–6, 504–9, 559–60, 567; WC, E2249, E1610-2 and 1656; WC, E1693; Dowe E. No. 2; Duncan E. No. 1; Hall (C. Ray) No. 3; Kantor E. No. 4.
14. Warren Report, p. 566; WC, E2168, pp. 1,2,5; North, *Act of Treason*, p. 425.
15. WC, E2168, p. 11.
16. Ibid.
17. Ibid., p. 13.
18. WC, E2168, p. 6.
19. Ibid., p. 10.
20. Ibid.
21. Ibid.
22. Ibid., p. 17.
23. Ibid.
24. Ibid., p. 19.
25. Ibid.
26. North, *Act of Treason*, pp. 434, 437.

Chapter 13

1. DMN, Jan. 18, 1962, I, p. 8; Center for American History, Austin, TX, Papers of Will Wilson, Wilson/Bigbee corr., Oct.–Dec. 1955; DMN, May 4, 1951, III, p. 1; Nov. 25, 1963, I, p. 20; Nov. 26, IV, p. 3; Nov. 30, I, p. 1; Dec. 24, 1963, I, p. 6; Jan. 21, 1964, I, p. 4; Jan. 22, 1964, I, p. 1; Jan. 26, 1964, I, p. 23; DMN Oct. 5, 1964, I, p. 18; DTH, Dec. 20, 1963, A, p. 27; DMN, Jan. 8, 1964, I, p. 4.
2. DMN, Dec. 4, 1963, I, p. 1; DMN, Jan. 18, 1964, I, p. 4.
3. Sam Campisi FBI interviews, Dec. 13, 1963 and Jan. 11, 1964.
4. DMN, Dec. 12, 1950, I, p. 1; DMN, Oct. 5, 1960, IV, p. 1.
5. DMN, June 1, 1962, I, p. 6.
6. U.S. v. John Eli Stone, et al., N. Dist. of Texas–Dallas, CR-3-63-86.
7. Blakey, *Plot to Kill the President*, p. 307.
8. *Texas Bar Journal*, Nov. 1965, p. 1027.
9. DMN, Sept. 15, 1951, III, p. 1; Nov. 23, 1963 (early city ed.), IV, p. 5; DTH, Nov. 25, 1963, A, p. 24.
10. DMN, Dec. 15, 1963, I, p. 13; DMN, Mar. 16, 1964, I, p. 1; DTH, Jan. 18, 1964, A, "Ruby's Lawyers, DA, Judge Meet."
11. DTH, Nov. 8, 1965, "Ruby Still Poor, Claims Burleson."
12. DMN, Mar. 29, 1964, I, p. 19.
13. WC, vol. 14, p. 399.
14. U.S. v. John Eli Stone, et al., N. Dist. of Texas – Dallas, CR-3-63-186; DMN, Dec. 14, 1963, IV, p. 1.
15. DTH, Nov. 28, 1963, I, p. 1.
16. DMN, Nov. 25, 1963, I, p.7; IV, p. 1.
17. DTH, Nov. 25, 1963, A, p. 4.
18. DTH, Nov. 25, 1963, A, pp. 4, 6, 9, 10, 24, 32; Nov. 25, B, 6; Nov. 26, "Ruby Possibly Avenging Tippit"; Nov. 27, C, p. 10; Nov. 28, A, p. 6; Nov. 29, A, pp. 16 and 24; Dec. 1, "Ruby Bid on Candy Strip Told" and "Ruby Busy Writing His Memoirs," C. 8, Dec. 8, "Officer Says He Saw Ruby, and Ruby Gets a Shampoo"; Dec. 15, 1963, A, p. 28; Jan. 5, 1964, "Jack Ruby Jail Mail Drops Off"; Jan. 7, "Wade Says Ruby Slipped by Guard"; Feb. 2, "Ruby Author of Life Story Sister Says"; Feb. 13, "Ruby Gets a Valentine"; Feb. 23, "Fate Gave Ruby a Fatal Moment"; Feb. 27, "Jack Ruby Gets Haircut"; Feb. 28, "Ruby Message Goes Undelivered"; April 15, A, 76; May 10, "More Dallas Headlines"; June 27, "Oswald Killed on Impulse, Ruby Claims"; July 8, "Did Oswald, Ruby Meet on Mail Runs?"; July 19, "Sheppard Ruling May Affect Ruby"; Sept. 28, A, 15; Nov. 15, C, p. 1; Nov. 24, A, p. 13; Nov. 24, 1964, "Killing Branded Stupid by Ruby"; April 7, "Ruby's Sister

Hits Prejudice in Job Search"; June 13, "Quick Search of the Mails," June 27, "The Ruby Family's Side"; Nov. 10, 1965, "Looking Again at Ruby Case"; Aug. 25, "Lawyers Following Ruby Trail"; Sept. 17, 1967, A, p. 25; April 12, "Unwritten Stories Are Yet to Be Told"; April 28, 1972, "Ruby's Safe"; April 30, 1975, "Ruby Unwitting Killer?"; May 13, 1975, "Jack Ruby: a Mysterious Type of Life Saver"; May 22, 1975, "FBI Eyes on Ruby Strippers in JFK Case"; June 23, "JFK Probers Accept Lone Assassin Finding"; July 4, 1976, A, p. 18; July 7, "Belli Says Jack Ruby Not in Any Plot to Kill JFK"; Dec. 9, 1976, "King of Torts Belli Doesn't Plan to Quit"; Dec. 8, 1977, "Coincidences Allowed Ruby to Kill Oswald"; Aug. 15, 1978, "Mattox Carries Ruby's Gun to Investigators"; Sept. 26, 1978, "Ruby Told Brother Oswald a Stranger"; Sept. 26, "Dying Ruby Still Denied Ever Knowing Oswald"; Nov. 14,1978, "Jack Ruby Business Card"; Feb.19, 1990, C, p. 3; Sept. 21, 1991, A, p. 19; DMN, Nov. 23, 1963, I, pp. 5 and 15; IV, p. 5; Nov. 24, I, p. 1; Nov. 25, I, pp. 3, 5, 6, 8; Nov. 26, "Club Owner Sought Class FBI Schedules Quiz of Ruby's Sister"; "Rubenstein at News at Time of Shooting"; November 26, I, p. 1; IV, pp. 1, 2, 4; Nov. 27, I, pp. 2, 8, 9; IV, p. 2; Nov. 28, "Data Show Oswald Rented Near Ruby"; I, p. 11; Nov. 29, "Ruby Enjoys Hearty Dinner"; Nov. 30, I, pp. 4 and 6; III, p. 8; Dec. 1, I, p. 12; Dec. 2, "Candy Spurns Ruby's Offer"; Dec. 5, I, p. 9; Dec 10, IV, p. 2; Dec. 24, 1963, I, p. 6; Jan. 3, 1964, "Ruby Gains Some Weight"; Jan. 7, IV, p. 1; "Suit Filed against Ruby"; Jan. 10, IV, p. 2; Jan. 21, "Doctor Testifies Ruby Sought Quick Dollar Notes: Ruby Nervous, Judge Stern in Court"; Jan. 23, "Well, Thanks for Calling"; Feb. 13, "French Letter Sets off Ruby Speech on Hatred"; "Ruby's Sister Speaks Mind Loud, Clear"; Feb. 14, "Ruby Says He Loves Dallas"; March 10, IV, p. 2; Mar. 24, "Ruby Signs Pauper Oath"; June 27, I, p. 1; July 8, "Wade Reveals He's Received Several Letters from Ruby"; Aug. 26, "Suicide Report on Ruby False"; Sept. 28, I, p. 17; Oct. 9,"Ruby Said Still Fearful of Plot Talk"; Nov. 18, "Decker Expresses Doubt Ruby Tried to Kill Self"; Nov. 21, IV, p. 2; Nov. 24, "Anniversary to Be Just Another Day"; Nov. 25, "Just Another Day in Cell for Ruby"; IV, p. 2; Dec. 2, I, p. 6; Dec. 3, I, p. 17; Dec. 6, 1964, "Organized Crime Said Main Target"; May 12, 1965, IV, p. 4; May 19, 1965, "Ruby Case Applied to New Trial Idea"; Dec. 18, A, p. 20; Dec. 18, 1966, "Ruby at Last Getting Sympathy He Sought"; Jan. 1, C, p. 3; Jan.3, "Disc Has Statement Ruby Made"; Jan. 4, "Believe Me, Jack Ruby Begged"; Feb. 3, "Subpoenas Issued in Ruby Case"; Feb. 21, I, p. 1; Nov. 5, 1967, "Widow Sues for Return of Letters Sent by Ruby'; May 7, 1972, "Carousel Club Mementos Go Fast at Athens Auction"; March 28, "Papers Link Ruby, Oswald"; May 20, A, p. 1; July 10, 'Ruby Role in Guns Studied"; July 12, "Ruby's Brother Wanting Inquiry of Death Charge"; July 15, "Witness Says Polygraph Cleared Ruby of Cuba Tie"; July 25, "Ruby Sought as FBI Informant, Group Claims"; Nov. 22, 1976, "Carousel Club"; Dec. 12, 1977, "Ruby's Access to Oswald Told"; July 9, 1978, "Watergate Burglar Claims Ruby, Castro Talked of Plot"; Aug. 15, "Ruby's .38 Taken to D.C."; Aug. 16, "Ruby's .38 Turned Over to House Panel by Mattox"; Aug. 18, "Jack Ruby's Gun Running to Castro Claimed"; Sept. 27, 1978, A, p. 8; Aug. 14, 1988, A, p. 42; March 22, 1992, C, p. 10; Feb. 20, 1994, J, p. 10; The Police Report, Dallas, Texas-1963, p. 47.

19. DMN, Aug. 31, 1963, II, p. 5; DMN, Sept. 12, 1963, IV, p. 1; DMN, Nov. 7, 1963, I, p. 14; *The Killing of President Kennedy: New Revelations Twenty Years Later*, (VidAmerica, Sydacast Serv., Inc., 1983).
20. DMN, Oct. 8, 1963, I, p. 12.
21. Alexander statement to Dallas FBI, Dec. 19, 1963, WC, E1628.
22. Sam Campisi FBI interviews, Dec. 13, 1963 and Jan. 11, 1964 (CE2274).
23. DMN, Nov. 26, 1963, I, p. 14; DMN Dec. 25, 1963, III, p. 1; DMN, Jan. 16, 1964, IV, p. 3; DMN Jan. 26, 1964, I, p. 16; DMN Feb. 14, 1964, I, p. 4; DMN Feb. 19, 1964, I, p. 1; *Atlanta Constitution*, Mar. 13, 1964, I, p. 12; DMN, Feb. 21, 1968, I, pp. 1 and 7.
24. DMN, Nov. 29, 1963, I, p. 1; April 24, 1964, I, p. 1; DMN April 28, 1964, I, p. 7; Blakey, *Plot to Kill the President*, p. 63.
25. Marrs, *Crossfire*, pp. 398–400.
26. DMN, Nov. 27, 1963, I, p .4.
27. Ibid.; DTH Nov. 27, 1963, "FBI Takes Over All Evidence Police Collected on Oswald."

Chapter 14

1. Warren Report, page ix; general assassination press coverage, Nov. 25 -29, 1963 for pressure and announcement.
2. Nelson Lichtenstein, ed., *Political Profiles: The Johnson Years* (NY: Facts on File, Inc., 1976), pp. 51, 133, 181, 375, 537, 491.

3. LBJ Library, Telephone Notes, The Pres. to Abe Fortas, Nov. 29, 1963, 1:15 p.m.; The Pres. To U.S. Sen. Richard Russell, Nov. 29, 1963, 4:05 p.m.
4. Scheim, *Contract on America* (Argyle Press), p. 197.
5. See note 3, LBJ-Russell phone conversation, 8:55 p.m.
6. Ibid.
7. Ibid.
8. Ibid.
9. DMN, May 25 and 26, 1952, I, p. 1; DMN, June 26, 1948, I, p. 2; DMN, July 30, 1949, I, p. 1; Aug. 2, 1949, I, p. 11; Aug. 3, 1949, I, p. 3; Aug. 5, 1949, I, p. 22; DMN, Jan. 24, 1950, I, p. 1; Dugger, *The Politician*, pp. 339-41.
10. DMN, Aug. 16, 1949, I, p. 5; DMN, Aug. 18, 1949, I, p. 5; Sept. 3, I, p. 4; Sept. 8, I, p. 7; Sept. 10, I, p. 1; Sept. 13, I, p. 9; Dec. 11, 1949, I, p. 15.
11. DMN, Aug. 4, 1939, I, p. 14; *Time*, Aug. 14, 1939, p. 14; Mar. 12, 1949, I, p. 2; May 22, 1949, II, p. 7.
12. DMN, March 13, 1959, I, p. 14; DMN Dec. 3, 1959, IV, p. 2; DMN May 22, 1959, I, p. 1 C.
13. DMN, Nov. 14, 1947, I, p. 1; Sept. 20, 1948, II, p. 5; Nov. 4, 1948, I, p. 2; DMN, March 23, 1947, I, p. 20; DMN, Feb. 24, 1948, I, p. 1; DMN, July 6, 1954, I, p. 5; DMN Oct. 3, 1962, IV, p. 4.
14. DMN, Feb. 21, 1954, I, p. 1.
15. Ibid; Warren confirmation to U.S. Supreme Court, FBI background report.
16. LBJ Library, Telephone Notes, The Pres. to Allen Dulles, Nov. 29, 1963, 5:41 p.m.; to U.S. Sen. John S. Cooper, 6:00 p.m.; to U.S. Rep. Gerald R. Ford, 6:52 p.m.
17. DMN, Mar. 31, 1958, I, p. 1.
18. DMN, Dec. 11, 1963, I, p. 19.
19. DMN, Jan. 21, 1964, I, p. 4.
20. Ibid., DMN, Dec. 24, 1963, I, p. 6; LBJ Library, Daily Diary, Sanders/LBJ entries, 1965-69 (49 entries).
21. Ibid.
22. DMN, Mar. 7, 1964, I, p. 1 (EC ed.); Mar.8, 1964, I, p. 17.
23. DMN, Dec. 6, 1963, IV, p. 1.
24. DMN, July 23, 1964, IV, p. 3.
25. Ibid.; Scheim, *Contract on America* (Argyle Press), pp. 113–14.
26. Ibid.
27. DMN, Nov. 23, 1963, I, p. 5; TT, July 7, 1962.
28. DTH, Nov. 27, 1963, B, p. 1.
29. Ibid.
30. WC, vol. 7, pp. 476-485; LBJ Library, Valenti to Cabell, Dec. 10, 1964; Moyers / Cabell, Nov. 6, 1964, LBJ / Cabell, Jan. 17, 1969.
31. LBJ Library, Parkhouse to LBJ, May 31, 1965.
32. DMN, Jan. 8, 1964, I, p. 5; DTH, Jan. 7, 1964, "Ruby

Interview by Panel Hinted"; LBJ, Library, Parkhouse to LBJ, Feb. 28, 1964.

33. WC, E1233; LBJ Library, McKee to LBJ, Dec. 9, 1963; Nov. 16, 1964.
34. Ibid.
35. DTH, Jan. 11, 1964, "McKee Urges Publication of All Facts"; April 12, 1964, "Citizenry Urged to Fight Crime"; July 31, 1964, "One in 10 May Be Victim of Crime"; DMN, Jan. 12, 1964, I, p. 19; Feb. 1, 1964, I, p. 12; May 16, 1964, "Grass-Roots Fight on Crime Urged"; Oct. 17, 1964, "McKee Urges Probe of Criminal Courts"; LBJ/ McKee letters, LBJ Library, LBJ correspondence.
36. LBJ Library, Pres. papers, Executive 5p3-236, PR8-1/c.
37. WC, Vol. 12, pp. 44, 49, 51, 52; DMN, Aug. 25, 1970, 8A.

Chapter 15

1. North, *Act of Treason*, pp. 339–40.
2. NYT, Jan. 16, 1964, p.7; Jan. 29, 1964, p. 1.
3. *Editor & Publisher*, Feb. 15, 1964, "Warren Commission Reports Are Routine."
4. *The Macon Telegraph*, Mar. 10, 1964, See ed. pg., "Staying On."
5. *Atlanta Constitution*, Mar. 11, 1964, p. 1.
6. LBJ Library, White House photos of Jan. 14 and 15, 1964 visit of Pres. Segni of Italy; Daily Diary, Jan. 14 and 15, 1964.
7. DMN, April 16, 1964, IV, p. 2.
8. DMN, May 20, 1964, I, p. 6.
9. LBJ Library, Master File Index, Jenkins to Wade, May 18, 1964; Memo, LBJ/ Watson, June 25, 1966, 11:00 a.m., re Yarborough on Wade; Jacobsen to Tonahill, Sept. 23, 1965, attached article, "Wade Considered a Top Contender"; DMN, Jan. 25, 1964, I, p. 8.
10. LBJ Library, Master File Index, Watson to Wade, Sept. 17, 1965; EX-PR-6-1/w.
11. WC, vol. 15, p. 243.
12. WC, vol. IV, pp. 431–440; DMN, Jan. 9, 1958, I, p. 10.
13. WC, Vol. 5, pp. 561–64.
14. Henry Hurt, *Reasonable Doubt* (NY: Henry Holt & Co., 1985), p. 398.
15. Ibid.
16. DTH, Jan. 14, 1964, A, p. 15; Texas AG, Supplemental Report, correspondence file, Dec. 6, 1963 letter, Guthman to Carr w/attachments.
17. Texas AG, Supplemental Report, corr. file, Dec. 6, 1963 letter, Guthman to Carr w/attachments; Carr to Warren, Dec. 5, 1963.
18. Texas AG, Supplemental Report, corr. file, Dec. 30, 1963 letter, Carr to Rankin.

19. Texas AG, Supplemental Report, corr. file, Feb. 4, 1964 letter, Carr to Rankin.
20. Ibid., Feb. 5, 1964.
21. Ibid., Carr to Warren, Feb. 14, 1964; Texas AG, Supplemental Report, corr. file, Aug. 14, 1964 letter, Carr to Rankin; Aug. 18 and 25, 1964, Rankin to Carr; DMN, Oct. 8, 1964, I, p. 12.
22. Ibid.
23. Activities of the Texas Attorney General's Office, 1963, See transmittal letter.
24. LBJ Library, Master File Index, Pres. Papers, Box 69, LBJ to Carr, Sept. 23, 1964; DMN, Oct. 8, 1964, I, p. 12.
25. DMN, Oct. 8, 1964, I, p. 12.
26. Dallas FBI, Philip S. Bosco, 182-14, sect. 2, sub file 162-292, Interstate gambling activity, correlation memo, Feb. 16, 1968, serial 28. Feb. 1964 interview Bosco.
27. *Washington Post*, April 17, 1964, A, p. 21.
28. DMN, May 31, 1964, I, p. 10; *Washington Post*, June 2, A, p. 3; June 3, A, p. 6; June 6, 1964, C, p.
15.
29. Ibid.
30. Ibid.
31. *Washington Post*, June 3, 1964, A, p. 2; June 4, 1964, B, p. 4; June 5, 1964, A, p. 2.

Chapter 16

1 NOTP, June 7, 1964, "Banister Found Dead at Home"; June 8, 1964, "W.G. Banister Funeral Today."
2. WC, vol. 5, pp. 196–98 and 210.
3. DMN, May 28, I, p. 15; May 29, I, p. 6; June 9, 1964, I, p. 9; FOIA CRM-961547F, Oct. 16, 1996, Mark North, DOJ June 15, 1964 letter, Stone to Hundley.
4. DMN, June 9, 1964, I, p. 9.
5. WC, vol. 5, p. 213; LBJ Library, Master File Index, Jenkins to Wade, May 18, 1964.
6. WC, E.1754.
7. U.S. v. John Eli Stone, et al., Robert M. Barrett Subpoena, May 25, 1964; Robert P. Gemberling, Subpoena, May 25, 1964.
8. WC, vol. 2, pp. 92–93, 131, 201.
9. Warren Report, p. 253; WC, E.3049.
10. WC, E.833, p. 15; Sylvia Meagher, *Accessories after the Fact* (NY: Vintage Books,1976), pp. 211-212.
11. WC, E.1748.
12. HSCA, vol. 9, pp. 419 and 1147 (notes 1192 and 1201).
13. Ibid.
14. WC, E.3021, DMN, Nov. 27, 1963, I, p. 8; *Lubbock Avalanche Journal*, Nov. 25, 1963, A, p. 2.15.
15. U.S. v. John Eli Stone, et al., Affidavits of SA's Kenneth E. Slane, Joseph D. Brandstetter, Charles E. Ballard, Aubrey C. Tomlin, B.A. Krueger, James O. Gann, Robert M. Crites, Joseph T. Houston, Kenneth

B. Carter of IRS Intelligence and ATF Divisions; Search Warrants, June 27, 1963; Affidavit of Charles A. Bus, June 27, 1963; Affidavit of Robert P. Gemberling, Dallas FBI; Comm. Doc. 101b.
16. Comm. Doc. 101; WC, E.1721, pp. 312-315; HSCA, vol. 9, pp. 1081–1085 and 1091; DTH, Dec. 5, 1963, A, p. 7; WC, E.1720, pp. 302-3.
17. *National Review*, June 30, 1964, p. 528.
18. Committee on Un-American Activities Annual Report for the Year 1963, 88th Cong., 2nd sess., Report No. 1739, Foreword, p.XII.
19. Ibid.
20. Ibid.
21. DTH, July 8, 1964, "Wade Reveals Ruby Letters."
22. DMN, Sept. 22, IV, p. 1; Nov. 22, I, p. 18; Annual Report of the AG of the U.S., 1965, pp. 205–6; *U.S. v. John Eli Stone, et al.*, Notice of Appeal of John Eli Stone; Stone sentencing appearance, p. 41.

Chapter 17

1. Harold Weisberg, *Whitewash: The Report on the Warren Report* (New York: Dell Pub. Co., 1965), p. 287; WC, vol. 6, p. 118; *Los Angeles Times*, May 29, 1999.
2. WP July 24, 1966, A, 10.
3. PCD, 1961, See 1500 block of Commerce; DMN, Jan. 6, 1950, I, p. 1; March 7, 1950, III, p. 2; April 27, 1952, III, p. 1; July 30, 1966, I, p. 1; August 5, 1966, I, p. 9; *Fort Worth Star Telegram*, August 11, 1966, p 10.
4. HSCA, vol. 9, 1155-6.
5. DMN, Aug. 5, 1966, A9.
6. DMN Aug. 11, 1966, A8.
7. Ibid.
8. Ibid.
9. Death Cert. of Joseph F. Civello.
10. DMN, Feb. 18, 1967, A6.
11. DMN, Dec. 6 and 7, 1966, I, p. 1; DMN Dec. 10, 1966, D5; Jan. 20, 1972, A8.
12. Ibid.
13. Ibid.
14. DMN, Jan. 4, 1967.
15. NYT, Feb. 18, 1967, p. 19.
16. NYT, Feb. 20, 1967, p. 28.
17. Blakey, *Plot to Kill the President*, p. 77.
18. NYT, March 1, 1967, p. 27.
19. Ibid., p. 1.
20. Ibid., LBJ Library, Papers of Ramsey Clark, Clark Resume.
21. NYT, March 1, 1967, p. 1.
22. John Eli Stone v. U.S., 390 U.S. 204 (1968).
23. Jules Witcover, *85 Days: The Last Campaign of Robert F. Kennedy* (New York: Ace, 1969), p. 54; NYT, March 5, 1968, p. 25.
24. DMN, March 9, 1968, A, p. 6; March 10, 1968, C2.
25. DMN, March 10, 1968, C2.
26. LBJ Library, Presidential Daily Logs, Aug. 3, 1964 and March 28, 1968, Foreign

Language Press, Editors and Publishers; LBJ-Gennaro correspondence.
27. DMN, March 9, 1968, A1.
28. See note 24.
29. JFK Library, Papers of Robert F. Kennedy, Tele. Messages, Desk Diaries; DMN, April 26, 1968, A, p. 3
30. DMN, Nov. 27, 1945, I, p. 6; March 14, 1959, III, p. 9; Ed Reid, *The Grim Reapers* (Chicago: Henry Regnery Co., April 1969), pp. 177–78; HSCA, vol. 9, 946.
31. Reid, *The Grim Reapers*, p. 178.
32. See note 30, HSCA; Scheim, *Contract on America*, p. 97.
33. HSCA, vol. 9, p. 1164, note 1970; Scheim, *Contract on America*, p. 275; FBI file, J.R. Patrono, July 30, 1966.
34. William C. Sullivan, *The Bureau: My Thirty Years in Hoover's FBI* (New York: W.W. Norton Co., 1979), p. 56.
35. See Scheim's *Contract on America*, Turner's *The Assassination of Robert F. Kennedy*, and Melanson's *The Robert F. Kennedy Assassination*, generally.
36. William W. Turner and John G. Christian, *The Assassination of Robert F. Kennedy* (New York: Random House, 1978), p. 24.

Chapter 18

1. G. Edward White, *Earl Warren: a Public Life* (New York: Oxford Univ. Press, 1982), pp. 307–313.
2. DMN, Oct. 3, 1968, A8; Jan. 14, 1969, 6A.
3. Ed Reid, *The Grim Reapers* (Chicago: Henry Regnery Co., April 1969), pp. 160 and 182.
4. Ibid., pp. 161 and 178.
5. DTH, March 5, 1969, p. 27; DMN, Jan. 20, 1972, A8.
6. Ibid.
7. Dallas FBI, Ross Musso, DL92-195, vol. II, Feb. 6, 1969 memo.
8. DMN, Oct. 26, 1969, 16A; HP, Oct. 26, 1969, I, p. 11.
9. Ibid.
10. DTH, Oct. 24, A1; Oct. 27, 1969, A22.
11. Death cert. of Joseph F. Civello.
12. DMN, Jan. 20, 1972, A8.
13. NYT, Oct. 16, 1970, p. 18; Organized Crime Control Act of 1970, (RICO)P.L. 91-452, Title II, Part V, Secs. 201 and 260.
14. Ibid.
15. Ibid.
16. Ibid.
17. DMN, Aug. 30, 1970, A1.
18. DMN, Aug. 31, 1970, D3; Death cert. of Robert Ward, #57716; HP Aug. 31, 1970, A20; NYT Aug. 30, 1970; NYT, Aug. 31, 1970, p. 27.
19. DMN, Dec. 11, 1970, A, p. 10.
20. NYT, Dec. 18, 1970, p. 79.
21. DMN, Dec. 20, 1970, 44A; Death cert. of Peter M. Tamburo.

22. DMN, Dec. 24, 1970, B8; Death cert. of Sam S. Campisi.
23. DMN, Jan. 19 and 20, 1972, A1.
24. Ibid.
25. *The Killing of President Kennedy: New Revelations Twenty Years Later* (VidAmerica, Sydacast Services, Inc., 1983).
26. DMN, Jan. 22, 1971, A2.
27. DMN, September 23, 1971, AA8; *San Antonio Express News,* Sept. 20, 1971, I, p. 1; *Washington Post,* September 23, 1971, B10; NYT, September 23, 1971, p. 38.
28. Ibid.
29. Ibid.
30. DMN, Sept. 23, 1971, D7.
31. DMN, Jan. 19 and 20, 1972, A1.
32. Ibid.
33. DMN, Mar. 30, 1972, D1.
34. Ibid.
35. DMN, March 30, 1972, A17.
36. DMN, April 4, 1972, D1.
37. LBJ Library, See Pres. Daily Diary, March 1, 1966; May 16, 1967; Sept. 26, 1968.
38. DMN, April 8, 1972, A1.
39. DMN, April 1, 1972, A19.
40. DMN, April 8, 9, 13 and 18, 1972, A1.
41. DMN, April 13, 1972, A1.
42. DMN, April 16, 1972, A1.
43. DMN, May 2 and 3, 1972, A1; May 6, 1972, A2.
44. DMN, May 2, 1972, A1.
45. DMN, May 3, 1972, A1.
46. DMN, May 6, 1972, A2.
47. DMN, March 28, 1974, A1.
48. DMN, Dec. 6, 7, 8 and 9, 1972, A1.
49. Ferrell, *Off the Record,* p. 37.
50. Donovan, *Conflict and Crisis,* p. 29.
51. DMN, Dec. 27, 1972, A1.
52. DMN, Jan. 23, 1973, A1.

Chapter 19

1. DMN, Jan. 12, 1946, II, p. 1; WCD-Dallas, 1944–'46, 1961–'64 (Polks), Robt. S. Strauss; NYT, Dec. 11, 1972, p. 28.
2. Ibid.
3. Ibid.
4. DMN, May 31, 1973, B15.
5. Ibid.; Death cert. of Joe Ianni.
6. See note 4; DMN July 18, 1973, A, p. 1.
7. DMN, Mar. 28 and 29, 1974, A1.
8. DMN, March 28, 1974, A1.
9. DMN, March 29, 1974, A1.
10. Ibid.; DMN, Nov. 6, 1974, D1.
11. DMN, Mar. 29, 1974, A1.
12. DMN, July 10, 1974, A1; DMN, Nov. 6, 1974, D1.
13. DMN, Nov. 6, 1974, D1; Tx. St. Bur. of Vital Stats, Austin, TX, Death cert. of Philip S. Bosco, Nov. 6, 1974.
14. U.S. v. John Eli Stone, et al., CR3-74-500, N. Dist. of Texas, (1974), See Criminal Docket.
15. Ibid., Interview, Robert C. Prather, May 29, 1996.
16. Ibid.
17. DMN, Jan. 30, 1975, A6.
18. Death cert. of Ross Musso; DMN, Jan. 31, 1975, D4.
19. DMN, March 8, 1975, E32; March 13, A3; March 16,

A15; March 27, A11; March 30, A10; May 3, A1, 1975.
20. Ibid.
21. DMN, March 5, 1975, A1; March 6, D1; March 7, 1975, A1.
22. Ibid.
23. Ibid.
24. Ibid.
25. DTH, Jan. 27, 1961; Sept. 4, 1961; Martin-Dell Hubell Legal Directory; St. Bar of Texas archives, Austin, TX, Kenneth J. Mighell file; DMN, March 6, 1975, A1.
26. Ibid.
27. DMN, March 6, 1975, A1.
28. Ibid.
29. Ibid.
30. DMN, Mar. 8, 1975, D1.
31. DMN, Mar. 9, 1975, A7 (early city ed.)
32. U.S. v. John Eli Stone, et al., N. District of Texas, CR3-74-500, Proceedings Docket.
33. DMN, March 9, 1975, A8.
34. DMN, May 6, 1975, A16.
35. See note 32.
36. DMN, May 7, 1975, D1.
37. DMN, May 16, 1975, D5.
38. DMN, May 16, 1975, A1.
39. DMN, May 24, 1975, D1.
40. Ibid.
41. DMN, May 18, 1975, A29; May 31, D1; June 2, A2; June 3, A2; June 6, A1; June 7, A3; June 10, A1; June 12, 1975, A42.
42. DMN, May 31, 1975, D1.
43. DMN, June 12, 1975, A42.
44. NYT, June 18, 1975, pp. 1 and 85.
45. DMN, June 5, 1975, A3; June 10, 1975, A2 (early city ed.); June 21, A3; June 22, A, 2 (early city, ed.); June 23, 1975, A1, (early city ed.)
46. DMN, June 17, 1975; See note 32.
47. See note 45.
48. Ibid.
49. DMN, June 21, 1975, A3.
50. John Davis, *Mafia Kingfish* (McGraw Hill, NY, 1989), p. 65.
51. DMN, June 25, 1975, A2.
52. See note 32, June 24, 1975.
53. DMN, July 1, 1975, D1.
54. Ibid.
55. See note 32, June 30, 1975.
56. DMN, July 1, 1975, D1; August 5, 1975, D1; U.S. v. Diadone, 558 F.2d 775 (1977); 98 S. Ct. 1239 (1978).
57. Ibid.

Chapter 20

1. DMN, Jan. 22, 1977, A15.
2. G. Robert Blakey, *The Plot to Kill the President* (NY: Times Books, 1981), page xii; DMN, June 14, 1977, 5D.
3. Silvia Meagher, *Master Index to the JFK Assassination Investigations* (NJ: Metuchen1980), pp. 308–9; HSCA Final Report.
4. DMN, July 29, 1988, B12; HSCA, vol. 9, pp. 406, 579, 1021-22; Death certs. of James W. Stone, Aug. 13, 1986, David L. Miller, July 28, 1988.
5. HSCA, vol. 9, pp. 1045–56 and 1061.
6. Death cert. of Isadore Miller, #034828-78.

7. DTH, Feb. 6 and 7, 1979; HSCA, vol. 3, pp. 642, 681, 686–87.
8. Ibid.
9. Ibid., HSCA, vol. 3, p. 643.
10. Ibid.
11. DMN, Mar. 30, 1979, A13; HSCA, Report, p. 10; Hearings before Comm. on Judiciary, 96th Congress, 1st sess., Serial No. 96-21, part 2, pp. 25, 27, 32 and 34.
12. Ibid.
13. Ibid.; Congressional Record, April 24, 1979, p. 8423.
14. HSCA, Report: Findings and Recommendations, March 29, 1979
15. Ibid.
16. NYT, March 31, 1981, p. 16.
17. *The Killing of President Kennedy: New Revelations Twenty Years Later* (VidAmerica Sydacast Services, Inc, 1983).
18. DMN, May 5, 1982, A1, A21, A33; May 7, 1982, A15, A27; April 25, 1985, A1.
19. Ibid.
20. Ibid.
21. Ibid.
22. Ibid.
23. DTH, Nov. 21, 1966, "Jack Ruby Says He's Sorry He Shot Down Oswald, But."
24. *The Killing of President Kennedy: New Revelations Twenty Years Later.*

Chapter 21

1. U.S. Bureau of Narcotics, Special Report, The Mafia, June 14, 1950 (Papers of Waggoner Carr, SW Collection, Texas Tech Univ.), Lubbock, TX.
2. DMN, Jan. 2, 1975, D 1.
3. Author's files, Ruby Campbell to author, April 19, 1996.
4. DMN, March 15, 1949, II, p. 1.
5. DMN, March 17, 1949, II, pp. 1 and 7; March 20, 1949, IV, p. 1; DMN, Jan. 22, 1950, I, p. 7; DMN, Feb. 17, 1950, III, p. 1; Nov. 29, 1950, I, p. 5; Dec. 1, 1950, III, p. 2; Dec. 2, 1950, III, p. 1.
6. TT, Dec. 21, 1957, p. 3; May 24, 1958, p. 2; June 28, 1958, p. 3; July 7, 1962, p. 3.
7. TT, July 7, 1962, p. 3; Blakey, *Plot to Kill the President*, p. 322.

Exhibits A -F

1. David E. Scheim, *Contact On America* (Silver Spring MD; Argyle Press, 1983), pp. 298-301. (Note, later editions of this book do not carry p.2 of Bobby Gene Moore dep., which names Phil Bosco.)
2. *Lyndon B. Johnson Library*, Presidential Papers, Box 64, FO 6-3-1 Foreign Publications; Box 69, PL/ST 43, LBJ/Gennaro letters; Box 75, "Genn," Perry to Gennaro, LBJ to Gennaro, Sinclair to Gennaro, August 10, to October 26, 1964; See Daily Diary Cards for Gennaro's March 1968 meeting with LBJ.
3. Henry Hurt, *Reasonable Doubt* (New York: Henry Holt & Co., 1985).

GLOSSARY OF NAMES

Bill Alexander: Assistant district attorney under Henry Wade during time of the Kennedy assassination. Believed Oswald was part of a conspiracy.

Guy Banister: Former Chicago FBI agent who worked for Louisiana Mafia boss Carlos Marcello. Died of a heart attack hours before the Warren Commission interviewed Jack Ruby.

Robert Barrett: Dallas FBI agent who oversaw bureau investigations of organized crime figures during the time of the Kennedy administration. Had detailed knowledge of Civello crime family.

Edward Becker: FBI informant who was present at the September 1962 private meeting with Carlos Marcello and others, during which Marcello declared his intention to have JFK assassinated.

Gilbert Beckley: Bookmaker to Carlos Marcello, Joe Civello, and the Montreal, Canada, mafiosi.

Lloyd Bentsen: U.S. senator (Texas). Ally of Lyndon Johnson and force behind the nomination of Barefoot Sanders to federal court in the Northern District of Texas in 1979.

Hale Boggs: U.S. representative from Louisiana (Marcello's district) placed on the Warren Commission by LBJ in order to contain any investigation of Marcello in the context of the JFK assassination.

Philip S. Bosco: Bookmaking associate of Dallas Mafia boss Joe Civello and Joe Ianni. Frequent guest of the Anonymous (a.k.a., Zuroma Club). Pall-bearer at the funeral of Filipo Civello, father of Joe Civello. Took the Fifth Amendment during October 1963 U.S. Department of Justice investigation of Dallas-area Mafia. One of the prime targets of RFK's Organized Crime Task Force.

Joe Brown: Dallas-area judge. Frequent guest of the Anonymous/Zuroma Club. Jack Ruby's trial judge.

Fred Bruner: Dallas attorney. Former assistant district attorney. Worked as part of Jack Ruby's defense team after Ruby murdered Oswald.

Phil Burleson: Dallas attorney. Former assistant district attorney, appeals expert. Worked as part of Jack Ruby's defense team.

Charles Bus: Agent of Bureau of ATF. Investigated the John E. Stone defendants in 1963 as part of RFK's Organized Crime Task Force operation against the Dallas Mafia.

Glenn Byrd: Dallas County official. Close associate of Henry Wade and Jack Ruby. Guest of the Anonymous/Zuroma Club. Died of heart attack in the months after JFK's assassination.

Earl Cabell: Mayor of Dallas. Frequent guest of Anonymous/Zuroma Club. Close ally of LBJ. Prevented the effort of the city council of Dallas to independently investigate the assassination. Later became U.S. representative with LBJ's help.

Ellis Campbell: Regional IRS director, Dallas. Coordinated with RFK's effort to investigate the Stone defendants and Jack Ruby in 1963. After the assassination, he was instructed by LBJ's people to contain the *Stone* case and prevent disclosure of Ruby's involvement with the defendants.

Joe Campisi: Involved in Dallas Mafia gambling operations. Associate of Joe Civello. Associate of Jack Ruby, visiting him in the county jail at Ruby's request shortly after Oswald's murder. Partner in Egyptian Lounge, purchased from John Grizzaffi. Guest of Anonymous/Zuroma Club.

Sam Campisi: Brother of Joe Campisi. Partner in Egyptian Lounge and associate of Joe Civello. Close associate of Jack Ruby. Guest of the Anonymous/Zuroma Club.

John Carcelli: Brother-in-law of Joe Ianni. May have been an informant to RFK's Organized Crime Task Force investigators in 1963. Was murdered gangland fashion in March 1963.

Waggoner Carr: Texas attorney general at the time of Kennedy's assassination. Expert on Dallas Mafia. Close ally of Lyndon Johnson. Coordinated closely with him after the assassination to prevent the filing of a conspiracy-based indictment against Oswald or state-level investigation of JFK's murder.

Cliff Carter: Personal aide to LBJ. Followed his directives after the assassination to prevent a conspiracy investigation of the murder. Also destroyed evidence which could have been used to investigate the assassination.

Charles E. Civello: Brother of Joseph F. Civello. Guest of Anonymous/Zuroma Club. Partners with Joseph in import businesses.

Joseph F. Civello: Member of Joseph Piranio's Sicilian mob family from latter 1920s onward. Convicted in 1926 for Prohibition (liquor) law violation. Arrested July 14, 1928, for murder. Killed Joe DeCarlo in St. Paul Drug Store with sawed-off twelve-gauge shotgun, fired at point-blank range into DeCarlo's stomach—later ruled "accidental."[1] Arrested January 8, 1937, for Federal Narcotics Act violation (trafficking in heroin and morphine). Pled guilty to avoid trial and disclosure of facts surrounding Piranio's regional narcotics distribution network. Sentenced to fifteen years in Leavenworth Penitentiary on April 2, 1937—served less than three and a half years. Upon release, returned to Dallas where he rose to lieutenant, then underboss in the Piranio crime family. Chief Deputy Sheriff Bill Decker appeared as a character witness for Civello in pardon hearings. Civello was voted into membership of the Anonymous Club on January 25, 1947.[2] Civello orchestrated weekly, floating poker game at the club from that point forward, in violation of Texas State gaming statutes. From latter 1940s to 1957, operated various Italian food and wine import businesses with brother Charles, brother-in-law Ross Musso, and Frank LaMonte.[3] On June 14, 1950, Civello was identified by the U.S. Bureau of Narcotics as one of four key Dallas mafiosi. Their report was given to the Texas House Special Committee to Investigate Organized Criminal Activites in Texas 1951–1953 (Little Kefauver Committee).[4] Civello became Dallas Mafia boss on October 27, 1956, with the "suicide" of Texas Mafia boss, Joe Piranio. Civello was arrested on November 14, 1957, in Apalachin, New York, with sixty-four other nationally known Mafia figures who had met to discuss the national distribution of illegal narcotics (heroin, morphine, cocaine, marijuana). Was called in for interview by Dallas Police department one month later.[5] Civello took the Fifth Amendment against self-incrimination before a Los Angeles, California, grand jury in March and April 1959, regarding West Coast operations of the Mafia. On March 24, 1959, he was identified to Dallasites by the U.S. Senate Labor Rackets committee as an associate of New Orleans mob boss Carlos Marcello. Was arrested again by federal authorities on May 21, 1959, in connection with the Apalachin raid. Civello's attorney was Lester May, the assistant U.S. attorney to Dallas until the mid-1950s.[6] Civello was convicted of obstruction of justice on December 18, 1959, in Apalachin conspiracy trial and sentenced to five years in prison. Retained Houston, Texas, Mob attorney Percy Forman and had conviction overturned in 1961.[7] Dallas media stated on January 14, 1960, that "Civello is linked with the [Mafia]." On October 7, 1963, again identified as "suspected Cosa Nostra chieftain."[8] Although interviewed by the Dallas FBI and discussed in various affidavits, Civello's name is not to be found in the Warren Commission report, hearings, or exhibits. In Commission Exhibit 1184, his name was altered to "Savella." Commission Exhibit 1536 discussed him as "Cirello," but that portion of the exhibit was suppressed by the Warren Commission prior to its inclusion in the published exhibits. Civello's January 14, 1964, FBI interview was suppressed in total, its existence unknown until 1981.[9] When Civello died on January 17, 1970, honorary pallbearers were members of the Anonymous (Zuroma) Club.[10]

Tom Clark: Former assistant Dallas district attorney. U.S. attorney general under Truman administration. As AG, accepted bribes from Dallas, New Orleans, and Chicago mafiosi to prevent their deportation by INS. Extremely close ally of Lyndon Johnson. Served on U.S. Supreme Court during LBJ administration.

Emmett Colvin: Assistant Dallas district attorney under Henry Wade. Left DA's office to work for Mafia defense attorney Charles Tessmer during RFK's investigation of Dallas Mafia.

John Connally: Close ally of LBJ. Governor of Texas during Kennedy administration. Essentially a creation of Johnson's and closely followed his directives after the assassination.

John Cooper: Member of Warren Commission. Initially promoted "lone nut" conclusion of the Warren Report but recanted before dying.

Frank Costello: New York Mafia kingpin. Mentor of Carlos Marcello. Prosecuted during Kennedy administration.

Vic Cotroni: Head of Cotroni mob in Montreal, Canada. Coordinated with Joe Civello and Carlos Marcello to import heroin and other hard narcotics into the United States through Texas and Louisiana. Was object of RFK Organized Crime Task Force investigation in Texas in the months leading up to the assassination. RFK's people succeeded in intercepting a one-quarter-billion-dollar heroin shipment Cotroni attempted to smuggle into the United States along the Texas border shortly before JFK's assassination.

Roger Craig: Dallas law enforcement official who saw an Oswald look-alike flee Texas School Book Depository after the assassination. Craig was later found shot to death, supposedly a suicide.

Jesse Curry: Dallas police chief at the time of JFK's assassination. FBI Academy graduate. Was controlled by FBI Director J. Edgar Hoover after the fact. After retiring, publicly expressed his belief in conspiracy surrounding JFK's murder.

Antoine D'Agostino: Narcotics trafficker who worked for Cotroni/Mondoloni heroin cartel, which was smuggling tons of hard narcotics into the United States annually through Texas. Was arrested in the mid-1950s in Mexico City and flown to Austin, Texas, where he was held by federal investigators. Significance of his arrest was hidden from the public by Lyndon Johnson and ally Price Daniel, both then U.S. senators to Texas.

Price Daniel: U.S. senator to Texas 1952–1956. Worked to trivialize the significance of Mafia narcotics smuggling operations in Texas in the 1950s. Then served as governor until leaving office in 1963. Replaced by John Connally. Both men were loyal servants to Lyndon Johnson.

Bill Decker: Dallas county sheriff in the decades leading up to JFK's assassination. Guest of Anonymous/Zuroma Club. Ignored growth of Dallas Mafia. Died in office in 1970, the year powerful anti-Mafia legislation (RICO) was passed by U.S. Congress.

Frank De Simone: Head of Los Angeles Mafia until January 1968. Close associate of Joe Civello.

Sig Dickson: Powerful Dallas-area bookmaker during JFK's administration. Was object of Organized Crime Task Force investigation.

James Dolan: Dallas-area bookmaker associated with the Civello mob and Jack Ruby.

Allen Dulles: Member of Warren Commission. Strong Hooverite. Defended lone-nut theory until the day he died.

Frank Dyson: Dallas police chief during post-assassination investigations of Dallas Mafia by federal authorities under RICO in the early 1970s. Reformed the Dallas PD along the lines of federal models.

Edward Epstein: JFK assassination investigator. Wrote early book calling for new investigation of Kennedy's murder, the first to do so.

Billy Sol Estes: Texas con man associated with LBJ and U.S. Agriculture Department scandal during the Kennedy administration.

Louis Ferrantello: 1950s-era Dallas mafioso and bookmaking associate of Jack Ruby. Took the Fifth Amendment over 100 times before the Texas House Crime Investigating Committee (Little Kefauver committee), June 2, 1951. Convicted for contempt, sentenced to one year in prison. Murdered July 17, 1956.

Gerald Ford: Warren Commission member. Loyal informant to J. Edgar Hoover. Stole commission's internal documents and delivered to Hoover to help LBJ control findings of the investigative body. Later used internal documents for personal profit. Lived in fear of prosecution for obstruction of justice. Became president of the United States 1974–77. Publicly defended the lone-nut conclusion of commission until dying day.

Abe Fortas: Worked for LBJ as interface with Warren Commission. Helped him control commission findings. Was rewarded with a U.S. Supreme Court judgeship by Johnson but was forced to resign because of corruption.

Will Fritz: Dallas Police Department homicide detective. Worked on Oswald's case until Oswald was murdered by Ruby.

Jim Garrison: New Orleans district attorney who was first to investigate the Kennedy assassination as a conspiracy. In latter 1960s publicly expressed conclusion that LBJ was involved in JFK's murder.

Robert Gemberling: Dallas FBI agent who worked on RFK's investigation of Dallas Mafia via the Stone prosecution. After the assassination, followed Hoover's directive to alter and destroy evidence which pointed to Oswald's innocence.

Joseph Gennaro: Publisher of *The Texas Tribune* (formerly *La Tribuna Italiana*), August 1951 to December 1962, when the *Tribune* ceased publication. Member of Anonymous/Zuroma Club. Documented the presence of Dallas-area law enforcement officials and members of the judiciary who were at the Anonymous Club with Joe Civello. Corresponded frequently with Lyndon Johnson during 1950s and '60s. Johnson assisted Gennaro with efforts on behalf of various Italians and their interaction with the Immigration and Naturalization Service (INS). Carried Johnson's U.S. Senate constituent column and endorsed his reelection bids. General chairman of the American-Italian Committee for Johnson, 1964 presidential campaign. Met with LBJ at the White House, August 3, 1964, and March 28, 1968.[11]

Sam Giancana: Chicago Mafia boss during the Kennedy administration. Loathed JFK. Coordinated with Cotroni mob in Montreal, Canada, and Civello and Marcello in the smuggling of tons of heroin into the United States. Participated in the plot to kill JFK. Was later murdered, possibly by a henchman of Marcello.

Louis Ginsberg: Depression-era Dallas mafioso who coordinated with the Piranio mob to smuggle heroin into the area.

Wesley Grapp: FBI special agent in charge in both Miami, Florida (1962), and later in Los Angeles, California (1968). A Hoover favorite.

John M. Grizzaffi: Considered by Dallas police and sheriff's departments as early as 1947 to be a "dope pusher" and "triggerman." Member of the Anonymous/Zuroma Club and Italian-American Civic Federation. Associate of Jack Ruby. Known to the Warren Commission but not questioned. Died August 17, 1993.[12]

Robert Groden: Photographic expert who computer enhanced the Zapruder film and had it nationally broadcast in 1975. Author on the JFK assassination.

Jerry Haynes: Dallas ABC affiliate reporter who, along with Jay Watson, scooped Kennedy's murder on November 22, 1963.

J. Edgar Hoover: FBI director. Close political ally of Lyndon Johnson. Had prior knowledge of Mafia contract on JFK, but withheld data from Secret Service for political gain. After the fact, conspired with LBJ to prevent the public from learning that President Kennedy had been a victim of a Mob hit. Died of a heart attack in 1972.

Tom Howard: One of Jack Ruby's defense attorneys. Worked to establish insanity defense in Ruby's killing of Oswald. Died at age forty-eight during Ruby's appeal of murder conviction.

Sarah Hughes: Longtime Dallas-area judge. Crony of LBJ. Obtained appointment to federal bench in U.S. District Court Northern District Court of Texas. Was handpicked by Johnson in 1961. Coordinated with him to blunt RFK's prosecution of Dallas Mafia, 1961–'64. Conspired with LBJ to prevent the public learning of Ruby's ties to the case after JFK was murdered.

Frank (Franceso) Ianni: Born in Calabria, Italy. Convicted of narcotics trafficking in 1925 in New Orleans, Louisiana. Arrested with Joe Civello in January 1937 and pled guilty to trafficking in heroin and morphine. Sentenced to Leavenworth Penitentiary. Joe Civello's attorney, Maury Hughes (a former Dallas DA), obtained in 1945 a pardon for Ianni from President Harry Truman for the 1937 conviction. Ianni again became a subject of deportation proceedings in Dallas in 1953. Used former assistant Dallas DA Angelo Piranio as his defense lawyer. Ianni was a cousin of New York mafioso Rocco Pellegrino. Rocco's son Peter assisted with control of Dallas Mafia operations in late 1950s. Ianni died January 9, 1958.[13]

Joseph Ianni: Son of Frank Ianni. Born in Calabria, Italy. In 1930s attended the University of Texas at Austin with LBJ's future wife, Claudia Alta Taylor. He was convicted in 1946 of a federal liquor law violation. Was subsequently arrested for murder in 1951, but was allowed to go unprosecuted by Dallas DA Henry Wade. Guest of the Anonymous/Zuroma Club and member of the American-Italian Committee for Johnson. Close bookmaking associate of Joe Civello and Phil Bosco. Possible suspect in the murder of his brother-in-law, John Carcelli, in 1963. Acted as official "informant" in the ruling of suicide by officials the same day of Carcelli's death. (Carcelli had been shot in the chest and then in the mouth.) Became head of Dallas Mafia after Joe Civello's death in 1970. Ianni died in May 1973.[14]

Lyndon Johnson: U.S. senator (Texas), January 1949 to January 1961. Assisted Dallas Italians during the 1950s to defeat INS deportation actions against them. Close ally of Dallas district attorney Henry Wade, Texas governor John Connally, U.S. attorney to Dallas Barefoot Sanders, FBI director J. Edgar Hoover. From 1948 onward, LBJ was a supporter of the Mafia-controlled Anonymous/Zuroma Club in Dallas. As part of the 1948 Senate campaign, he undoubtedly appeared as a guest of the club, along with close ally Pete Tamburo. Vice president under John Kennedy. Conspired with Mafia to have JFK murdered in Dallas on November 22, 1963, in exchange for presidency and cessation of Justice Department investigations into his corruption. Created and controlled Warren Commission. Orchestrated the cover-up in the Mafia killing of JFK. Died of heart attack January 22, 1973, after U.S. government began investigation in his corrupt relationship with Hoover.

Robert Jones: 1930s-era Dallas police chief. Ex-FBI agent and favorite of Hoover's. Stalked and then murdered an unarmed man in downtown Dallas in front of eyewitnesses on a busy street. Avoided conviction with the aid of Dallas officials as a gesture of their support for Hoover and the reputation of FBI.

Nicholas Katzenbach: U.S. attorney general under LBJ.

John F. Kennedy: U.S. president, 1961–1963. Assassinated in Dallas, Texas, by Mafia contract killers hired by Louisiana Mafia boss Carlos Marcello through foreign drug cartel associates. Killed in order to stop his brother's war on Marcello, heroin traffickers, and Joe Civello's Dallas-based gambling and heroin distribution operations.

Robert F. Kennedy: U.S. attorney general, 1961–64. Attempted to destroy Mafia operations in the United States. Attempted to discredit Vice President Lyndon Johnson for his corruption in office. Was stopped by his brother's assassination and LBJ's seizure of the presidency on November 22, 1963.

Edward Levi: U.S. attorney general under Gerald Ford.

Nick Licata: Los Angeles Mafia boss in 1968. Associate of Joe Civello.

Evelyn Lincoln: JFK's secretary.

Gaetano Lucchese: Boss of Lucchese mob in New York. An object of RFK's war on the Mob. Associate of John Ormento.

Henry Luce: Owner of *Life* magazine. Purchased Zapruder film and then suppressed it in cooperation with LBJ and Hoover. Died of a heart attack at the outset of Garrison's investigation in New Orleans over fear that film would have to be turned over as evidence. It was.

Carlos Marcello: Mafia boss of Louisiana. Deported and then prosecuted by RFK upon return to United States. In August 1962, put out Mob contract on JFK. Conspired with Mob bosses Joe Civello and Sam Giancana and LBJ to orchestrate murder of the president in Dallas, Texas.

Russell Mathews: Dallas mobster and associate of area bookmakers, including Jack Ruby.

John McClellen: U.S. senator who worked closely with RFK to break the Mafia during the Kennedy administration.

John McCloy: Member of Warren Commission. Ardent supporter of cover-up in cooperation with LBJ and Hoover. Died March 11, 1989.

John McKee: Dallas Crime Commission president during the Kennedy administration. Fanatical supporter of LBJ. Loathed RFK. Cooperated with Johnson after the fact to contain the truth about Kennedy's murder. Navy deserter who lived under an assumed name. Later exposed and disgraced.

Albert Meadows: Dallas-area bookmaker. Associate of Joe Civello. Pursued and indicted by RFK's Organized Crime Task Force in Dallas in 1963.

Kenneth Mighell: Assistant U.S. attorney to Dallas, handpicked by LBJ and Barefoot Sanders in 1961. Viewed Zapruder film on November 22, 1963. Supporter of the lone-nut conclusion of the Warren Commission.

Herbert Miller: Head of Criminal Division of U.S. Department of Justice under RFK. Was placed in charge of the situation in Dallas after JFK's murder. Knew little of organized crime. Cooperated with Sanders and Sarah Hughes to stop Stone prosecution. Died November 21, 2009.

David Miller: Brother of Dallas mobster Isadore Miller and an associate of Jack Ruby. Co-owner of Enquire Shine and Press Shop. Worked with Jack Ruby to promote bookmaking business at Ruby's night club, located two doors down from the Enquire in downtown Dallas. His Dallas FBI file was suppressed in total under the JFK Assassination Records Collection Act of 1992.

Isadore Miller: Brother of David Miller. Bookmaker working with John Eli Stone and the Dallas Mafia. Prosecuted by RFK as a defendant in the Stone gambling tax case in 1963. Died of a heart attack during U.S. House Select Committee on Assassinations hearings in May 1978.

Paul Mondoloni: French heroin trafficker. Member of Cotroni mob family. Object of RFK's efforts to destroy foreign heroin cartels associated with Marcello's and Civello's domestic narcotics operations. Murdered in Marseille, France, on July 29, 1985.

Ross Musso: Born in Salaparuta, Italy. Subpoenaed February 28, 1937, in connection with Joe Civello's heroin trafficking prosecution. Musso was Civello's brother-in-law and business partner. From 1937 onward, they were neighbors in a duplex in West Dallas. Member of Anonymous Club. Was initially denied citizenship for "concealing arrests." Died January 30, 1975. Honorary pallbearers were members of the Anonymous /Zuroma Club.[15]

Bill Newman: JFK assassination witness. Was standing with his family between grassy knoll and Kennedy's limousine at the moment of Kennedy's death. Fatal round fired from knoll passed over his head. Interviewed by ABC affiliate minutes after JFK's death.

Warren Olney: Eisenhower's organized crime chief at Department of Justice.

John Ormento: Heroin trafficker in New York Lucchese mob. Object of RFK's war on Mafia. Convicted, sentenced to forty years in prison. Close criminal associate of Joe Civello. Died in 1974.

Lee Oswald: Employee of Texas School Book Depository and former U.S. Marine. Was unwittingly drawn into Mafia contract on JFK's life. Was subsequently falsely accused of murder of JFK and Dallas police officer J. D. Tippit. Oswald was murdered by Dallas mobster and bookmaker Jack Ruby to prevent trials and acquittals. Oswald was a victim of right-wing mass hysteria prevalent in Dallas at the time of Kennedy's assassination. Hysteria was exacerbated by FBI Director Hoover's injection into the case at LBJ's order.

George Parkhouse: Powerful Texas state senator for Dallas area. Close ally of Lyndon Johnson. Guest of Anonymous/Zuroma Club. Chaired legislative committee on mental health. Worked closely with LBJ after the assassination, using his position to promote an insanity defense for Ruby. Also worked to project Oswald as a "lone nut." Died in office on August 24, 1967.

Leonard Patrick: Chicago-area mob contract killer and associate of Jack Ruby. Died March 16, 2006.

John Ross Patrono: Dallas mobster and bookmaker. Close associate of Joe Ianni and Jack Ruby. Frequent guest of Anonymous/Zuroma Club. Warren Commission identified him only as "Johnny Ross" in order to conceal Ruby's involvement with the Dallas Mafia.[16]

Nofio Pecora: Lieutenant under Carlos marcello. Guest of Anonymous/ Zuroma Club. In close communication with Jack Ruby during the months leading up to the JFK assassination.

Rocco Pellegrino: New York–area Mafioso. Cousin of Frank Ianni (Joe ianni's father). Object of RFK's war on Mafia.

Angelo Piranio: Nephew of Texas Mafia boss Joseph T. Piranio. Assistant Dallas county district attorney, 1930–1932 and 1941–1946. Assisted Dallas-area Italians with immigration to United States. Frequently gave private barbeques for Dallas county grand jury. One-time law partner with Mafia defense attorney Maury Hughes. Member of Anonymous Club. Died of cerebral hemorrhage, May 2, 1957.[17]

Joseph T. Piranio: Born in Corleone, Sicily, immigrating to the U.S. and Dallas area in 1904. Head of Texas Mafia until his death. Member of Anonymous Club from 1939 until 1956. Died October 27, 1956. Pallbearers included Dallas mafiosi Joe Civello and Ross Musso.

Joe Pool: Dallas-area Texas state representative and then U.S. representative during the Kennedy administration. Guest of Anonymous/Zuroma Club. Worked on the House Un-American Activities Committee after the assassination, which tried to convince the public Oswald was a crazed Marxist. Died July 14, 1968.

John Quigley: FBI agent who worked in both New Orleans and Dallas field offices prior to the assassination. Was knowledgeable about Mafia in both cities. Interviewed Oswald in New Orleans in 1963 regarding his public pro-Castro demonstrations.

J. Lee Rankin: General counsel to Warren Commission. Hooverite and governmental sycophant. Responsible for Warren Report in published form. Died June 28, 1996.

Sam Taliaferro Rayburn: U.S. Speaker of the House from Texas. Mentor of LBJ. During his time as speaker, 1950s and early 1960s, anti-Mafia legislation stalled. Died November 16, 1961.

Jack Ruby: Chicago mafioso who moved to Dallas after World War II. Became a local strip club owner and bookmaker. Worked with the Civello mob in the 1950s and 1960s via his club to expand bookmaking operations. Close criminal associate of John Eli Stone and Miller brothers. Was object of RFK's war on the Dallas Mafia in 1963. Would have been indicted after completion of Stone prosecution. Killed Oswald as part of the Mafia contract on JFK. Participated in the assassination plot to avoid prosecution by RFK. Friend of Henry Wade and other local law enforcement figures.

Probable guest of Anonymous Club. Died of cancer in the Dallas county jail while awaiting a new trial, his original conviction having been overturned. Died January 3, 1967.

Richard Russell: U.S. senator. Member of Warren Commission. Knew JFK was killed by conspiracy, but cooperated with Johnson to prevent the public learning the truth. Confessed prior to his death, recanting the lone-nut conclusion of the commission. Died January 21, 1971.

Barefoot Sanders: Dallas-area lawyer. Texas state representative prior to the Kennedy administration. Guest of Anonymous Club. Was fanatical supporter of LBJ. Was appointed U.S. attorney to Dallas by Johnson in 1961 in exchange for unquestioning loyalty. Tried to stop RFK's prosecution of Civello bookmakers in 1963. Publicly denied existence of the Civello crime family. Worked closely with presiding judge Sarah Hughes to eliminate serious charges against defendants after JFK was killed. Ultimately became chief judge of U.S. District Court for the Northern District of Texas, following in Sarah Hughes's footsteps. Ardent supporter of the Warren Report. Died September 21, 2008.

Charles Sansone: Dallas police officer and detective, 1933 to 1968. Frequent guest of Anonymous/Zuroma Club, becoming member in June 1959. Resigned from force in 1968 after arrest on illegal gambling charges.

Lucien Sarti: Corsican heroin trafficker, contract killer, and close associate to Paul Mondoloni. Operated out of Mexico City, where he was killed in a shoot-out with police on April 27, 1972. Possibly one of the hit men who assassinated JFK.

Sam Savalli: Dallas-area mobster associated with Civello crime family and Anonymous/Zuroma Club. Convicted murderer. Turned to Johnson for help against INS in mid-1950s and was successful. Died in Dallas in 1970.

Gordon Shanklin: Dallas FBI SAC, placed in charge in April 1963. A Hoover loyalist, he worked closely with the director after the assassination to prevent the public's learning of the Mafia contract on JFK. Orchestrated alteration and destruction of evidence to hide FBI's awareness of Oswald and falsely implicate him as JFK's assassin. Remained Dallas SAC until 1975. Died July 13, 1988.

Mike Shapiro: Manager of ABC television affiliate in Dallas. Viewed Zapruder film the day of the assassination but did not air the film. Later worked to prevent it from being shown to Dallas-area viewers in 1975 when it was shown on national television for the first time. Died April 27, 1987.

Salvatore Shillitani: Heroin trafficker in Lucchese mob. Target of RFK's war on Mafia drug cartels.

Arnold M. Stone: Assistant U.S. attorney under the Kennedy administration. Placed in charge of RFK's Organized Crime Task Force investigation of Civello mob's Dallas gambling operation, 1962–'64. Secured indictment of Civello bookmakers, John Eli Stone, James Stone, and Isadore Miller in latter 1963. His efforts were undercut by LBJ's people after the assassination.

James Stone: Brother of John Eli Stone. Prosecuted by RFK.

John Eli Stone: Dallas bookmaker associated with Joe Civello and Phil Bosco. Prosecuted by RFK Organized Crime Task Force. Convicted on minor charges in 1964. Prosecuted again in mid-1970s. Died in Las Vegas, Nevada, on October 17, 1990.

Robert Strauss: Chairman of Democratic National Party, early to mid-1970s. Former Dallas FBI agent. LBJ supporter.

Peter Tamburo: Dallas-area Italian-American activist and loyal LBJ supporter dating back to 1940s. Honorary member of the Anonymous/Zuroma Club. Died in 1971.

Claudia Alta Taylor (Lady Bird Johnson): Wife of LBJ.

Charles Tessmer: Dallas-area mob defense attorney. Served as counsel to the Stone defendants in 1963-64.

Albert Thomas: U.S. representative Texas (Houston area). Close ally of Lyndon Johnson. Played key role in bringing JFK to Texas in November 1963. Died February 15, 1966.

Clyde Tolson: Associate FBI director. J. Edgar Hoover's lover. Hated Kennedys. Died April 14, 1975.

John Tower: U.S. senator from Texas. Knew of RFK's attempt to break the Civello mob via the Stone prosecution in Wichita Falls, Texas, in 1963. Favored Warren Report. Died April 5, 1991.

Santo Trafficante: Florida Mafia boss. Target of RFK's war on the Mob. By the fall of 1962, he knew of Marcello's contract on the life of JFK. Died March 17, 1987.

Joseph Valachi: New York mafioso who turned informant during Kennedy administration. Assisted RFK with exposure of Mafia before a national television audience in October 1963. Died on April 3, 1971, in a Texas prison.

Henry Menasco Wade: Dallas district attorney, 1951–'87. Fanatical supporter of LBJ. Played key role in framing Oswald for Kennedy and Tippit murders. Sought political gain from Johnson before and after the assassination. Ardent supporter of the Warren Report. Guest of Anonymous/Zuroma Club. Under his tenure, Civello mob's narcotics and gambling operations exploded in Texas. Associate of Joe Civello and Jack Ruby. Close ally of key Dallas mafioso and murderer Joe Ianni. Through his malfeasance in office, promoted Mafia's national distribution of hard narcotics to several generations of American citizens. Died March 1, 2001.

Robert Ward: Assistant U.S. attorney to Dallas, handpicked by LBJ and Barefoot Sanders. Worked to derail RFK's effort to prosecute the Stone defendants in 1963–1964. Died of heart failure the same day as Dallas county sheriff Bill Decker, August 29, 1970.

Earl Warren: Chief justice of the U.S. Supreme Court. Chair of Warren Commission. Knew JFK had been killed by a Mafia hit but cooperated with LBJ and Hoover to hide the truth from the American people. Did so, in part, to spare Supreme Court from scandal. If the Dallas Mafia had been exposed, the public would have learned of Associate U.S. Supreme Court Justice Tom Clark's promotion of that crime family's illegal operations during the 1940s and early 1950s. Warren died July 9, 1974, during Justice Department's second prosecution of John Eli Stone. Warren's Court had previously thrown out Stone's original conviction by RFK.

Jack Wasserman: Former U.S. attorney. Member of Board of Immigration Appeals. Defense counsel for Carlos Marcello. Died in 1980.

Jay Watson: Dallas-area journalist who worked for ABC affiliate. Along with Jerry Haynes, he quickly launched key reporting on JFK's assassination the afternoon of November 22, 1963.

Irwin Weiner: Chicago-area bail bondsman called by Jack Ruby in October 1963. Ruby was facing indictment by RFK's Organized Crime Task Force in 1964 and panicked after the October 21, 1963, Dallas indictment of his close bookmaking associate Isadore Miller.

Will Wilson: Former Dallas district attorney and Texas attorney general. Strong opponent of LBJ.

David Yaras: Chicago-area mobster and associate of Jack Ruby.

Abraham Zapruder: Dallasite who filmed JFK assassination.

BIBLIOGRAPHY

Freedom of Information Act (FOIA) Demands

U.S. Dept. of Justice – Immigration and Naturalization Service, April 3, 1996, Philip S. Bosco, et al. Dallas: DAL96000813 - 96000817, 96001724 - 960001725; Washington DC: CO96002513 - 96002517.

U.S. Dept. of Justice – FBI, April 12, 1996, Philip S. Bosco, Joseph Ianni, Johnny Ross Patrono, et al.: 408986-87, 408989, 408997, 409001, 409002, 409005.

U.S. Dept. of Justice – Criminal Division, Oct. 16, 1996: CRM-961547F.

U.S. Dept. of Justice – Executive Office for U.S. Attorneys, Oct. 29, 1996: 96-2766.

U.S. Dept. of Justice – Office of Information and Privacy, Nov.26, 1996: AG/96-R0593.

U.S. Internal Revenue Service, Nov. 4, 1996, U.S. v. John Eli Stone, et al.: CR-3-63-186 (Certified letter #PSS0991069; IRS made no response).

Interviews: Former Federal and Texas Officials

Blakey, G. Robert, Chief Counsel, U.S. House Select Committee on Assassinations 1977-1979. Interview, Sept. 13, 1996.

Carr, Waggoner, State Representative – Lubbock, vice-chairman of Meredith Crime

Committee, Speaker of the House 1951 to 1960; Attorney General, Jan. 1963 to Jan. 1967. Interview, fall 1992, Dec. 12, 1994.

Mauzy, Oscar, State Senator – Dallas. Interview, Feb. 4, 1994.

Murphy, Charles, State Representative – Houston, member of Meredith Crime Committee 1951-1953. Interview, April 6, 1994.
Prather, Robert, Assistant U.S. Attorney – Dallas 1974-1981. Interview, May 29, 1996.
Schwartz, A. R., State Senator – Galveston. Interview, Feb. 4, 1994.
Stone, Arnold M., Assistant U.S. Attorney, Organized Crime Section, Kennedy Administration. Interview, August 21, 1995.
Wade, Henry M., Assistant District Attorney – Dallas, Jan. 1947 to Dec. 1949; District Attorney – Dallas, Jan. 1951 to Dec. 1986. Interview, July 31, 1995.
Wilson, Will R., Sr., District Attorney – Dallas, Jan. 1947 to Dec. 1950; Texas Attorney General, Jan. 1957 to Jan. 1963. Interview, Aug. 7, 1995.

Author's Files

Letter to G. Robert Blakey, Certified letter #P245-724-838, Sept. 4, 1996.
Letters to Dallas PD, Feb. 28 and May 7, 1994 (arrest records of Sicilian-Americans).
Letter from Joe Gennaro to Mark North, May 6, 1996.
Letters to/from Leavenworth Penitentiary, 1994, (imprisonment records of Joseph F. Civello and Frank Ianni).
Letter to U.S. Senator Edward M. Kennedy, Certified letter #P245-725-466, Sept. 13, 1996.
Letter to U.S. District Court Judge Barefoot Sanders, Certified letter #P300-972-018.
Letters to/from Texas Department of Criminal Justice, April 23, 1996 (re Ross Musso).
Letter to Henry M. Wade, Sr., Certified letter #P300-972-019, Sept. 3, 1996.

Government Documents: Federal

Annual Report of the Attorney General of the United States, 1962-1966.
Committee on Un-American Activities, Annual Report for the Year 1963, 88th Congress, 2nd Session, Report No.1739.
Congressional Directory, 78th Congress, 1st Session, May 14, 1943; 79th Congress, 1st Session, 1945.
Congressional Record, 84th Congress, 1st Session, 1955; 87th Congress, March 28, 1962; June 29, 1962; April 24, 1979.
Congressional Quarterly Almanac, 87th Congress, 1st Session, 1961.
Federal Bureau of Investigation, Uniform Crime Reports, 1936-1968.

Hearings before the Committee on Interstate and Foreign Commerce, U.S. House of Representatives, 87th Congress, 2nd Session (Gambling Devices), Jan. 16,18-19, 1962.

Hearings before the Committee on the Judiciary, U.S. Senate, 87th Congress, The Attorney General's Program to Curb Organized Crime and Racketeering, June 6, 1961.

Hearings before the Committee on the Judiciary, U.S. Senate, 96th Congress, 1st Session, Selection and Confirmation of Federal Judges, (Serial No. 96-21, pt.2) March 29, 1979.

Hearings before the Permanent Subcommittee on Investigations of the Committee on Government Operations, U.S. Senate, 87th Congress, 1st Session (Gambling and Organized Crime), 1961.

Hearings before the Permanent Subcommittee on Investigations of the Committee on Government Operations, U.S. Senate, 88th Congress, 1st Session (Organized Crime and Illicit Traffic In Narcotics), Sept. 25, 1963.

Hearings before the President's Commission on the Assassination of President Kennedy, (Warren Commission Hearings, Exhibits, and Report), 1963-1964.

Hearings before the Select Committee on Assassinations of the U.S. House of Representatives, 95th Congress, 2nd Session (HSCA, Hearings and Report), 1978-1979.

Hearings before the Select Committee on Improper Activities in the Labor or Management Field, 86th Congress, 1st Session (McClellan Hearings), 1959.

Hearings before the Special Committee to Investigate Organized Crime in Interstate Commerce, U.S. Senate, 81st Congress, 82nd Congress (Kefauver Hearings, 1st, 2nd, 3rd Interim Reports), 1950-1951.

Hearings before Subcommittee No.5 of the Committee on the Judiciary, House of Representatives, 87th Congress, 1st Session (Organized Crime), Serial No.16, 1961.

Hearings before the Subcommittee on Improvements in the Federal Criminal Code of the Committee on the Judiciary - Illicit Narcotics Traffic, U.S. Senate (Daniel Committee Hearings and Preliminary Report – the Illicit Narcotics Traffic, No.1440, Jan. 23, 1956; No.2483, July 9, 1956), 1955-1956.

Ianni v. Harris, et al., 111 F.2d. 833.

John F. Kennedy Presidential Library, Boston, Mass., WHCF (Thomas, Valenti files).

Lyndon B. Johnson Presidential Library, Austin, Texas.

National Commission on Law Enforcement, Report on Lawlessness in Law Enforcement – the Third Degree (Washington DC: GPO, 1931).

National Commission on Law Observance and Enforcement of the Prohibition Laws – Survey of Texas, 1930.

Organized Crime Control Act of 1970, P.L.91-452.
Prohibiting the Transportation of Gambling Devices in Interstate Commerce, U.S. Senate, 87th Congress, 1st Session, Report No.645, July 27, 1961.
Prohibiting the Transportation of Gambling Devices in Interstate Commerce, U.S. House of Representatives, 87th Congress, 2nd Session, Report No.1828, June 15, 1962.
Report of the Committee on Government Operations, Permanent Subcommittee on Investigations, U.S. Senate, 87th Congress, 2nd Session (Gambling and Organized Crime), March 28, 1962.
Stone v. U.S., 357 F.2d 257 (1966).
Stone v. U.S., 390 U.S. 204 (1968).
Stone v. U.S., 98 S. Ct. 1239 (1978).President Harry S. Truman Proclamation 3000.
U.S. Bureau of Narcotics, Special Report, The Mafia, June 14, 1950, (Papers of Waggoner Carr Southwest Collection, Texas Tech University), Lubbock, Texas.
U.S. Bureau of Narcotics, Traffic in Opium and Other Dangerous Drugs (annual reports), 1932-1968.
U.S. Census, Fourth through Fourteenth – Texas: Dallas, Houston, Galveston, Karnack; Louisiana: New Orleans, West Baton Rouge, Shreveport; Alabama: Autauga County; Georgia; (Enumeration District Sheets, Soundex cards).
U.S. Code, 18 USC 241, (1958 ed.), (1964 ed.), Titles 5 and 28.
U.S. Department of Justice, FBI National Academy, Directory of Graduates, 1991.
U.S. District Court, Northern District of Texas – Dallas, Naturalization Docket, 1910-1950, NationalArchives, SW Region, Fort Worth, Texas.
U.S. v. Diadone, et al., 558 F.2d 775 (1977).
U.S. v. Edward V. Driscoll and Albert Meadows, CR-3-63-174, U.S. District Court, Northern District of Texas – Dallas, Oct. 1, 1963, (gambling) National Archives, SW Region, Fort Worth, Texas.
U.S. v. John Eli Stone, et al., CR-3-63-186, U.S. District Court, Northern District of Texas – Dallas, Oct. 21, 1963, (gambling) National Archives, SW Region, Fort Worth, Texas.
U.S. v. Smith, et al., #8848, U.S. District Court, Northern District of Texas – Dallas, Jan. 14, 1937, (narcotics) National Archives, SW Region, Fort Worth, Texas.
U.S. v. Texas Meat Packers, Inc. and American Produce and Vegetable Company, CR-3-63-192,
U.S. District Court, Northern District of Texas – Dallas, Nov. 15, 1963, (ICC violations) National Archives, SW Region, Fort Worth, Texas.

Government Documents: State of Texas

Activities of the Texas Attorney General's Office (annual report), 1963.

General Investigating Committee Report to the House of Representatives, 57th Legislature of Texas (Murray Hearings), 1961.

Journal of the House of Representatives of the 52nd Legislature, State of Texas, Jan. 9, 1951.

Journal of the Senate of Texas, 44th Legislature (Beck Report), Jan. 8, 1935.

Legislative Messages of the Honorable James V. Allred, Governor of Texas, 1935-1939.

Municipal Police Administration in Texas, No.3843 (Austin, TX.: University of Texas, 1938).

Official Report of the House General Investigating Committee to the House of Representatives of the 58th Legislature of Texas, Part II, Basketball Investigation, 1963.

Papers of Waggoner Carr (Texas State Rep., Speaker of House, Attorney General), Southwest Collection, Texas Tech University, Lubbock, Texas.

Papers of Will Wilson (Dallas District Attorney, Texas Supreme Court, Attorney General), Center for American History, Austin, Texas.

Paul Rowland Jones v. State of Texas, #23837, Texas State Archives, Austin, Texas.

President John F. Kennedy Assassination Files, Texas Court of Inquiry, Dallas Police Report, Texas State Archives, Austin, Texas.

Proclamation by the Governor of Texas (Coke Stevenson), No.37-7760, January 31, 1945.

(Savalli reprieve), Texas State Archives, Austin, Texas.

Supplement to Texas House Journal, 53rd Legislature, Regular Session, March 10, 1953, Crime Investigating Committee – Final Report; Hearings, June 2, 1951 (Meredith Committee).

Texas Attorney General Will Wilson, Address to United Citizens For Law Enforcement, Inc., Beaumont, Texas, Aug, 22, 1961.

Texas Attorney General Will Wilson, Letter to U.S. Senate, Permanent Subcommittee on Investigations, Sept. 20, 1961.

Texas Attorney General Will Wilson, Biennial Report, Texas Attorney General Will Wilson to Governor Price Daniel, Dec. 14, 1962, Legislative Reference Library, Austin, Texas.

Texas Bar Journal (memorials), 1930-1995, Austin, Texas.

Texas Bureau of Health, Bureau of Vital Statistics, (death certificates of Philip Bosco, Sam S. Campisi, Joseph F. Civello, Louis and Leon Civello, Philip Civello, Sam Civello, Joe and Frank Ianni, Isadore Miller, Carlo T. Piranio, Joseph T. Piranio, Charles Satarino, Peter M. Tamburo), Austin, Texas.

Texas Criminal Reports, Court of Criminal Appeals, vol.151 (1948).

Texas Dept. of Criminal Justice (TDCJ).
Texas House Journal, 1957; May 12, 1959.
Texas State Bar Association (Paul E. Coggins, Sarah T. Hughes, Kenneth J. Mighell, Barefoot Sanders, Henry Wade files) Austin, Texas.
University of Texas at Austin, Student Directories, Catalogs 1930-1934.
Vernon's Annotated Code of Criminal Procedure of the State of Texas (Kansas City, MO:
Vernon Law Book Co., 1954).
Vernon's Annotated Penal Code of the State of Texas (Kansas City, MO: Vernon Law Book Co.,1952).
Vernon's Annotated Revised Civil Statutes of the State of Texas (Kansas City, MO: Vernon Law Book Co., 1958, 1962).
Vernon's Texas Codes Annotated (St. Paul, Minn.: West Pub., Co., 1986).

Government Documents: City and County of Dallas, Texas; Cities of Austin and Houston, Texas

Calvary Hill Cemetery, 3235 Lombardy Lane, Dallas, Texas (Catholic Arch Diocese); Date of Burial Records.
Dallas County Crime Commission Reports, 1959-1966.
Dallas County Sheriff's Department, 1846-1982, Commemorative Edition.
Dallas Police Department, Records Department (arrest records).
Dallas Public Library, Texas History Center, Media files: Gambling, Narcotics, JFK assassination,
Jack Ruby, John McKee, Henry Wade, Bill Decker, Earle Cabell; Index to Naturalization Records, Dallas County Court.
Greater Dallas Telephone Directories, 1920 - 1994.
Morrison & Forny's City Directory, Austin, Texas, 1944-1956.
Morrison & Forny's City Directory, Houston Texas, 1946-1951.
The Police Report, Dallas, Texas (annual reports), 1938-1965.
Polk's City Directory, Dallas, Texas, 1958-1969.
Worley's City Directory, Dallas, Texas, 1921-1957.

Directories: Texas Public Officials

A Roster of Texas City Officials
Directory of Texas City Officials
Martin-Dell Hubell Legal Directory (1996)
Texas State Directory
The Texas Legal Directory

Newspapers: Texas

Austin American-Statesman
Beaumont Enterprise
Daily Texan [University of Texas at Austin]
Daily Times Herald [Dallas]
Dallas Journal
Dallas Morning News
Fort Worth Star-Telegram
Houston Chronicle
Houston Post
La Tribuna Italiana [Dallas, 1924-1941]
Lubbock Avalanche-Journal
San Antonio Express-News
Texas Tribune [Dallas, 1941-1962], formerly *La Tribuna Italiana*
Texas Tribune Bowling News [Dallas]
Waco Times Herald
Wichita Falls Times

Newspapers: Out of State

Atlanta Constitution
Avanti [Rome, Italy]
Chicago Tribune
Los Angeles Times
Macon Telegraph [Georgia]
New Orleans States Item
New Orleans Times-Picayune
New York Times
State-Times [Baton Rouge, LA]
Washington Evening Star
Washington Post

Books

Bainbridge, John. *The Super Americans.* New York: Doubleday & Co., Inc, 1961.

Belfiglio, Valentine J. *The Italian Experience in Texas.* Austin, TX: Eakin Press, 1983.

Benton, Wilbourn E. *Texas: Its Government and Politics.* New Jersey: Prentice Hall, Inc., 1961.

Black, George F. *The Surnames of Scotland.* New York: The New York Public Library, 1962.

Black's Law Dictionary, 5th ed. West Publishing Co., 1983.

Blackwell, Barri and David Mattingly. *An Atlas of Roman Britain.* Cambridge, Mass.: Basil Blackwell, Inc., 1990.

Blakey, G. Robert and Richard N. Billings. *The Plot to Kill the President.* New York: Times Books, 1981.

Caro, Robert A. *Means of Ascent: The Years of Lyndon Johnson.* New York: Alfred A. Knopf, 1990.

Caro, Robert A. *The Path to Power: The Years of Lyndon Johnson.* New York: Random House, 1981.

Cinel, Dino. *The National Integration of Italian Return Migration, 1870-1929.* Cambridge: Cambridge University Press, 1991.

Cormier, Frank. *LBJ: The Way He Was.* New York: Doubleday & Company, 1977.

Curry, Jesse E. *JFK Assassination File.* Dallas: American Poster and Printing Co., Inc., 1969.

Dallas Morning News. *Texas Almanac, 1930-1994.* Dallas: A.H. Belo Corp., Inc.

De Felice, Emidio. *Nomi E. Cultura, Societa Servizi Ausiliari E. Ricera Informatica P.A. Pomezia.* 1987.

Dobson, David. *Directory of Scots in the Carolinas, 1680-1830.* Baltimore, Maryland: Genealogical Pub., Inc., 1986.

Dugger, Ronnie. *The Politician: The Life and Times of Lyndon Johnson.* New York: W.W. Norton & Co., 1982.

Epstein, Edward J. *Inquest: The Warren Commission and the Establishment of Truth.* NY: Viking , 1966.

Faber, Doris. *The Presidents' Mothers.* New York: St. Martin's Press, 1978.

Fucilla, Joseph G. *Our Italian Surnames.* Baltimore, MD: Genealogical Pub., Co., 1993.

Goldman, Eric F. *The Tragedy of Lyndon Johnson.* New York: Alfred A. Knopf, 1969.

Gosch, Martin A. and Richard Hammer. *The Last Testament of Lucky Luciano.* Boston: Little, Brown & Co., 1974.

Gulley, Bill and Mary E. Reese. *Breaking Cover.* New York: Simon & Schuster, 1980.

Harwood, Richard and Haynes Johnson. *Lyndon.* New York: Praeger, 1973.

Hoare, Alfred. *A Short Italian Dictionary.* Cambridge, Mass.: The MacMillan Co., 1946.

Hurt, Henry. *Reasonable Doubt.* New York: Henry Holt & Co., 1985.

Iorizzo, Luciano J. and Salvatore Mondello, *The Italian Americans.* Boston: Twayne Pub., 1980.

The Italian Texans. San Antonio, TX: Institute of Texan Cultures, UTSA, 1973.

Jansen, Clifford J. *Italians in a Multicultural Canada*. Lewiston, NY: The Edwin Mellen Press, 1988.
Johnson, Sam H. *My Brother Lyndon*. New York: Cowles Book Co., 1969.
Kantor, Seth. *Who Was Jack Ruby?* New York: Everest House, 1978; retitled as *The Ruby Cover-Up*.
Kearns, Doris. *Lyndon Johnson and the American Dream*. New York: Signet, 1976.
Kennedy, John F. and Edward Claflin. *JFK Wants to Know: Memos from the President's Office, 1961-1963*. New York: Morrow, 1991.
King, Rufus. *Gambling and Organized Crime*. Washington DC: Public Affairs Press, 1969.
Lait, Jack and Lee Mortimer. *U.S.A. Confidential*. New York: Crown Pub., Inc., 1952.
Lichtenstein, Nelson. *Political Profiles: The Johnson Years*. New York, NY: Facts on File, Inc., 1976.
Mafia: The Government's Secret File on Organized Crime. New York: Collins, 2007.
Marrs, Jim. *Crossfire: The Plot That Killed Kennedy*. New York, Carroll & Graf Publishers, 1989.
McClellan, John L. *Crime Without Punishment*. New York, Duell, Sloan and Pierce, 1962.
Meagher, Sylvia. *Accessories after the Fact*. New York: Vintage Books, 1976.
Meagher, Sylvia. *Master Index to the JFK Assassination Investigations*. NJ: Metuchen, 1980.
Melanson, Philip H. *The Robert F. Kennedy Assassination*. New York: Shapolsky Pub., 1991.
Moldea, Dan E. *The Hoffa Wars*. New York: Paddington Press, Ltd., 1978.
Montgomery, Ruth. *Mrs. LBJ*. New York: Holt, Rinehart & Winston, 1964.
Mooney, Booth. *LBJ: an Irreverent Chronicle*. New York: Thomas Crowell, 1976.
Phipps, Joe. *Summer Stock: Behind the Scenes with LBJ in 48*. Ft. Worth: Texas Christian University Press, 1992.
Powers, Richard G. *Secrecy and Power: The Life of J. Edgar Hoover*. New York: The Free Press, 1987.
Reid, Ed and Ovid Demaris. *The Green Felt Jungle*. New York: Pocket Books, Inc., 1964.
Reid, Ed and Ovid Demaris. *The Grim Reapers*. Chicago: Henry Regnery Co., 1969.
Reston, James, Jr. *The Lone Star: The Life of John Connally*. New York: Harper & Row Pub., 1989.

Rolle, Andrew. *The Immigrant Upraised.* Norman, OK: University Of Oklahoma Press, 1968.
Scheim, David E. *Contract on America.* Silver Spring, MD: Argyle Press, 1983 and New York: Shapolsky, 1988.
Schlesinger, Arthur M., Jr. *Robert Kennedy and His Times.* Boston: Houghton Mifflin Co., 1978.
Schneider, Stephen. *Iced: The Story of Organized Crime in Canada.* Mississauga, Ont.: Wiley, 2009.
Sherill, Robert. *The Accidental President.* New York: Grossman Pubs., 1967.
Smith, Marie. *The President's Lady.* New York: Random House, 1964.
Steinberg, Alfred. *Sam Johnson's Boy.* New York: The Macmillon Co., 1968.
Sullivan, William C. *The Bureau: My Thirty Years in Hoover's FBI.* New York: W.W. Norton, 1979.
Truman, Harry S. and Robert H. Ferrell. *Off the Record: The Private Papers of Harry S. Truman.* New York: Harper & Row, 1980.
Turner, William W. and John G. Christian. *The Assassination of Robert F. Kennedy.* New York: Random House, 1978.
Valentine, Douglas. *The Strength of the Wolf.* New York: Verso, 2006.
Waldron, Lamar and Thom Hartmann. *Ultimate Sacrifice: John and Robert Kennedy, the Plan for a Coup in Cuba, and the Murder of JFK.* New York: Carroll & Graf, 2005.
Weisberg, Harold. *Whitewash: The Report on the Warren Report.* New York: Dell, 1965.
White, Edward G. *Earl Warren: a Public Life.* New York: Oxford Univ. Press, 1982.
Who Was Who in America. Marquis Who's Who, Inc. Vol. 4, 1968.
Who's Who in the South and Southwest. Chicago, IL: Marquis Who's Who, Inc. (8th through 11th editions) Witcover, Jules. *85 Days: The Last Campaign of Robert F. Kennedy.* New York: Ace, 1969.
Witcover, Jules. 85 Days...
Woods, Richard D. and Grace Alverez-Altman. *Spanish Surnames in the Southwestern United States: a Dictionary.* Boston: G.K. Hall & Co., 1978.

Magazines and Articles

Atlantic Monthly, April 1962.
"Something Is Rotten in the State of Texas." *Colliers.* June 9, 1951.
"The Law and Henry Wade." *D Magazine.* June 1977.
"Warren Commission Reports Are Routine." *Editor & Publisher.* Feb. 15, 1964.
Family Weekly. Jan. 26, 1964; Jan. 17, 1965.

Life. June 19, 1950; Jan. 25, 1960; Feb. 1, 1960; Jan. 26, 1962.

Look. Oct. 1, 1957.

National Review. June 30, 1964; April 21, 1964.

Newsweek. Oct. 22, 1945; June 14, 1954; June 6, 1960.

Texas Observer. Feb. 23, 1996.

Texas Police Journal [Dallas]. 1954-1962.

Time, Aug. 4, 1939; Jan. 12, 1953; Aug. 25, 1961; Sept. 8, 1961; Jan. 12, 1962; Sept. 30, 1996.

John C. Taylor, "The First Hundred Years," *TPA Messenger*, June 1980.

Television News Reports and Documentaries

Investigative Reports, "The Men Who Killed Kennedy (The Forces Of Darkness)," Bill Kurtis, 1988.

The Killing of President Kennedy: New Revelations Twenty Years Later. VidAmerica, Sydacast Services, Inc., 1983.

KRLD TV (Dallas, CBS affiliate) November 22, 1963, Dan Rather footage.

One on One, KVUE 24, Austin, TX (ABC affiliate), Judy Maggio interview with Claudia (Lady Bird) Johnson, May 22, 1996.

"Lyndon Johnson," *American Experience*, PBS, 1991.

20/20, ABC TV, Claudia Johnson Interview, March 24, 1995.

WFAA TV (Dallas, ABC Affiliate) November 22, 1963, Jay Watson footage.